Japan in
Global Ocean
Politics

Japan in Global Ocean Politics

TSUNEO AKAHA

UNIVERSITY OF HAWAII PRESS

AND

LAW OF THE SEA INSTITUTE
UNIVERSITY OF HAWAII

HONOLULU

Library of Congress Cataloging-in-Publication Data

Akaha, Tsuneo, 1949–
  Japan in global ocean politics.

  Bibliography: p.
  Includes index.
  1. Economic zones (Maritime law)—Japan.
  2. Economic zones (Maritime law)   I.   Title.
JX4144.5.A53   1985   341.4'48   85–16432
ISBN 0–8248–0898–3

To my wife Janet
and to the memory of my mother
Shime Akaha
(1915–1984)

Contents

Tables

Figures

Preface

ONE of the lasting questions among observers and practitioners of international politics is: How successfully do nations cope with and adapt to changes in their global environment? Applied to Japan, the question often invokes apparently contradictory answers depending on who is doing the answering. There have been a plethora of criticisms in Japan about the "short-sightedness," "lack of initiative," "lack of ingenuity," "passivity," and "defensiveness" of Japanese foreign policy behavior. Japanese policymakers themselves have virtually accepted the negative verdict by expressing pessimistic and sometimes even fatalistic views on world politics and emphasizing the complexities of the global system that are beyond their control and the uncertainties in the system that render long-range policies virtually impossible. On the contrary, to outsiders Japan appears to have been a much more resilient and amazingly adaptable political system worthy of such laudatory phrases as the "Japanese miracle," the "Japanese challenge," and the "Japanese model for success."

The present study is an attempt to examine Japan's "defensiveness" and "resilience" in an area critically important to the welfare of this nation, that is, global ocean politics. Poor in natural resources and dependent on international regimes to help them secure necessary resource supplies, Japan has developed maritime activities, particularly fishing and shipping, more extensive than those of any other nation in the world, but its success in conducting those activities is critically dependent on the presence of a stable, liberal international regime that imposes few constraints on ocean activities of coastal states such as Japan. National ocean enclosure, the movement of the post-World War II period that engulfed virtually all nations of the world, coastal and landlocked, developed and developing, capitalist and Communist, first challenged and then re-placed the traditional rules of law in the seas, rules that had provided a stable and liberal international regime for major maritime powers. This is a study of Japan's struggle to first resist and then adapt to that change.

This is also a study of domestic politics and bureaucratic policy making in Japan. A part of the answer to the puzzle presented by the domesti-cally negative and externally positive assessments of Japanese foreign pol-icy behavior will be found, as this study argues, in the manner in which important policy problems are discussed and decisions made by the rele-vant government agencies and domestic groups. Certainly, the interests and concerns of the Japanese ocean community and the Japanese govern-ment's effort to accommodate them have had an important bearing on the nation's ability to cope with the painful sacrifices it has had to make in response to the transformation of the international ocean regime. Equally important, however, have been the manner in which the domestic inter-ests and concerns were placed on the policy agenda of the government and the way relevant government agencies, following their established pattern of behavior, approached the policy problems thus presented.

Moreover, this is a study of Japan's effort to strike a balance between its domestic policy and its foreign policy. Because of the nature of the ocean, policies regarding the use of its space and its resources are, for Japan and for other coastal nations, both domestic and foreign policies. Japan's decisions about its shipping and fishing interests immediately affect other countries' ocean-based activities and vice versa. In the drama of global ocean politics, the words of one major actor have a rippling effect on the whole scene.

Throughout the study, the English style is used for Japanese names, that is, the given name first and family name last. The spelling of Japa-nese names follows the Hepburn style. English translations of informa-tion originally in Japanese language sources are mine unless otherwise noted. Wherever appropriate and helpful for readers who are not familiar with the Japanese language, I provided English translations for Japanese terms, laws, book and article titles, and names of organizations.

This study developed through three phases, and in each phase I received assistance from many people and I am grateful to them. The ini-tial phase began with my participation in the Ocean Policy of Japan (OPJ) Project, funded by the National Science Foundation (Grant No. OCE 77–26776) and administered by the University of Southern California

Institute for Marine and Coastal Studies. As the project's field research coordinator, I was able to conduct extensive information gathering and interview activities in Japan in 1979 and 1980. The first phase came to an end when the project was completed in 1981. I would like to extend my gratitude to the six colleagues who participated in the project and gave me valuable comments on my work. They are Professors Robert Friedheim and George Totten of the University of Southern California (co-principal investigators of the project); Professor Haruhiro Fukui of the University of California, Santa Barbara (whose thorough and critical evaluation was essential to my work); and in Japan Professor Mamoru Koga of Aichi University of the Arts, Nagoya; Mr. Hiroyuki Nakahara of the Research Institute for Ocean Economics, Tokyo; and Professor Masayuki Takeyama of Chuo University, Tokyo (all of whom assisted me in making interview contacts during my field research trips in Japan). Thanks are also due to Clinton Atkinson (formerly Fisheries Attaché in the U.S. Embassy in Tokyo), Dr. Henry Birnbaum of the University of Southern California (formerly National Science Foundation representative in the U.S. Embassy), both of whom provided me with suggestions for interview contacts in Japan. I thank also the individuals who offered their valuable time answering my interview questions and whose names appear in this study.

The second phase involved building on and expanding my OPJ technical report into a Ph.D. dissertation. I would particularly like to thank Bob Friedheim, who helped me through this phase as chair of my dissertation committee and read the first "uncut" version and the revised version of the dissertation, providing me with intellectual critique and moral support. I am also grateful to the other members of the dissertation committee. Professors Richard Ashley of Arizona State University and Roger Dingman of the University of Southern California also read earlier versions of the present study in their entirety and provided critical and helpful suggestions. During the first and second phases, my study also benefited from the helpful suggestions for refinement of Dr. Ann Hollick of the U.S. Department of State (an authority on U.S. ocean policy and politics), Professor Lauriston King of Texas A&M University (formerly with the Office of the International Decade of Ocean Exploration), Professor Arvid Pardo of the University of Southern California (the "father of the modern law of the sea"), and Professor Choon-ho Park of Korea University (an authority on Asian international law and policy). The third and final phase required extensive updating, rewriting, and refining of the earlier work. This task was made manageable with the skillful assistance of the editorial staff at the University of Hawaii Press. Particularly my thanks go to Damaris Kirchhofer for her professional editorial work. I would also like to thank the anonymous reviewers of the manuscript.

Finally, I am thankful to my wife in many ways. I am certain this study would never have been possible had it not been for her understanding, encouragement, and dedication. She spent countless late evening hours typing my dissertation drafts and the entire first manuscript of the current study before it was submitted to the University of Hawaii Press. I am deeply thankful to her.

Despite the many debts I have recorded here, I am responsible for all factual information and interpretation contained in this study.

TSUNEO AKAHA

Introduction

NATIONAL enclosure of the world's oceans and their resources has been one of the most important global trends during the second half of the twentieth century. Increasing awareness of the real and potential value of the ocean space and resources and recognition of the growing scarcity of natural resources on land have prompted nation-states to claim and exert control over wide areas of the hitherto unclaimed oceans and their riches. Littoral states have laid unilateral claims over their coastal waters and resources, met bilaterally to settle competing and overlapping claims, and negotiated multilaterally a new law of the sea.

At the heart of these global trends has been the question: Who gets what, how, and at what cost, as well as why?[1] Views on this central problem have varied widely. Some have argued for the natural right of coastal states to lay sovereign proprietary claims to their coastal waters and resources, and jurisdictional claims to regulate and, if necessary, exclude other nations' activities within their claimed areas. Others have asserted that ocean space should not be appropriated or subjected to exclusive national jurisdiction and that traditional users of the seas should be allowed to continue their ocean activities unhampered by new coastal state claims and restrictions. Still others have asserted that the ocean and its riches belong to every nation and that not only traditional users but also newcomers to ocean activities and future users should be accorded equal rights to the ocean space and resources on an equitable basis.

Developing coastal states and other "newcomers" to maritime affairs have favored expanded coastal state jurisdiction in order to correct what they consider the past injustices in ocean politics—the principle of freedom of the seas, they claim, has benefited almost exclusively those with the capital and technology to exploit the marine resources and navigate the global oceans. Traditional maritime powers have maintained that international management of the seas should be on the basis of free access to and use of their riches.

Amid this complex matrix of claims and claimants has been one of the biggest maritime users of the world—Japan. Its extensive participation in worldwide ocean activities, that is, fishing and shipping, has made Japan one of the most fortunate beneficiaries of the traditional ocean regime. Its lasting interest in the traditional uses of the ocean and in the development of modern technological capabilities with which to expand its ocean use into new areas, such as deep-sea mining and ocean energy development, has made Japan one of the most extensive users of the ocean space and resources.

What accounts for Japan's past and continuing interests in the maritime activities? The answer is rather obvious—its economic dependence on the ocean space and its resources. For example, it is estimated that Japan gets almost one-half of its animal protein intake from its fisheries products, the bulk of which come from foreign coastal waters.[2] As of 1977, this maritime power accounted for over 15 percent of the world's total fishery production.[3] Its fishery production has been the largest in the world since the anchovy disaster in Peru in the early 1970s deprived that Latin American country of the number one spot. Japan's dependence on coastal as well as blue-water fishing will certainly continue into the foreseeable future.

Japan's dependence on foreign mineral supplies, for which maritime transportation is essential, is also well known. In 1980, for example, Japan imported 96 percent of its copper needs, 100 percent of its nickel, 68.5 percent of its zinc, 98.7 percent of its iron ore, 83.9 percent of its lead, 98.4 percent of its tin, 100 percent of its aluminum, and 100 percent of its cobalt.[4] In the same year, Japan also imported 81.8 percent of its coal supply, 99.8 percent of its petroleum, and 90.7 percent of its natural gas.[5] Heavy dependence on foreign mineral supplies has caused Japan to be keenly interested in the mining of deep-sea manganese nodules. It is estimated that the sea bottom holds mineral deposits in the amount of about 500 billion tons, with a potential reserve of copper as large as 16 times the land-site reserve, 132 times for nickel, 250 times for manganese, and 1,250 times for cobalt.[6] Despite the enormous capital and technological investment that is necessary to make such minerals available for industrial use, Japanese observers believe that it is feasible in the near future to actually start exploiting them.[7] In fact, in December 1980 the Ministry of International Trade and Industry (MITI) decided to invest ¥200 million in a National Research and Development Program to develop deep-sea mining technology over the next nine years. Japan's genuine interest in manganese nodule development is further indicated by its establishment in July 1982 of a Law on Interim Measures for Deep Seabed Mining to promote government-industry cooperation in research and development in this area.[8]

It is estimated that transportation costs account for as much as 20 to 30 percent of the import prices of iron ore, coal, and crude oil used in Japan.[9] Increased shipping regulations and environmental restrictions on ocean transportation are certain to raise these shipping costs. Japan is equally dependent on imports of agricultural items such as soybeans (constituting 95.8 percent of the country's needs), corn (100 percent), and wheat (90.5 percent).[10]

It is quite understandable, then, why the recent trends toward national ocean enclosure have caused officials and observers in Japan to sound off such alarmist notes as "Can Maritime-Nation Japan Survive?"[11] "Japan, Squeezed Out of the Sea,"[12] "North Pacific Fishing Faces a Crisis of Complete Devastation,"[13] and so on. Particularly, coastal states' declarations of the 200-mile fishery or economic zone in the 1960s and 1970s have had both symbolic and real impacts on Japanese ocean interests. Not only has the government had to abandon its long-standing position of favoring the 3-mile territorial sea limit as the international norm; it has extended its own territorial sea to twelve miles. At the same time, Japan has also extended its fishery jurisdiction from twelve miles, which it had maintained since 1965, to two hundred miles.

The present study describes and explains the Japanese government's decision-making process leading to its final decisions in January and March 1977, respectively, to extend the country's territorial sea limit from three to twelve miles and to establish its 200-mile fishery zone. It covers the period from 1958, when the First United Nations Conference on the Law of the Sea (UNCLOS) took place, through 1977, when the two maritime decisions were translated into domestic legislation, to the early 1980s, when Japan learned how to operate under the new international ocean regime, with the major focus on developments leading up to the 1977 decisions. What happened to Japan during this crucial period that caused the abandonment of its earlier, adamant defense of the traditional principle of freedom of the seas? Who participated in the decision-making process and whose interests were considered in the final decisions? How did the government define its role in the national debate on this crucial issue? Were there conflicts within Japan regarding various objectives and approaches with respect to Japan's ocean interests in foreign as well as its own coastal areas? If there were, how were they resolved? Were Japan's decisions internally determined, that is, were they primarily a response to changes in the domestic debate, or were they calculated responses to changes in the international environment? While answering these questions that are specific to the current case, the study also addresses broader themes.

First, a society whose internal needs are being met by a status quo in the international political-economic system will respond to a disruption in that order in a manner designed to uphold it. The assumptions are that every national society has a means of identifying and defining its internal needs, that it attempts to satisfy such needs by gaining access to and utilizing resources available at home and abroad, and that it supports an international order that allows it to maintain its access to externally available resources.

Second, a society's interaction with what it perceives to be the existing international order tends to be highly structured and routine. The assumptions are that an international status quo is relatively stable over time and that the society's linkage to it is also rather stable as long as internal needs remain the same, or nearly the same, over time. Under such circumstances, it is unlikely that the society will reevaluate its relationship to the external environment.

Third, when the existing order that a society supports and benefits from is challenged by other members of the international community, it will attempt to protect the status quo by adhering to the approach it has traditionally followed vis-à-vis the environment. That is, rather than quickly abandoning its rather established approach and introducing a new one, the society will exert greater energy than before in carrying through the existing approach. But this time it will do so more self-consciously and more vehemently than before. The assumption is that a challenge to the status quo will cause the society to become more acutely aware of its internal needs and to strengthen its strategic ties with the challenged order.

Fourth, if the challenge to the existing arrangement becomes insurmountable in the sense that the society's support can no longer help maintain it, the society will reevaluate its relationship with the changing environment. In other words, the pressure on the status quo passes a threshold in the perception of the society such that its policy toward the international system itself becomes a subject of reassessment and reevaluation. The assumptions are that a society benefiting from the established order will perceive a threat to that order as a threat to its own internal needs and that the society has a mechanism that translates its perception of such a threat into a reevaluation of its approach to the status quo.

Fifth, when it becomes clear that the continuation of the status quo is no longer possible, the society will reformulate its policy. It will do so in light of what it perceives to be the emerging order. If no clear order is in sight, however, the society's policy reformulation process will be tentative at best and immobilized at worst. The assumptions are that a change in the status quo necessarily calls for a different set of strategies and that each society has a mechanism whereby it can innovate strategies to link its internal needs with the emerging new order. What is important is that the mechanism cannot function effectively if there are great uncertainties about the emerging order. If uncertainties should persist for long, internal divisions will emerge between those groups whose immediate needs cannot be satisfied because of the inability of the society to reformulate a new approach, on the one hand, and others whose interests are not seriously or immediately challenged by the change in the international environment, on the other. A prolonged period of uncertainty will not be tolerated by some politically significant members of the society whose needs are on the national agenda.

Finally, only when a transformation of the international political-economic system imposes on the society a reordering of its internal priorities and interests will it begin to reshape its internal needs. That is, only when a new status quo makes it impossible for the society to pursue its traditionally defined needs will it question the viability and appropriateness of those needs and begin to deemphasize those needs and give priority to other needs that it can more successfully satisfy within the new international order.

In the Japanese case, the traditional status quo is the international ocean regime under the principle of freedom of the seas. The emerging order is one in which coastal states will enjoy far more extensive jurisdictional rights to their coastal waters and resources than has been the case under the former status quo. As far as Japan is concerned, great uncertainties have existed regarding the exact nature of the new ocean regime and its implications for the nation's activities in fishing, maritime transportation, energy and mineral development, scientific research, pollution control, and so on. How have such uncertainties affected Japan's policy and policy making? This is the crux of the present study.

I first define the nature of the ocean and ocean policy problems facing Japan and other participants in global ocean politics (chap. 1). Second, I provide a review of the history of the international debate on the global ocean regime (chaps. 2–4). In that section, I focus on the multilateral debate of the First and Second UNCLOS and in the UN Seabed Committee, which presented important policy problems to Japan. A look at Japan's behavior in its bilateral fishery negotiations with other Pacific-rim countries in the 1960s provides an insight into the nature and direction of its reaction to the gradual but irrevocable demise of the traditional ocean regime.

The third section (chaps. 5–7), gives a detailed analysis of the process of Japanese decision-making starting in 1973 in response to the commencement of the Third UNCLOS and culminating in the 1977 decisions to extend the country's fishing jurisdiction and territorial sea limits. The focus is on (1) the manner in which the competing and conflicting interests, concerns, and views of various participants in the process found their way into the government's decision-making process; (2) the influence of developments outside Japan on its decision-making system; (3) the process whereby the various government agencies responded to pressures going in different and incompatible policy directions; and (4) how the government eventually unified and formalized its policy on the fishery jurisdiction and territorial sea questions. Finally, some general observations about Japan's behavior thus analyzed and its likely approach to the new global order of the sea are provided.

1

The International Political Economy of Ocean Management and Japan

THE ocean covers about 70 percent of the earth's surface. This vast space and the resources in and under it have been and will continue to be used for a variety of purposes.

Navigation for commercial as well as noncommercial purposes is one of the most traditional uses of the ocean space. Fishing is another traditional ocean activity. Fishery products, at about 70 million metric tons a year, provide about 3 percent of the total amount of protein for human consumption and about 10 percent of the animal protein.[1] Extraction of raw materials from seawater is another use of the ocean, providing about 30 percent of the world's salt, 70 percent of its bromine, 60 percent of its magnesium metal, 5 percent of its magnesium compounds, and 60 percent of its water supply.[2] The ocean is also a supplier of hydrocarbons such as petroleum and natural gas, energy, and hard minerals. It has also been used for recreational purposes. Finally, although often overlooked, the ocean has served as the depository of pollutants.

To sustain these uses of the ocean, its users must bear some costs. Navigation requires measures for ensuring safety and environmental conservation. Fishing must be accompanied by fishery resource conservation if resource depletion is to be avoided. Safety and environmental concerns also apply to the extraction of nonliving resources from the sea as well as, of course, to the use of the ocean as a waste receptor. In short, virtually all uses of the sea entail both benefits and costs. This gives rise to the necessity of managing the uses of the sea. Particularly important is ocean management in areas where the various uses compete with one another and/ or where the ocean users lay competing claims.

Ocean Management

At the international level, there are basically three possible regimes for the management of the oceans: (1) open access and free use, (2) national management, and (3) international management.[3] The regime of open access and free use renders most of the ocean space and resources accessible to all nations, and no nation is charged a fee for its use. This laissez-faire regime was espoused by Hugo Grotius toward the end of the seventeenth century to justify the rights of the Dutch East India Company. In opposition to the Spanish and Portuguese division of the world's oceans into their spheres of dominance, Grotius asserted in his *Mare Liberum* that the ocean belonged to everyone *(res communis)* or to no one *(res nullius)*. The implication was that whoever wanted and was able to use it could do so freely.

The Grotian principle of freedom of the seas was not without detractors. It was attacked by John Seldon who, in his *Mare Clausem,* argued that nations had the right to enclose portions of the ocean and exclude from them others' fishing, navigation, landing, and taking of gems. The attack eventually lost to the Grotian doctrine, which dominated maritime thinking during the following centuries. In part to codify the principle of freedom of the seas and in part to put an end to disagreement over the extent of territorial sea claims of coastal state, the League of Nations called a conference on these questions in 1930. However, the thirty-eight nations attending the conference at The Hague failed to reach agreement on the breadth of the territorial sea.

Since then, the laissez-faire ocean regime has been subjected to mounting opposition. Criticism has been leveled against three assumptions upon which the Grotian doctrine was predicated, namely that the ocean is infinite and therefore not appropriable, that its resources are inexhaustible, and that it is perpetually pure and therefore not degradable by man. As long as these assumptions were an approximate and adequate description of the properties of the ocean and of man's relationship to it, the doctrine of freedom of the seas served as a normative regime or as a descriptive view of ocean affairs. However, those assumptions are no longer accurate or appropriate.[4] Due to technological advancement, economic needs, and political aspirations, more and more areas of the ocean have been appropriated by national claimants in the last thirty years; marine resources, both living and nonliving, are recognized today as exhaustible; and degradation of the ocean environment has progressed due to increasing concentrations of industrial and residential uses of the narrow coastal land areas and increasing maritime traffic congestion and energy development in the coastal sea areas of the world.

As the principle of freedom of the seas has become inappropriate as a norm and inaccurate as a description, the other two management schemes have gained in importance—national management and international management. They have been proposed as alternatives to the traditional regime of open access and free use.[5] Both are aimed at enclosing the ocean. National management encloses the ocean in a decentralized manner; international management in a centralized manner.[6] The former divides the world's ocean into portions to be appropriated among the members of the international system, and the latter treats the world's ocean as a "common" and transfers its functional ownership to the international community, its use to be determined collectively. The international community has so far accepted a mixed system, as evidenced by the Third UNCLOS's 1982 adoption of the Convention on the Law of the Sea, which combines recognition of coastal states' expanded territorial and jurisdictional claims with collective scheme for managing the development of the deep seabed beyond the limits of national jurisdiction.

National enclosure has accelerated since the end of World War II, beginning with the Truman Proclamation on the Continental Shelf of 1945, which asserted the United States' sovereign rights over the mineral resources offshore, and the Proclamation Concerning the Policy of the United States with Respect to Coastal Fisheries in Certain Areas of the High Seas, which established a new fishery conservation zone outside the U.S. 3-mile limit and recognized other states' rights to fishery jurisdiction up to twelve miles from their coasts.

These decisions were soon followed by similar and more extensive claims by other littoral states. In 1951 Ecuador, Romania, and Bulgaria established 12-mile territorial seas. Other countries followed suit in the following years, and by 1958 sixteen states had made territorial sea or fishery jurisdiction claims or a combination of both extending to twelve miles. These states included the Soviet Union and Guatemala, the latter having claimed a 12-mile territorial sea and beyond it a 6-mile fishery zone before the Second World War. Chile, Peru, Costa Rica, El Salvador, and Ecuador established either a 200-mile territorial sea or a 200-mile fishery zone during this period. In addition, Guinea claimed a 130-mile territorial sea.[7] By September 1977, as many as sixty-two states had claimed 12-mile territorial seas, and twenty-six states had established ter-

ritorial sea limits exceeding twelve miles, including thirteen countries
claiming 200-mile territorial waters. In comparison, there were thirty-
three countries with territorial sea claims of less than twelve miles, including twenty countries with 3-mile territorial seas. Furthermore, as many as
forty-six countries had set up 200-mile economic or fishery zones.[8] In
short, the postwar history of the ocean regime has been one of sweeping
transformation.

What caused the expansionist coastal state claims? Why did such a
large number of states opt for national rather than international management to replace the traditional laissez-faire regime? While different
observers emphasize different factors, the following list includes those
that are the most frequently discussed: (1) the increase in the expected
value of ocean resources and the resulting competition for them; (2) the
revolutionary development of marine technology; (3) the rise of environmental consciousness; (4) the new demands for redistribution of the
world's wealth; (5) the East-West political and ideological conflict; (6) the
dynamics of multilateral negotiations on the regime of the sea; and (7)
the decentralized world political system.

First, the ocean is a real and potential supplier of large quantitites of
both living and nonliving resources. The current exploitation of fishery
resources and offshore petroleum and natural gas and the expected development of the mineral deposits on the deep seabed have raised the level
of expectations among all countries, including those that have only limited ocean capabilities. The importance of coastal areas as a reserve of
renewable and nonrenewable resources can be readily understood. About
65 percent of the world's total fishery resources lie within two hundred
miles of the coast.[9] Ninety-five percent of the known submarine petroleum reserves are also within two hundred miles of the coast.[10] As of
1969, offshore petroleum production accounted for 17 percent of the
total oil production by the non-Communist countries.[11] These and other
statistics testify to the potential contribution of ocean resources to the
food, energy, and other resource supplies of both developed and developing countries.

This general observation must be qualified, however, because a number of biogeographical marine attributes lower the level of expectations
for some countries with regard to the ocean resources. There are fifty
landlocked and shelf-locked states that will gain little or nothing from the
national enclosure of the ocean.[12] Sixty-eight coastal states can be considered relatively disadvantaged in the sense that they will gain fewer areas

of the sea than the global average when they extend their jurisdiction to its maximum within the 200-mile limit.[13] Furthermore, the natural distribution of living and nonliving resources of the sea is quite skewed. For example, the average production of aquatic organisms in the Far East between 1974 and 1976 amounted to 11.2 million tons, as compared with 3.9 million tons in Africa, 0.8 million tons in the Near East, 4.1 million tons in North America, and 7.7 million tons in Latin America.[14] One estimate places the level of production in the year 2000 at 18.1 million tons in the Far East, 6 million tons in North America, and 10.2 million tons in Latin America.[15] These statistics indicate that the amount of benefits coastal states can expect from extending their resource jurisdiction varies greatly.

Furthermore, there are resources that lie mostly beyond the limits to which coastal states have extended or are likely to extend their jurisdiction. For example, the most promising known deposits of manganese nodules lie in the deep-seabed areas well beyond any state's 200-mile economic zone.[16] This indicates that for most countries national enclosure itself will add to their mineral resource base only petroleum, natural gas, and polysulfides.

The additional factor that determines the contributions that decentralized ocean management will be able to make to national economies is the availability of technology that can be directly applied to the exploitation of nationally appropriated resources. There is an obvious gap in this area between the developed and developing countries. The former can expect immediate gains, while the latter cannot, at least without the former's support. However, it is not only the expectation of short-run returns that has induced coastal states into national ocean enclosure. Expectations of future potential benefits are also an important factor that has pushed many technology-poor countries toward jurisdictional expansion. Even when they themselves are not capable of exploiting the resources they have claimed, less developed coastal states can still extract value from them. For example, they can lay title to their coastal fishery resources and extract revenues from foreign fishing counties that want to harvest those resources. As of 1977, Brazil required license fees of US $1,215 per vessel annually, Mexico charged US $18 per capacity ton, Ecuador received a US $700 registration fee and US $60 per net registered ton for fifty days or one full load, and Peru extracted a US $500 registration fee annually and US $20 per net registered ton for 100 days.[17] To cite a few Japanese examples, as of 1979 Japanese fishermen were charged US $400,000 to operate

470 boats in the newly established 200-mile exclusive economic zone (EEZ) of Palau Islands, US $2 million for 900 vessels in Micronesia's 200-mile zone, and US $400,000 in the Marshall islands' 200-mile economic zone.[18]

Furthermore, by allowing foreign vessels to harvest fish in their economic or fishery zones, developing coastal states can avoid their own investment in fairly capital- and technology-intensive industries. They can also expect a transfer of fishery-related technologies, to build a fishery industrial infrastructure with foreign assistance, to train and provide employment for their nationals in fishery-related industries, and to earn foreign exchange by export of fishery products.[19] The importance of fishery resources to some developing countries cannot be understated because approximately 64 percent of the world's potential fishery resources are found off the coasts of the developing countries.[20] Again, this statement must be qualified because the economic value of fishery resources, both real and potential, varies greatly, depending on the market situation for the particular stock and the cost of harvesting it. For example, according to one estimate, as of 1973, the value per metric ton of fish landing in Africa was US $125 per ton, whereas in North and Central America it was US $331, in South America US $132, in Europe US $57, in Asia US $307, and in Oceania US $766.[21]

The second major factor that has contributed to the national enclosure of the ocean is the revolutionary technological development in the field of ocean resource exploitation. Technological advancement makes possible exploration and exploitation of marine resources that have hitherto escaped access. Such resources include the deep-sea minerals, the most important of which are manganese nodules, much of the offshore petroleum and natural gas, and, for developing coastal states, still relatively underexploited fishery resources in their offshore areas. Expectations of new economic values can now be translated into real assets by means of technology.

Technological development also provides incentives for national enclosure indirectly. The fear that advanced countries will exploit and possibly deplete less developed nations' coastal ocean resources before the latter can develop their own capabilities may be sufficient to push them toward national enclosure. In short, resource conservation for their own future use has been an important consideration in the decision by coastal states to resort to unilateral ocean enclosure.

Third, national ocean enclosure has accelerated because of the increasing awareness of the impact that human activities on land and at sea have on the ecology of the ocean, including both the seawater itself and the living resources in and under it. Although not all human-produced substances that eventually end up in the "ultimate sink" are harmful to ocean ecology, there is no denying that even small quantities of certain substances and large amounts of others degrade the quality of the ocean environment. For example, heavy metals such as mercury, lead, and cadmium; certain chemicals such as DDT and polychlorinated biphenyls; radioactive materials; and other toxic materials are harmful to the ocean environment.

Petroleum products are perhaps the most controversial pollutants because of their salience. It is estimated that 2 to 5 million metric tons of oil directly enters the ocean each year.[22] Some of it is discharged into the ocean intentionally, for example, in the process of the pumping of bilges, the discharge of ballast by tankers, and the cleaning of oil tanks. Some of it escapes into the ocean by accident, such as in vessel collisions, spillage from tankers at sea, and spillage due to accidents on offshore oil rigs. Some of the most sensational cases of oil pollution at sea include the oil spill by the British supertanker *Torrey Canyon* in 1967, the oil spill by the Union Oil Company's rig in the Santa Barbara Channel in 1969, the Ekofisk Bravo blowout in the North Sea in 1977, and the spill by the Liberian tanker *Amoco Cadiz* off the Brittany coast in 1978. In addition to the direct contamination of the marine ocean environment by oil, there is also an indirect and largely uncontrollable escape of hydrocarbons into the ocean. According to a report by the U.S. National Academy of Sciences, as much as 90 million metric tons of oil escape into the ocean through the atmosphere.[23]

International awareness of these sources of marine pollution has been translated into cooperation and coordination of marine environmental programs through such multilateral organizations as the Inter-Governmental Maritime Consultative Organization (IMCO), the Food and Agriculture Organization (FAO), the Inter-Governmental Oceanographic Commission (IOC) of UNESCO, and the Joint Group of Experts on the Scientific Aspects of Marine Pollution (GESAMP). Of course, problems of marine pollution have been an important item on the agenda of UNCLOS. International conferences are another forum through which international consciousness about the marine environment is raised. An example is the United Nations Conference on Human Environment held in Stockholm in 1972. It adopted the General Guidelines and Principles for the Preservation of the Marine Environment and also resulted in the creation of the Governing Council for Environmental Programs.

Marine environmental concerns have also found their way into national legislation in many countries.[24] The designation of sea-lanes and traffic separation schemes for passage through straits used for international navigation and through archipelagic waters and the establishment of environmental and safety laws and regulations exemplify coastal states' safeguards against marine hazards and pollution.

The debate on the international regime of the sea and the trends toward decentralized marine management must also be understood in the context of the international political-economic situation. One of the most profound debates about the international political-economic system in the last two decades is that over the structure of the world economic system. The less developed countries assert that the postwar international economic system is structured in favor of the industrialized North and against the developmental needs of the developing countries in the South. Current patterns of international trade, monetary relations, foreign investment, technology transfer, economic aid, resource development, and international information flow are all targets of the less developed countries. In their view, while the developed countries are enjoying the benefits of symmetrical interdependence through international interactions in these areas, the less developed countries are suffering from growing disparities, asymmetries, and dependencies that they believe have been imposed on them by the world economic system. The developing countries demand major changes in the production, transfer, and consumption of economic values. They demand a New International Economic Order (NIEO) and a New World Information Order (NWIO).

Within this grand debate, the developing countries demanded the establishment of a new international regime of the sea that would eliminate the inequalities in marine resource exploitation and in the use of ocean space for transportation—inequalities that, they argue, have been maintained under the traditional regime of freedom of the seas. Their first attempt, therefore, was to destroy the traditional ocean regime and create a new one under which they would be assured greater and equitable shares of the riches of the sea. Thus, during the First and Second UNCLOS, the developing countries sought to alter the regime.[25] For example, they argued for territorial sea limits beyond the traditional 3-mile limit. The Communist bloc countries by and large supported the demands of the less developed countries on this question. They too supported proposals for a 12-mile territorial sea and adamantly opposed attempts to set a uniform breadth at any lesser distance.[26] The informal coalition between the Eastern bloc countries and the developing countries demanded expanded jurisdictional rights to coastal fisheries so as to protect them against exploitation by large foreign distant-water fishing vessels.[27] On the other hand, as I will discuss in the next chapter, the traditional users of the ocean in the developed parts of the world wanted to maintain the freedom of the seas and argued for broad high seas and narrow territorial seas and contiguous zones.

Although neither the North nor the South is a monolithic group of countries with identical ocean interests, there is no denying that the North-South conflict at the global level was interjected into the UNCLOS debate.

The East-West political-ideological conflict and the dynamics of multilateral negotiations on the regime of the sea have contributed to the acceleration of the trend toward national enclosure in an indirect way—indirect in the sense that these two factors per se do not cause coastal states to expand their jurisdiction, but they have induced many coastal states to take unilateral expansionist actions. More specifically, the conflict between Communist bloc members and capitalist countries during the cold war and the dynamics of complex multilateral negotiations among more than 150 nations participating in the UNCLOS debate slowed down the process of global consensus formation, frustrating the expansionist attempts by many coastal states.

As I pointed out earlier, the question of the breadth of the territorial sea and contiguous zone divided the delegations at the first two UNCLOS between the developed capitalist maritime powers on the one hand and the Communist bloc members and the developing coastal states on the other. As I will discuss later, Communist bloc states supported proposals for a 12-mile territorial sea, whereas the Western maritime powers such as Japan, the United States, and Great Britain opposed them and instead proposed a 3-mile territorial sea and, subsequently as a compromise, a 6-mile territorial sea limit.

The East-West cleavage was also seen on cold war–related issues such as the question of the use of the high seas for nuclear testing or as a dumping ground for atomic wastes and the controversy over whether UNCLOS should take any position on the credentials of the Hungarian delegation in the aftermath of the Hungarian revolution.[28]

These East-West disagreements during the early phases of the

UNCLOS negotiations held back consensus formation on the ocean regime, with the result that a number of coastal states, frustrated by the slow progress, resorted to unilateral actions to extend their territorial sea limits as well as the limits of their resource jurisdiction. However, as the cold war gradually waned in the 1960s and with the advent of U.S.-Soviet détente, the superpowers began to take positions on some law of the sea questions that indicated a convergence on some ocean interests. For example, both have been particularly concerned with the implications of national ocean enclosure for their military activities in, under, and over the ocean. In this context, the status of straits used for international navigation and the question of passage through foreign territorial waters have been a particular concern for the superpowers. Their strong commitment to the preservation of unimpeded transit through straits used for international navigation has even made them give in, as a trade-off, on the question of the coastal states' right to establish a 200-mile economic zone. Their defense of relatively free passage through international straits and their opposition to broad definitions of such concepts as "innocent passage" and "archipelagic waters," which I will describe later, have been seen by others as an attempt to limit their natural sovereignty. The superpowers' opposition to the 200-mile economic zone until around 1973 was also seen as an attempt to defend the traditional regime of the sea. Seen in this light, the superpowers' positions on these questions during the 1960s and the early years of the 1970s added to the dissatisfaction and frustration among the developing coastal states intent on defeating the traditional regime of the sea.

The other political factor, that is, the dynamics of multilateral negotiations on the law of the sea, has been an additional source of frustration for coastal states—both most developing countries and many developed —inclined toward expansionist ocean claims. The Third UNCLOS took over ten years before it finally adopted, in April 1982, the culmination of its work, the Convention on the Law of the Sea.

The difficulty in reaching a universally acceptable legal regime is structural. Some 150 countries have participated in this attempt. They have included developed and developing countries, traditional marine users and newcomers to ocean activities, coastal states, and landlocked and shelf-locked states. Their marine interests are almost as diverse as the political, economic, and ideological perspectives they represent. Their coalition behavior in regional caucusing groups, informal negotiating groups, and groups organized around specific issues of the law of the sea

adds to the complex network of interactions among the UNCLOS delegations. The issues they have discussed have been equally varied and intri-
cately intertwined. They have encompassed the breadth of the territorial
sea; the rights and duties of coastal and other states within territorial
waters; the extent and nature of resource jurisdiction of coastal states; the
rights and duties of littoral states and fishing states concerning high seas
fisheries; coastal states' rights and responsibilities regarding marine safety
and environment; deep-seabed mineral development; the rights and
duties of coastal states and others regarding marine scientific research;
and the settlement of international marine disputes. What emerges is a
picture of dynamic complexity. There is no question that the process has
been one of the most complex negotiations that the international community has ever undertaken.[29] It is not surprising at all, therefore, that
the multilateral debate on the new ocean regime has taken as long as
it has.

Finally, while the debate in the UNCLOS forum has set some important trends in the emergence of a new international law of the sea, much
trend-setting has also been done outside the framework of the multilateral debate. Much of this can be explained as a natural, logical consequence of the decentralized world political system that renders collective
management of the ocean more nonrational than rational from the perspective of its individual members. In the absence of a global authority
that can consolidate and exercise a collective will of the world community,
sovereign nation-states are ultimately responsible to themselves. Just as it
is rational for an individual nation-state to build up its arms to defend
itself from potential external aggression, so it is in the nationally defined
interest of each individual state to determine its own policy toward the
management of ocean uses rather than allowing others to determine its
interests and policy. However, as Garret Hardin's "tragedy of the commons" and Mancur Olson's "logic of collective action" have illustrated,
what may be rational for individual states may not be rational for the
whole community of states.[30] As individual security leads to collective
insecurity, so decentralized, national management of ocean uses may lead
to a collective, global disaster.[31]

Arvid Pardo, "the father of the modern law of the sea," has lamented
that the vast "common heritage of mankind" has been appropriated by
nation-states, which individually are in no position to rationally manage
the fish and pollutants that do not recognize national authority and
national boundaries.[32] There is one area, however, in which the common

heritage approach, or the centralized management scheme, has been adopted, although its workability is yet to be tested. UNCLOS has adopted a new regime for the development of deep-seabed minerals beyond the limits of national jurisdiction. The International Seabed Authority, with its commercial arm, the Enterprise, and with its decision-making organs of the Assembly and the Council, is expected to represent the will of the international community as it allocates seabed minerals and the revenues they generate among the participants in this scheme. Even though the United States under the Reagan administration and a handful of other states have so far rejected this scheme while accepting almost all of the other parts of the new convention, the vast majority of the international community, including Japan, has accepted the centralized management of the international seabed resources.

In summary, national rather than international enclosure has been the principal replacement of the traditional laissez-faire ocean regime, with the exception of deep-seabed mineral development, where a centralized management scheme has been set up, and on the high seas, where the traditional freedoms are still in operation albeit under increasing international and regional restrictions.

Japan and National Ocean Enclosure

Where does Japan fit in these global trends? Prior to the Second World War, Japan had four major ocean interest sectors: fishing, shipping, shipbuilding, and the navy. Since Japan's defeat in World War II, however, fishing, commercial shipping, and shipbuilding have been its most important maritime preoccupations. Of these, shipping and fishing are the most seriously affected by the decentralized ocean enclosure.[33] In addition, there are a few relatively recent ocean activities that are likely to be influenced in important ways by the demise of the traditional regime of the sea. They are continental shelf petroleum development, deep-sea minerals exploitation, and scientific research.[34]

The importance of shipping to the Japanese economy is well known. Japan's dependence on foreign imports of raw materials, sources of energy, and foodstuffs has already been pointed out. Supporting the importation of these economic necessities for this resource-poor country is its international shipping. In 1981, for example, 15 percent of all the oil shipped in the world, as measured in terms of weight and mileage, was transported to and from Japan, as was 46 percent of the coal and 50.8 percent of the iron ore.[35] To support the country's GNP, which constitutes about 10 percent of the gross world product, shipping to and from Japan plays a very important role, carrying well over 20 percent of the world's total cargo transport.[36] Japan's share in the world's total ship bottom also indicates the extent of Japanese shipping interests. Of the total ship bottom of the world in 1977—393,678,000 tons—Japan accounted for as much as 40,036,000 tons, second only to Liberia's 79,983,000 tons.[37]

These statistics clearly indicate the substantial degree to which Japan's economic needs are linked to the world economy through international shipping. Disruption of major shipping routes and the increased cost of marine transportation are important concerns to Japanese shipping interests. Particularly problematic are the status of straits used for international navigation and the status of the so-called archipelagic waters that lie between the sources of Japanese imports and Japanese ports. Oil from the Middle East supplies over 70 percent of Japan's oil imports. A disruption of the passage of its shipment through the Straits of Malacca and Singapore and the Sunda–Lomboc Straits would force tankers to navigate around Australia. According to one estimate, this would increase the shipping cost by 60 percent.[38] The importance of these straits and the archipelagic waters of Indonesia and the Philippines cannot be overemphasized because over 70 percent of the oil passing through the Malacca–Singapore Straits is bound for Japan, over 19 percent of Japan-bound oil passes through the Indonesian and Philippine archipelagic waters, and 20 percent of the oil moving through the Strait of Hormuz is bound for Japan.[39]

Fishing plays a major role in Japan's economy. The country's post–World War II fisheries development depended heavily on the availability of fishery resources outside its narrow 3-mile territorial sea. When Japan was defeated, it was placed under severe navigational and fishery restrictions. On August 20, 1945, the Supreme Commander, Allied Powers (SCAP), issued the *Okiai Kōkō Kinshirei,* the order that banned virtually all navigation of Japanese ships in the offshore area of the country, severely limiting Japanese fishing operations. This was followed on September 27, 1945, by the establishment of the so-called MacArthur Line, which limited the area in which Japanese fishing was allowed to about 630,000 square miles. Until it was repealed on April 25, 1952, it severely limited Japan's marine fisheries. As the restrictions were gradually lifted, however, fishery activities slowly recovered, and by 1952 the total fishery production had surpassed the prewar record.[40] During the thirty years after the war, Japanese fishery production recorded a nearly sixfold increase.

In the early postwar years of fishery recovery, fishing efforts were concentrated in Japan's immediate coastal waters, but, in part to prevent the depletion of some coastal stocks and in part to expand the country's food supplies, fishing efforts were gradually expanded into offshore areas and further into the coastal waters of other countries. The government's fishery policies also encouraged the development of offshore and distant-water fisheries.[41] The growth of these fisheries during the 1960s and early 1970s was remarkable. Offshore production increased from 1,931,000 metric tons in 1956 to 3,984,000 tons in 1973, and to 4,924,000 tons in 1977, while distant-water production rose from 808,000 metric tons in 1956 to 3,988,000 tons in 1973 and to 6,112,000 tons in 1977.[42] By comparison, the relative importance of coastal fisheries gradually diminished in the 1950s, its total production fluctuating up and down around the 1,800,000- to 2,000,000-ton levels until about the middle of the 1960s.[43]

The unmitigated expansion of offshore and distant-water fisheries continued until the early 1970s. However, two major developments in the first half of the 1970s began to change the picture. The oil shock of 1973–1974 resulted in the doubling of fuel costs for Japanese fisheries between 1973 and 1975. This caused price increases of other principal fishery supplies in proportions never before experienced. Particularly hard hit were the distant-water fisheries whose postwar development had been made possible by the availability of large quantities of inexpensive fuel.[44] One of the most important consequences of the oil shocks of 1973–1974 and 1978–1979 has been the realization in Japan of the importance of its own coastal fishery resources, which it had sometimes neglected in favor of offshore and distant-water fisheries.[45]

Another development that has increased domestic attention in Japan to its own coastal fishing grounds in recent years is the global phenomenon of ocean enclosure. There is a grave concern about the impact of national ocean enclosure on fishery supplies for human consumption. During the 1955–1960 period, as much as 78 percent of the animal protein consumed by the average Japanese came from fish and fish products. Although the share of fish and fish products has gradually declined since then, it is still one of the most important sources of animal protein in Japan. In the 1971–1975 period, for example, the Japanese depended on fish and fish products for an average of 51 percent of their animal protein intake.[46] Since Japan depends heavily on imported foodstuffs, it wishes to minimize overseas dependence in the fishery area.

The most direct impact of decentralized ocean enclosure has been felt by Japan's distant-water fisheries. In 1974, Japan caught as much as 43.7 percent of its total marine fish measured in weight within two hundred miles of foreign coasts. Particularly extensive were the catches in the coastal waters of the United States and the Soviet Union, respectively accounting for 16.3 percent and 16.7 percent of the country's total marine fishery production. Since 1974, however, Japanese catches within two hundred miles of foreign coasts have clearly declined. In 1977, for example, they accounted for 29.9 percent of the total marine fishery production.[47]

The fishing industry in Japan is spearheaded by its national organization—the Japan Fisheries Association. Its membership encompasses all private fishery organizations and all major fishing companies in the country. Although it is not a monolithic group in terms of the interests it coordinates and represents at the national level, the association is the dominant fishery group in the country and exerts substantial influence in fishery policy-making in the government. As of 1979, its membership numbered 414 enterprises representing all phases of the fishery industry, including production, processing, marketing, fishing machinery and tool manufacture, and fishery shipbuilding.[48]

The association has fifteen standing committees on a wide range of fishery concerns such as planning, fishery resource development, finances, international fisheries problems, seamen's labor problems, marketing, taxation, and so forth. Its functions include coordination of views and opinions of member fishermen, companies, and organizations on questions of general importance to the industry; studies of fisheries problems; formulation and implementation of private-level measures concerning domestic and international fisheries problems; submission of the industry's requests and petitions to the government, Diet members, and political parties; public relations campaigns; and promotion of information exchange with interested parties both at home and abroad. Furthermore, the association administers government fishery programs such as the disbursement of government-funded subsidies and government-supported loans. The association's leadership also participates in private-level international fisheries negotiations. The group has sent its representatives to the Third UNCLOS since its first session in New York in 1973, indicat-

ing the concern of the industry about the impact of the demise of the traditional ocean regime on the Japanese fishery interests.

Although the Japan Fisheries Association presumably represents the
interests of the fishery industry as a whole, it is often strongly influenced
by the distant-water fishery interests and the major fishing companies.
The interests of coastal (and predominantly small-scale) fisheries are
nationally represented by the National Federation of Fisheries Cooperatives. Coastal fishermen are organized into some 2,500 local fisheries
cooperatives throughout the country. The local cooperatives send their
representatives to their prefectural associations, which are in turn represented at the national federation level.

The two nationally organized fishery groups do not necessarily prefer
the same fishery policies. For example, until 1976 the Japan Fisheries
Association, dominated by the distant-water fishery interests, bitterly and
persistently opposed national ocean enclosure, be it by other countries or
by Japan, whereas the position of the National Federation of Fisheries
Cooperatives was more ambivalent. Fishery cooperatives in the northern
and northeastern coastal areas of Japan preferred early extension of
Japan's territorial sea limit from three to twelve miles. They were also
more eager to see Japan's own 200-mile fishery zone established than
were the fishermen in the southern and southwestern parts of Japan. The
disagreement between these groups of coastal fishery groups presented
some difficulty for government-level decision making on these questions
in 1976 and 1977.

In discussing Japan's fishery interests, one cannot overlook the important ties between the fishery industry and the national government. It
was close government-industry policy coordination that helped increase
fishery production in the postwar years of food shortages, unemployment
problems, and low income levels. The industry, represented by both
national organizations, has several channels through which to influence
the government's fishery policy. First, it directly submits appeals, requests, and petitions to the Fisheries Agency and the Ministry of Agriculture, Forestry, and Fisheries. Second, it sponsors annual fishery promotion conferences to which high-ranking government officials and
representatives of the pro-fishery members of the Diet and of the ruling
Liberal Democratic Party (LDP) are invited. Third, there are personal
links between the Fisheries Agency and the industry in that many former
agency officials find employment in top-level positions in the industry
after retirement from the public sector. Fourth, the industry often

endorses parliamentary candidates and actively supports their election bids. Fifth, the industry sends its representatives to the meeting of the LDP Policy Affairs Research Council's Fishery Division. Sixth, sometimes representatives of the industry are invited to appear before parliamentary hearings to present the industry's views and opinions on major fishery legislation. Seventh, the industry, particularly the Japan Fisheries Association, often sponsors informal meetings and social events attended by Cabinet-level government representatives, high-ranking bureaucrats, and LDP representatives. Finally, the industry conducts opinion-making campaigns through the mass media, the industry's periodicals, and occasional publications. We will see how the industry used these channels to influence government-level decision making regarding ocean policy.

2

The First and Second
United Nations Conferences
on the Law of the Sea

JAPAN knew what its immediate stakes were when the enclosure and the antienclosure forces met head-on in Geneva in 1958 and then again in 1960. It joined the other traditional maritime powers of the West against the expansionist claims by the Communist bloc members and the developing coastal states led by some extremist Latin American countries. It fought single-handedly, however, when the other traditional maritime partners began showing a more accommodating attitude as the debate proceeded.

The First UNCLOS

On February 21, 1956, the General Assembly of the United Nations in its eleventh session adopted a resolution (Resolution 1105 [XI]) calling upon its members to convene a conference to

> examine the law of the sea, taking account not only of the legal but also of the technical, biological, economic, and political aspects of the problem and embody the results of the work in one or more international conventions or such other instruments as it may deem appropriate.[1]

In accordance with the resolution, eighty-six states, including Japan, participated in the First United Nations Conference on the Law of the Sea (UNCLOS) in Geneva from February 24 to April 28, 1958. Earlier, the International Law Commission had held six sessions of discussions on the legal aspects of the law of the sea and in its eighth session in 1956 produced a report including seventy-three draft articles with commentary.[2]

This report then served as the working paper of the first law of the sea conference except for the question of landlocked states, which was placed on the conference agenda at the last minute by the General Assembly.[3] Since Japan had not participated in the commission's work because it did not become a member of the Untied Nations until December 18, 1956, the Geneva Conference was the first formal opportunity for Japan to present its views and listen to the others'.

The basic work of the conference was divided among four committees: First Committee—the Territorial Sea and Contiguous Zone; Second Committee—the High Seas Regime; Third Committee—Fishing and Conservation of Living Resources of the High Seas; and Fourth Committee—the Continental Shelf. There were major conflicts and disagreements on all central issues of the law of the sea. Most pronounced, however, was the division on the question of the breadth of the territorial sea and contiguous zone—the question that the League of Nations had failed to settle in 1930. The territorial sea is the belt of water off the coastal state over which the state exercises sovereign rights, subject to limitations imposed by international law. In, over, or under this belt of water, no other nation can sail, fly, or lay cables unless otherwise approved by the coastal state. Should coastal states extend their territorial sea limits beyond three miles, the Western maritime nations feared, the traditional freedoms of navigation, fishing, flight, and laying of submarine cables would be curtailed to the detriment of their security and economic interests.

The maritime nations of the West—for example, the United States, Great Britain, Holland, Belgium, Greece, France, West Germany, and Japan—wanted to preserve the 3-mile limit. It was the United States that led the fight against extension of territorial sea limits beyond three miles. Arthur H. Dean, chairman of the United States delegation to the conference stated that an "extension of the territorial sea threatens the security of the United States by reducing the efficiency of its naval and air power, and by subjecting it to increased risk of surprise attacks."[4] Locked in the cold war confrontation with the Soviet Union, the People's Republic of China, and other Communist bloc members, the United States was concerned that extended territorial seas of neutral nations would dramatically increase the striking power of enemy submarines and that the extension of the breadth of territorial seas in areas such as the Mediterranean Sea and off the coast of Mainland China would reduce the high seas area in which the United States fleet could operate.[5]

Another serious consequence of territorial sea extension beyond the traditional 3-mile limit related to straits areas of the world. The United States wanted to preserve both ships' right of innocent passage in straits connecting paths of the high seas, even though the straits were entirely territorial seas, and aircrafts' right to overflight.[6] The United States was also concerned that new bilateral treaties and other agreements would have to be negotiated, that commercial shipping might be forced to take longer and more costly routes, that ships' movements might be interrupted or delayed, that freight and passenger aircraft might similarly be hampered or disrupted, and that international disputes over unintentional violation of foreign territory by aerial overflight might increase.[7] With these concerns, the United States argued that the 3-mile limit was firmly established in international law and that the limit was a proper compromise between the interests of the coastal states and the principle of freedom of the seas. Lest there be no agreement, however, the superpower indicated it was willing to consider other proposals.[8]

It soon became clear that no proposal, either for or against the 3-mile limit, would secure the required two-thirds vote in the plenary session. Thereupon, the United States put forth a compromise proposal that the territorial sea limit be extended to six miles and beyond that the coastal state could exercise the right to regulate fishing up to another six miles. A proviso was attached to the proposal. It stated that if a foreign country's vessels had been fishing within the 12-mile limit for five or more years prior to the date of signature of a new convention incorporating the U.S. proposal, they could continue fishing there.

In the plenary session, the compromise proposal of the United States received more votes than any other proposal on the territorial sea question. It was supported by all NATO members except Iceland, by Greece, Italy, Spain, Pakistan, South Vietnam, Turkey, by all British Commonwealth members except Canada, and by some Middle Eastern countries such as Iran and Lebanon. However, the affirmative votes were seven short of the requisite two-thirds majority.[9]

Japan abstained from voting on the compromise proposal. The Japanese delegation asserted that three miles was the maximum breadth of the territorial sea that any state could legitimately claim on the basis of the existing international law.[10] The 3-mile limit, in the Japanese view, was the very embodiment of the principle of freedom of the seas. The Japanese head delegate proclaimed:

Freedom of the high seas was established for the purpose of serving the interest and welfare of the entire international community. Extension of the territorial sea would result in an encroachment upon the area of the high seas open to all nations. Should this Conference decide to take such course of action, it would run counter to the development of international law. I sincerely hope that this Conference will be able to reach an agreement on a uniform limit of three miles for the width of the territorial sea.[11]

When the United Kingdom put forth a compromise proposal for a 6-mile territorial sea, however, the Japanese delegation did concede that it was ready to agree to the proposal if it would help to bring the conference to a fruitful conclusion, even though it would involve much sacrifice on the part of the Japanese people.[12]

The strategy of the Japanese delegation was rather simple. It was to oppose territorial sea extension beyond three miles by emphasizing the universal benefit of preserving the 3-mile limit and freedom of the high seas and, if and only if no position was likely to bring the conference to a successful conclusion—that is, agreement on a uniform breadth of the territorial sea—to show a conciliatory posture but to minimize its concession, perhaps accepting the 6-mile territorial sea limit but nothing beyond that. This strategy meant that the delegation abstained from voting on the U.S. proposal, voted against the Canadian proposal for a 6-mile territorial limit plus a 12-mile exclusive fishing zone, and reluctantly agreed to the British compromise formula.

No proposal on the breadth of the territorial sea received a two-thirds vote in the plenary session, and the conference failed to agree on a uniform limit. Therefore, Japan decided, as did other pro–status quo states including the United States, to adhere to the 3-mile limit as the recognized rule of international law.[13]

Another crucial issue related to the territorial sea question was that of the contiguous zone. The International Law Commission's draft provided that "The coastal state may exercise the control necessary to (a) prevent infringement of its customs, fiscal or sanitary regulations within its territory or territorial sea; (b) punish infringement of the above regulations committed within its territory or territorial sea."[14] The Polish delegation proposed that to exercise control in a high seas area contiguous to its territorial sea, "the coastal state may take the measures necessary to prevent and punish infringements of its customs, fiscal or sanitary regulations, and violations of its security."[15] The proposal was adopted by the First Committee by a vote of 33 to 27 with 15 abstentions.[16] However, it was rejected by the plenary meeting primarily because of the objection of major maritime powers, including Germany, Great Britain, and the United States, to the term "violations of its security." Instead the International Law Commission's draft was adopted by a vote of 60 to 0 with 13 abstentions. Japan voted in favor of it.[17] The adopted article stated: "The contiguous zone may not extend beyond twelve miles from the base line from which the breadth of the territorial sea is measured" (Article 24).[18]

Another instance of Japan's attempt to check coastal states' territorial sea expansion was seen in its proposal concerning the rule for defining the baseline from which the territorial sea was to be measured. In 1951 the International Court of Justice, in the case involving a fishery dispute between Norway and England, had upheld the Norwegian practice of drawing a baseline that followed the general direction of its coast rather than following the sinuosities of the extraordinarily indented coastline. Special geographical circumstances were taken as a legitimate reason for the coastal state to adopt this straight baseline rule instead of the generally accepted low-water mark as the baseline. Following this precedent, the International Law Commission adopted the straight baseline rule in its draft article, which stated, inter alia that such baselines should not depart from the general direction of the coast and that the sea areas lying within the lines must be sufficiently closely linked to the land domain to be subject to the regime of internal waters.[19] As a means to prevent possible abuse of this procedure, Japan proposed that as a general rule, the maximum permissible length for a straight baseline be ten miles, that straight baselines be drawn between headlands of the coastline or between a headland and an island less than five miles from the coast, and that longer baselines be allowed only if no point on such lines was more than five miles from the coast. Japan subsequently withdrew its proposal containing this provision but cosponsored with Germany, Greece, and Italy a joint proposal with a provision virtually identical to it.[20]

The Japanese delegation explained that "unless a maximum permissible length for the straight baseline is fixed, there is always the possibility that a considerable area of the sea might be placed within such lines, amounting to the coastal State subjecting a part of the high seas to their sovereignty."[21] The proposal was later amended to limit the maximum length of baselines to fifteen miles but was rejected by a vote of 30 to 13 with 12 abstentions.[22] Finally, the conference adopted a text virtually identical to the International Law Commission draft.[23] It did not set a maximum limit but nonetheless specified geographical conditions under which a coastal state could draw straight baselines.

Another practice objectionable to Japan was the enclosure by some coastal states of large areas of open bays on the basis of the concept of the historic bay. The concept had been used by the Soviet Union to justify its 1957 decree incorporating the Peter the Great Bay as part of its internal waters. To counter the practice by the Soviet Union and possibly by others, the Japanese delegation proposed a strict definition of "historic bay" as "those bays over which a coastal state or states have effectively exercised sovereign rights continuously for a period of long standing, with explicit or implicit *recognition* of such practice by *foreign states*" (emphasis added).[24] Since Japan would not recognize Soviet sovereignty over the Peter the Great Bay, the Soviet Union's claim would not be justifiable. At the end of the conference, the issue remained unsettled, although trends against Japan appeared.

Another set of law of the sea issues on the agenda of the conference related to the regime of the high seas. In the Second Committee, the Japanese head delegate, Akira Oe, explained his government's policy:

It is hardly necessary for me to dwell upon the fact that the freedom of the high seas was established by the wisdom of man for the purpose of promoting the interest and welfare of mankind, and it is our great satisfaction that the freedom of the high seas, the cardinal principle of international law of the seas, is well provided for in Article 27 of the draft articles prepared by the International Law Commission. As stated clearly in this article, no state may validly purport to subject any part of the high seas to its sovereignty.[25]

Here again it is clear that Japan's basic concern was to preserve as much freedom of the seas as possible and to refer to this principle as part of the "interest and welfare of mankind." Japan's national interest was unmistakably indentified with the status quo. Any attempt to challenge the established order would be rejected by Japan. Such a position was in general accord with those of other major maritime powers, such as the United States and Great Britain. However, as far as the regime of the high seas was concerned, Japan's policy ran counter to that of the United States on an important security issue, namely nuclear testing on the high seas. The atomic bombs dropped on Hiroshima and Nagasaki in August 1945 engendered in the Japanese people and their government an emotional and philosophical aversion to nuclear weapons. Their attitude was further intensified when the United States conducted an atomic bomb test at Bikini Atoll in the Pacific in March 1954, resulting in radioactive contamination of a Japanese tuna boat and a fatal injury to one of its crew members.

The Japanese position on this issue was made explicit in the Second Committee:

> Nuclear tests should not be permitted so far as they obstruct the freedom of the use of the high seas by nationals of other states. . . . [A]s far as the problem of the relationship between nuclear tests and the freedom of the high seas is concerned, the Government of Japan is of the same opinion as that enunciated in the Commentary of Article 27.[26]

The commentary read: "States are bound to refrain from any acts which might adversely affect the use of the high seas by nationals of other states."[27] Herein lay the fundamental problem of freedom of the seas. Should nuclear testing be considered a freedom when it clearly infringed upon the use of the ocean by others? If it was, as the superpowers argued, whose freedom was the international community to protect? In essence, the whole modern law of the sea debate was to find some universally acceptable solution to the problem of the clash of "freedoms" that resulted from the advancement of technology, be it weaponry, fishing, mining, transportation, or science. When Japan's freedom to fish was seen by coastal states as an encroachment on their resources, Japan failed to recognize (or if it did, it did not admit) that freedom is only relative, but when the superpowers' freedom to conduct military research and development infringed upon Japan's fishing interests, it accused them of violating Japanese rights. The conflicts are different in impact and substance but the same in principle. Japan's call to incorporate into the new law of the sea a ban on nuclear testing on the high seas failed, however, when two proposals by Yugoslavia and Poland to this effect were rejected and instead the Indian move to refer this matter to the General Assembly for appropriate action was adopted by the committee and by the plenary session.[28] The vote on the Indian proposal was 51 to 1 with 14 abstentions in the committee and 58 to 0 with 13 abstentions in the plenary session. Japan was one of the thirteen countries abstaining.[29]

Japan's defense of narrow territorial seas and contiguous zones and broad high seas was predicated on its two axiomatic economic interests:

fishing and shipping. The Japanese head delegate described the importance of the fishing industry and the country's dependence on fisheries resources as follows:

> Because Japan is surrounded by some of the world's richest fishing grounds and since its sea-faring people have attained by extensive study and years of experience, a high degree of fishing techniques, Japan has become the leading fishing country of the world with its total annual catch reaching roughly five million tons, which amounts to almost 20% of the world's entire catch. In order to realize this catch, a vast number of people, most of them operating on a small scale, are engaged in fishing activities, employing about 400 thousand fishing vessels. Since the development of livestock industry is naturally restricted on account of the small limited territory, the Japanese people obtain almost 90% of their animal protein requirements from the living resources of the sea. Moreover, the fishing industry plays an important role in Japan's foreign trade, because a part of the fishing products is exported, enabling Japan to import foodstuffs and raw materials which are not available domestically.[30]

He also defended Japan's interest in maritime transportation:

> In view of the geographical situation and shortage in resources, Japan is dependent to a high degree on its foreign trade to maintain its national economy and to secure the basis of its industry. Consequently, it is the natural outcome of such a situation that shipping should be one of the most important industries in Japan. This industry suffered a serious blow during the last war, but it has since recovered to the extent that the gross tonnage of the ships [has] reached some four million five hundred thousand (4,500,000) tons. Shouldering the task of carrying out Japan's export and import activities, its merchant vessels, today, visit leading ports in all corners of the world, contributing, at the same time, to the development of world trade. Therefore, shipping forms a valuable source of Japan's foreign exchange for financing the import of the necessary foodstuffs and raw materials.[31]

The Japanese delegation put up stiff resistance in the Third Committee to all attempts that would have restricted the freedom of high seas fishing in the name of resource conservation. While indicating concern for fishery resource conservation measures to be established on the high seas, Japan rejected the notion that coastal states were entitled to a special status concerning the conservation of marine living resources and instead supported conservation measures that would give a great deal of discretion to the fishing countries.[32] Thus, in response to the International Law Commission's draft article calling upon fishing nations to adopt conservation measures, the Japanese delegation proposed an amendment that would leave it up to the states "whose nationals are engaged in fishing *certain stock or stocks of fish or other marine resources* in any area of the high seas where the nationals of other states are not thus engaged" to adopt regulatory measures "when necessary."[33] Japan was concerned that the original draft article without the phrase italicized above could be interpreted to mean that states whose nationals did not engage in fishing the stock or stocks in question would have the right to participate in conservation decisions. The Japanese proposal was incorporated into a joint proposal cosponsored by other major fishing countries—namely, France, Germany, Italy, the Netherlands, the United Kingdom, and Yugoslavia— and was unanimously adopted by the plenary session and written into Article 3 of the Convention on the Fishing and Conservation of the Living Resources of the High Seas.[34]

Japan's fight against the extension of coastal states' resource jurisdiction extended elsewhere. To counter a move in the committee to recognize special interests of coastal states in the management, research, regulation, and conservation of fishery resources in the high seas areas adjacent to coastal states' territorial seas, Japan submitted a proposal that would have given equal recognition to the special interests of both fishing and coastal states.[35] The Japanese delegation withdrew this measure, however, when Sweden submitted a set of proposals containing the same provision. Japan, Sweden, Germany, the Netherlands, Italy, and Greece supported the Swedish proposal, but the committee defeated it.[36] As a result, the Convention on Fishing and Conservation of the Living Resources of the High Seas accorded coastal states a special status as to the ocean areas adjacent to their territorial waters. More specifically, the provision entitled them to participate in any system of research and regulation for resource conservation purposes regardless of whether their nationals engaged in fishing in the areas concerned.[37] Furthermore, according to the convention, coastal states could demand that states fishing near their shores agree on conservation measures and, if necessary, enter into agreement or arbitration arrangements with them.[38]

Japan was opposed to other major attempts by a number of coastal states to expand regulatory mechanisms for conservation purposes. One such attempt came from the United States and Canada, which sponsored the so-called principle of abstention. According to this principle, where the nationals of a coastal state, alone or with the nationals of other states, were fishing a stock in an area of the high seas adjacent to the coastal states' territorial waters to the extent that a further increase in fishing efforts would not result in a substantial increase in the yield maintainable year after year, and where the maintenance of an improvement upon the current yield depended on a conservation program of those states, states that had not fished the stock in question on a regular basis or within a reasonable length of time in the past should abstain from fishing that stock. The principle would not apply, however, to the coastal state with respect to fishing any stock in waters adjacent to its own territorial sea. This time Japan's effort to defeat the proposal was successful, thanks to support from other major distant-water fishing states, including the Soviet Union, Norway, Sweden, the Netherlands, France, Portugal, Bulgaria, Poland, Spain, Germany, the United Kingdom, and Italy.[39]

Japan's persistent defense of the freedom of the seas extended to its delegation's position on another set of law of the sea questions, the continental shelf regime, debated in the Fourth Committee. The two questions that concerned Japan more than anything else in this issue-area were the outer limit of the continental shelf and the definition of "continental shelf resources." On the first question, the International Law Commission had not been able to adopt a uniform draft provision and instead posited competing means of defining the limit of the continental shelf side by side. One proposal defined the continental shelf as the seabed and subsoil of the submarine areas adjacent to the coast but outside the areas of the territorial sea, to where the depth of the superjacent waters admitted of the exploitation of natural resources—the so-called "exploitability" criterion. An alternative definition would have limited the continental shelf to the seabed and subsoil of the submarine areas to the depth of two hundred meters. The fear that "exploitability" could be extended by technological advancement to the detriment of states operating in foreign coastal waters led Japan to support the French proposal based on the 200-meter depth criterion.[40] Neither definition could marshall enough support, however, and the conference decided to adopt a definition that combined the exploitablity criterion and the depth criterion. According to this definition, the continental shelf refers to:

(a) the seabed and subsoil of the submarine areas adjacent to the coast but outside the area of the territorial sea, to a depth of 200 meters, or beyond that limit, to where the depth of the superjacent waters admits of the exploitation of the natural resources of the said areas; (b) the seabed and subsoil of similar submarine areas adjacent to the coasts of islands.[41]

The conference also adopted the principle of median line for drawing the boundary of the continental shelf appertaining to coastal states whose coasts are adjacent to the same continental shelf or are opposite each other, unless some other boundary is drawn by agreement.[42]

In the continental shelf thus defined, the coastal state would exercise sovereign or exclusive rights with regard to the exploitation of natural resources. What then was the definition of "natural resources" on the continental shelf? Should living resources as well as mineral resources be included in the definition? The International Law Commission stated in its commentary on the draft resolution on the continental shelf that attempts were made but failed that would have included in the definition those natural resources permanently attached to the seabed or all marine life living in constant physical and biological relationship with the seabed. The commission did not take a stand on whether the continental shelf resources would include shrimp and other crustaceans.[43] In response to a proposal to distinguish between sedentary and nonsedentary species, with the former to be included in the definition of continental shelf resources that would be placed under coastal states' monopoly, the Japanese delegation pointed out that whether a species was fixed to the seabed or not was a relative question and was an inappropriate standard to be applied as a legal criterion. Japan's argument apparently lacked sufficient support, for the conference decided to make the sedentary/nonsedentary differentiation and judged organisms in constant physical contact with the seabed or the subsoil, such as pearl oysters, to belong to the sovereignty of the coastal states.[44]

In the end the conference adopted four conventions: the Convention on the Territorial Sea and Contiguous Zone; the Convention on the High Seas; the Convention on Fishing and Conservation of Living Resources of the High Seas; and the Convention on the Continental Shelf.[45] Japan voted in favor of the first two conventions, abstained from voting on the third, and voted against the last. Japan became a party to the Convention on the High Seas on July 10, 1968. By then, the convention had gone into effect with sufficient signatories (on September 30, 1962). By the time Japan became a party to the Convention on the Territorial Sea and the Contiguous Zone on July 10, 1968, this convention had also gone into force (on September 30, 1964). Japan did not join the Convention on the Continental Shelf, which went into force on June 10, 1964, nor the Convention on Fishing and the Conservation of Living Resources of the High Seas, which went into force on March 20, 1966. In addition to the four conventions, an Optional Protocol of Signatures Concerning the Compulsory Settlement of Disputes was adopted by the conference, and Japan endorsed the document.[46]

As we have seen above, the international community's attempt to agree on a uniform breadth of the territorial sea was unsuccessful. Japan was one of the countries that contributed to that failure. It persistently attempted to block other countries' efforts to extend coastal jurisdiction beyond the traditional 3-mile limit.

The Second UNCLOS

The United Nations General Assembly adopted a resolution on December 10, 1958, calling upon member states to meet again to take up several law of the sea problems that had not been settled by the First UNCLOS, including the breadth of the territorial sea and the establishment of fishing zones by coastal states in the areas of the high seas beyond the territorial sea. All but one of the states, Afghanistan, that had participated in the First Conference, and two new countries, Cameroon and Guinea, attended the Second Conference in Geneva in 1960.[47]

A number of proposals submitted to the second conference, if adopted, would have had important consequences for Japan's position on both the territorial sea and the fishing zone. The first such proposal, co-sponsored by Canada and the United States, allowed the coastal state to establish a fishing zone extending out to twelve miles and to grant itself exclusive jurisidiction over all living resources within the limit. The proposal had one qualification, which was to suspend coastal states' exclusive fishing jurisdiction and allow fishing by other states with "historic rights" between six and twelve miles from the coast for ten years starting on October 31, 1960. It recognized historic rights for states that could show their fishing vessels had made a practice of fishing in the area between January 1, 1953, and January 1, 1958. Past the ten-year grace period, foreign nationals would not be allowed to fish in the 12-mile fishing zone unless otherwise permitted by the coastal state by agreement.[48]

The Soviet Union submitted the second important proposal. It would have permitted each state to choose for itself any territorial limit from three to twelve miles, plus a 12-mile fishing zone measured from its baseline.[49] This proposal would also have increased pressure upon coastal states to extend their territorial sea limits to twelve miles, for if one state extended its territorial sea limit to twelve miles and the sea limit of its adjacent state remained at three miles, the latter would not have been allowed to fish anywhere in the former's fishery zone, while the former could fish anywhere beyond the latter's 3-mile limit. Under such circumstances, the latter would be inclined to extend its territorial sea limit to twelve miles to be on an equal footing with the other.[50]

Mexico, Indonesia, the Philippines, Ethiopia, Ghana, Guinea, Iran, Iraq, Jordan, Lebanon, Libya, Morocco, Saudi Arabia, Sudan, Tunisia, the United Arab Republic, Venezuela, and Yemen put forth what became known as the "18-Power" proposal. It provided that any state that had fixed its territorial sea or contiguous zone limit at fewer than twelve miles from its coast would be entitled, vis-à-vis any other state with a wider delimitation, to exercise its sovereignty or rights with respect to fishing and the exploitation of the sea's living resources up to the same limit fixed by the other state.[51]

The fourth major proposal was cosponsored by Mexico, Venezuela, Indonesia, Lebanon, Morocco, Saudi Arabia, Sudan, the United Arab Republic, and Yemen. This proposal called upon all UNCLOS participants that had declared their independence prior to October 24, 1945—the date the United Nations Charter went into force—to abstain from extending their present territorial sea limits pending the consideration of this question by the General Assembly or by another conference that might be convened in the future but in the meantime to recognize the 12-mile fishing zone.[52] Presumably, those states that became independent after October 24, 1945, could extend their territorial sea limits as they chose.[53]

Of these competing proposals, the third and the fourth were rejected by the Committee of the Whole, and the Soviet proposal was withdrawn.[54] The Canada-U.S. proposal for the 6 + 6-mile limit with a ten-year grace period almost made it. It was adopted by the Committee of the Whole by a vote of 43 to 33, with 12 abstentions and submitted to the plenary session, where several attempts at compromise were made, a few proving successful.[55] One such attempt was designed to reconcile, on the one hand, the desire on the part of Latin American countries (such as Argentina, Peru, and Cuba) and Iceland to accord themselves preferential fishing rights beyond twelve miles off their coasts and, on the other hand, the objection to such preferential rights by Japan, the Western European fishing states, the United States, and Canada.[56]

The United States proposed that the dispute settlement procedure under the auspices of an international commission that had been set up by Article 9 of the 1958 Convention on Fishing and Conservation of the Living Resources of the High Seas should apply to coastal states' claims regarding preferential fishing rights on the high seas and that the international commission should hear evidence to be submitted by both foreign and coastal states to pass on the scientific justification for such preferential rights beyond the 12-mile limit.[57] When the United States approached Canada, Western European, and Latin American countries with this proposal, Brazil, Cuba, and Uruguay responded positively by submitting to the plenary session a formal proposal of amendments to the original Canada-U.S. joint proposal. The Latin American proposal provided that coastal states could claim preferential fishing rights on the high seas adjacent to their exclusive fishing zones when they could scientifically establish that the exploitation of the living resources in the area was of fundamental importance to their economic development or food supply. According to the proposed amendments, the international commission would make decisions on the basis of technical, geographical, biological, and economic evidence presented by the coastal and fishing states. The Latin American proposal also provided that the provisions in the Canada-U.S. proposal regarding historic fishing rights and the ten-year grace period should not apply or might be varied, as between states that concluded bilateral, multilateral, or regional fishery agreements.[58]

When the proposed amendments received over two-thirds of the votes in the plenary session (58 for, 19 against, 10 abstentions), Japan abstained because of the fishing industry's objections.[59] Japan continued to advocate unrestricted high seas fishing beyond the 3-mile territorial sea limit. The most it could accept, with great reluctance, was the original Canada-U.S. proposal for the 6-mile territorial sea coupled with the 6-mile fishing zone beyond it.

Chile and Ecuador had indicated that they intended to abstain on the Canada-U.S. joint proposal as amended by the successful Brazil–Cuba–Uruguay proposal, but at the last minute they decided to vote against it.[60] As a result, the proposal fell one vote short of the requisite two-thirds majority in the plenary session. The final count was 54 votes in favor, 28 opposed, with 5 abstentions.[61] The affirmative votes came from every

Western European country except Iceland; from Thailand, Laos, Vietnam, Ceylon, Pakistan, and Malaya; and from the other members of the British Commonwealth of Nations, except India.[62] The negative votes were cast by India; the Soviet Union and its eight allies; Yugoslavia; seven Arab states including Saudi Arabia, Yemen, the United Arab Republic, Libya, Morocco, the Sudan, and Iraq; and Mexico, Panama, Venezuela, Ecuador, Peru, Chile, Guinea, Burma, Indonesia, and Iceland. The five abstaining states were Japan, Cambodia, El Salvador, Iran, and Lebanon.[63]

Again, Japan's adherence to the principle of freedom of the seas and opposition to any attempt to accord coastal states preferential fishing rights, much less territorial claims, beyond the 3-mile limit contributed to the defeat of attempts at compromise. This proved to be critical, for following the unsuccessful Second UNCLOS one coastal state after another resorted to unilateral actions to expand their territorial sea and fishery jurisdictional claims.

3

Japan's Fight Against the Proliferation of Expansionist Coastal States' Claims

The Trend Toward National Enclosure

IT has been clearly demostrated in the foregoing discussion that Japan was a strong advocate for the traditional ocean regime with the freedom of the seas as its cardinal principle. Particularly on the issues of the breadth of the territorial sea and contiguous zone and high-seas fishing, Japan's defense of the existing order was more persistent and more systematic than that of any other beneficiary of that order. On one issue—the territorial sea and fishing zone—Japan's inflexibility, as manifested by its abstention from the vote on the Canada–United States joint compromise proposal at the Second UNCLOS, had a decisive impact on the outcome of the conference. Instead of adopting a convention setting a uniform territorial sea limit of six miles and a 12-mile fishing zone, the conference adjourned without agreement in this area. Some observers in Japan criticized the apparent obstinence of their government as a sign of shortsightedness and attributed much of the proliferation of unilateral claims that followed the Second UNCLOS to this "diplomatic failure." They argued in effect that had Japan's affirmative vote resulted in the adoption by the UNCLOS of the 6 + 6 proposal, the expansionist aspirations of the less developed coastal states would have been quelled.[1] In my view, however, the sources of national enclosure discussed in chapter 1 could not have been substantially reduced, much less eliminated by a 1960 UNCLOS agreement on uniform rules for territorial or fishery zone delimitation. Such an agreement may have delayed some coastal states' unilateral moves, but technological advancement, intensified competition for resources—"resource nationalism," as some would call it—environmental concerns, and so forth, all of which have contributed to the trend toward national enclosure, are long-term, irreversible historical forces that would not have been readily contained by a political-legal adjustment, however noble and desirable such attempts might have been from the collective, global perspective.

It cannot be denied, however, that unilateral claims proliferated after the Second UNCLOS. The number of countries claiming a 12-mile territorial sea limit jumped from six in 1955 to twenty-seven in 1965 and then to thirty-nine in 1970. By 1965, 12-mile fishing zones had been established by twenty-one states and by the beginning of the 1970s, twenty-four, as compared with only two in 1955. There were as many as ten countries with 200-mile territorial sea or fishery zone claims by 1970 but only four such states in 1955. In contrast, the number of countries claiming a 3-mile territorial sea dropped from thirty-three in 1955 to twenty-one in 1965 and then to only nine 1970. Likewise, states with a territorial sea limit between four and ten miles decreased from eighteen in 1955 to eleven in 1965 and then to seven in 1970.[2] Furthermore, as of June 1970, there were five states that claimed various types of rights over fishing beyond a 12-mile limit.[3] Moreover, ten countries claimed territorial sovereignty or fishery jurisdiction to even greater distances. Table 1 shows the number of states that established territorial sea limits and/or fishery zones extending beyond three miles before the Second World War, between the war and the Second UNCLOS, and between the Second UNCLOS and June 1970.

TABLE 1
Territorial Sea and Fishery Zone Claims by Period

Claim	Pre-WW II	Pre-UNCLOS II (1945–1960)	Post-UNCLOS II (1960–1970)	Total
12-mile territorial sea	2	10	33*	45
12-mile fishery zone	1	1	16	18
25-mile territorial sea	0	0	1	1
130-mile territorial sea	0	0	1	1
200-mile territorial sea or fishery zone	0	5	5	10

SOURCE: Kenzo Kawakami, *Sengo no Kokusai Gyogyō Seido* [The postwar international fisheries regime], p. 790.
*Including five states claiming fishery jurisdiction beyond and in addition to the 12-mile territorial sea limit.

Expansion of territorial or fishery jurisdiction beyond the traditional 3-mile limit was global. In North America, Canada established a 9-mile fishery zone beyond its 3-mile territorial sea limit in 1904 and further extended its territorial sea claim out to twelve miles in 1970. The United States also set up a fishery zone extending nine miles beyond its 3-mile territorial sea limit in 1966. Mexico promulgated a law in 1967 establishing a 9-mile territorial sea and a fishery zone extending three miles beyond it. In 1969, its territorial sea limit was further extended to twelve miles.[4]

In Central America, Costa Rica had laid a 200-mile fishery zone claim as early as 1948, followed by an El Salvadorian claim in 1950 of a 200-mile territorial sea and 200-mile fishery zone in 1955. Nicaragua's 200-mile fishery zone was established in 1965. In 1967, Panama promulgated a law laying territorial claim out to 200 miles from its coast. As of 1970, Guatemala and Honduras remained the only countries in Central America that had not followed their neighbors' examples.[5]

In South America, by 1970, six of the eight coastal states had established either a 200-mile territorial sea (Ecuador, 1966;[6] Argentina, 1967; Uruguay, 1969; Brazil, 1970), or a 200-mile fishery zone (Chile, 1947; Peru, 1947).[7]

In Africa, eighteen coastal states maintained a 12-mile territorial sea and four claimed a 12-mile fishery zone as of 1970.[8] Guinea set up a 130-mile territorial sea in 1964. In addition, Ghana laid a 100-mile fishery zone claim beyond its 12-mile territorial sea, and Senegal and Namibia asserted 6-mile fishery jurisdictional claims beyond their 12-mile territorial sea limits.[9]

In Western Europe, twelve coastal states concluded a fishery agreement in 1964 to set up their respective 12-mile fishery zones.[10] Earlier, Iceland and Norway—not parties to the European fishery agreement—had already established 12-mile fishery zones in 1958 and 1961, respectively. In Eastern Europe, the Soviet Union, Rumania, and Bulgaria had declared 12-mile territorial seas by 1951. Yugoslavia set up a 10-mile territorial sea in 1965. Poland joined the European fishery agreement, thus becoming a member of the 12-mile club.[11]

In the Near and Middle East, before or immediately after the Second UNCLOS, a number of countries unilaterally established 12-mile territorial seas, including the United Arab Republic (1958), Saudi Arabia (1958), Iraq (1958), and Iran (1959). Turkey established a 6-mile fishery zone beyond its 6-mile territorial sea in 1964. Syria, Cyprus, Kuwait,

Yemen, and South Yemen asserted 12-mile territorial sea claims in 1963, 1964, 1967, 1967, and 1970, respectively.[12]

In Asia, Cambodia claimed a 7-mile fishery zone beyond its 5-mile territorial sea in 1957 but extended the territorial sea limit to twelve miles in 1969. Indonesia began planning its 12-mile territorial sea in 1957. After the Second UNCLOS, six Asian states established 12-mile territorial seas, including Thailand (1966), Pakistan (1966), India (1967), Burma (1968), Malaysia (1969), and Ceylon (1970).[13] Elsewhere, New Zealand and Australia each maintained 3-mile territorial seas and, beyond them, 9-mile fishery zones.[14]

From the Japanese perspective unilateral actions continued ad nauseum throughout the 1960s. A prominent Japanese legal scholar and advisor to the Japanese UNCLOS delegation, Shigeru Oda, concluded in 1972 that by then the 12-mile fishery zone had become an accepted rule of international law.[15] While the multilateral debate addressed principles that were to be universalized, Japan's arguments against pro-enclosure principles were by necessity couched in general, legal terms bordering on philosophical espousal; its fight against the expansionist claims of the Pacific-rim states during the following decade was considerably more pragmatic and specific. This was primarily because the problem Japan faced in bilateral negotiations with Pacific coastal states was a more urgent one that required an immediate and concrete response. At stake in these talks was Japanese access to distant-water fisheries in high seas areas under a threat of "nationalization" by Pacific-rim states that included South Korea, the United States, Mexico, New Zealand, and Australia. The threat was no longer one of a general, philosophical nature that could be countered by legal arguments alone; it had to do with the real issue of the size of Japan's fish catch and the food supply for Japanese consumers.

The essence of the challenge was whether Japan should recognize the legitimacy of unilaterally established fishery zones. Japan met this challenge head-on as it negotiated with South Korea from 1952 to 1965, with the United States in 1967, with New Zealand in 1967, with Mexico in 1968, and with Australia in 1968.

The Japan–South Korea Fishery Agreement

The Japan–South Korea fishery agreement concluded in June 1965 was a product of fourteen years of arduous and often hostile negotiations between the two countries made necessary by the 1952 Korean "Presidential Proclamation of Sovereignty Over the Adjacent Sea." President Syngman Rhee's declaration established what became known as the Rhee Line, which extended from twenty to almost two hundred miles from the Korean coast.[16] Within this line, the proclamation stated, Korea had exclusive sovereign jurisdiction over and control of the preservation, protection, conservation, and utilization of all natural resources. The proclamation was followed in 1953 by the promulgation of the Fisheries Resources Protection Act to implement the new policy. The implementation involved seizure of foreign fishing vessels and detention of fishermen who violated the law. As a result, by 1965, when diplomatic relations between the two countries were normalized and a fishery agreement was concluded, 326 Japanese fishing vessels had been seized and 3,904 Japanese fishermen detained by Korean authorities.[17] Japan protested what it considered were unlawful acts on the grounds that the presidential proclamation and the accompanying domestic legislation ran counter to the principle of the freedom of the high seas that had long been established in the international community and also that they were inconsistent with the basic principle of international cooperation for the development and protection of high seas resources.[18]

A bilateral fishery committee to discuss the fishery problems between Japan and Korea had been set up in February 1952. It was one of several committees established to conduct negotiations for the eventual normalization of diplomatic relations, which had been severed by the Japanese annexation of Korea in 1910. No sooner had the committee begun its work than it became evident that the respective claims of the two governments were irreconcilable. Japan proposed that the two governments establish and implement on an equal basis joint measures to maintain a maximum sustainable yield of the fishery resources in which both countries had a common interest, that trawl fisheries be banned for a specific time period in those areas where scientific data would warrant such action, and that a joint committee be established to conduct a scientific survey and research concerning preservation and effective utilization of fishery resources of mutual concern.[19] Korea proposed that such measures as were proposed by Japan be established on the high seas outside the Korean fishery zone, beyond and adjacent to its territorial sea. This was clearly intended to establish the legitimacy of Korean jurisdiction within the Rhee Line.[20] The proposals were so far apart that there was no possible ground for agreement, and the negotiations were discontinued on April 25.

The second round of talks in May–June 1952, the third round in October 1953, and the fourth round in October 1958 all failed. The Korean side insisted throughout that Japan recognize the Rhee Line and Korean jurisdiction within the zone, and the Japanese flatly refused to do so. What further complicated the already strained fishery relations between the two countries was the establishment in September 1952 of a "defense zone" inside the Rhee Line by the international forces under the united command of the United States as part of their Korean War efforts. The Rhee government took this opportunity to step up its coastal patrol and increase the seizure of Japanese fishing vessels within the Rhee Line.

The relationship between the two countries deteriorated to the extent that in February 1953, a Japanese fishing boat was fired on and one fisherman was killed by Korean authorities. When the defense zone was eliminated on August 27, 1953, after a ceasefire agreement was signed on the Korean Peninsula on July 27, the Rhee government ordered all Japanese fishing vessels to move outside of the Rhee Line by September 8. When many Japanese boats ignored the order and continued their operations, Korean authoirties seized, searched, and forced them out of the Korean-claimed area; there was even firing at some.[21] These incidents and the unbridgeable gap between the two governments' claims regarding the Korean fishery zone led to the discontinuation of the third round of negotiations in 1953. Fishery negotiations were not resumed until 1958. The fourth round of talks began in October 1958, only to be broken off again in December. They were resumed in October 1959, but were again suspended soon afterward when the two sides could not find grounds for compromise.[22]

The April Nineteenth Uprising of 1960 brought about the downfall of the Rhee government, and a new government emerged under Chang Myon. Chang's regime came to an abrupt end when the government was toppled by a military coup on May 18, and Korea entered a period of military rule that was to last until December 1963. The military government agreed to the resumption of the overall bilateral negotiations in October 1961, and the fishery committee met for a sixth round of talks. In the beginning of 1962, when the two governments had moved closer on other issues, particularly on the war reparations question, the main focus of the negotiations shifted to the fishery relations between the two countries. In December, Japan indicated that it would be willing to consider a settlement similar to the 6 + 6 proposal proposed by Canada and the United States at the Second UNCLOS in 1960. According to the scheme, a foreign country whose nationals had been fishing for five years or more in a newly established fishery zone would be able to continue fishing in the zone for another ten years.

For specific regulatory measures, the Japanese negotiating team proposed the following:

1. Japan would recognize the establishment of a Korean high seas fishery zone extending twelve miles from Korea's coast in which Korea would exercise the same rights over fishing as it did in its territorial sea.

2. Korea would recognize the continuation of Japanese fishing in the outer 6-mile area of the fishery zone for ten years after the bilateral agreement went into force.

3. Within this area, fishing boats of both countries would be subject to their respective governments' enforcement jurisdiction.

4. Japan possessed the right to establish a fishery zone according to the same conditions as in item 1.[23]

The Korean side countered by stating, first, that fishery conservation measures were necessary not only within the 12-mile limit but also beyond it in view of the worsening resource situation due to Japanese fishing and, second, that the Geneva Convention on the High Seas Fisheries provided for the special interests and preferential fishing rights of coastal states. The Korean team also pointed out that the Japan–U.S.– Canada and Japan-Soviet fishery agreements also provided for the preferential rights of the coastal states concerned and that the same rights should be recognized for Korea.[24] Japan's response was basically that a 12-mile fishery zone was the maximum compromise that it could accept. When Korea later submitted a proposal that included a provision for a 40-mile Korean fishery zone, the Japanese negotiating team could not accept it even though it was clearly smaller than the area enclosed by the Rhee Line.[25]

Besides the 40-mile provision, the new Korean proposal called for joint regulatory measures in specified areas outside of its fishery zone, a ban on trawl fisheries in areas already designated by the respective countries' domestic laws, and the establishment of a joint committee to conduct resource research in these areas and to settle fishery disputes between the nationals of the two countries.[26] Japan agreed to discuss these measures but rejected the 40-mile fishery zone provision. A Japanese counterproposal—dubbed as a "private position" of its chief negotiator—showed readiness to agree to some joint regulatory arrangements in the 12-mile zone.[27] The Korean side responded with its own "private position," according to which eventually all Japanese fishing would be excluded from a joint regulatory zone outside the Japanese-proposed 12-mile zone.[28] Although subsequent negotiations showed some progress, the two countries could not reach agreement, and negotiations were again suspended in April 1964.[29]

In the meantime, on December 17, 1963, a new civilian government had been installed under General Park Chung Hee, and with renewed energy the two governments got on with the task of reconciling their differences on diplomatic and economic issues, including fisheries. The seventh round of overall negotiations resumed in December 1964 and continued through the summer of the following year. The fishery committee also met during this period. To break the deadlock in the negotiations, the two sides decided to upgrade the talks to the ministerial level. The Japanese agriculture and forestry minister and the Korean fishery agency director-general met ten times from March 3 to 24 and produced a general agreement. After all necessary technicalities were worked out, the two governments finalized the agreement in June 1965. Together with other agreements dealing with the bilateral relations and the status of Korean residents in Japan, the fishery agreement was ratified by each country and went into force on December 18, 1965. At the same time, a private-level fishery agreement that dealt with the safety of fishing operations of Korea and Japanese nationals went into effect.[30]

As the preamble of the government-level agreement stated, its objectives were (1) to maintain a maximum sustainable yield of fishery resources of mutual interest to Japan and Korea; (2) to contribute to the preservation and rational exploitation and development of the resources; (3) to respect the principle of freedom of the high seas except in areas otherwise specified by the agreement; (4) to eliminate causes of conflict stemming from the geographical proximity and the intersection of fishing activities of the two countries; and (5) to cooperate for the development of the two countries' fisheries.[31] The Japanese side referred to the third objective as grounds for *de facto* abolishment of the Rhee Line because both parties accepted freedom of the high seas as a general rule unless otherwise agreed by the two parties and so specified in the agreement, and no such agreement existed with reference to the controversial fishery zone.[32]

Japan did agree, however, that each party to the agreement had the right to establish an exclusive fishery zone (Article 1). In establishing its fishery zone, according to a note exchanged between the governments, Korea would use the straight baseline formula but would do so only after it consulted and received consent from Japan. In this connection, an interesting agreement, according to a note exchanged between the foreign ministers, was that Korea would not draw a straight baseline but rather, as a provisional measure, would designate an area around Saishūtō Island (Cheju, in Korean)—located between Japan and Korea—which lies beyond twelve miles from the Korean coast, as part of the Korean fishery zone. This agreement became necessary when a dispute occurred because Japan insisted that Korea draw the outer limit of its fishery jurisdiction as measured from the low tide line and Korea claimed it had the right to draw a straight baseline for measuring its 12-mile fishery zone, including the area surrounding the island.[33]

Another set of provisions of the agreement related to the establishment of a joint fishery regulation zone beyond the Korean fishery zone. In this zone provisional regulatory measures would be implemented, including the fixing of the maximum number and size of fishing vessels engaged in trawl, purse seine, and angling fisheries, the size of trawl nets and purse seines, the power of fish attraction lamps, and so on.[34] Article 4 of the agreement stated that the enforcement and judicial powers beyond the fishery zone rested with the flag state. Therefore, within the joint fishery zone each country would be in charge of enforcing regulatory measures with respect to the fishing vessels of its own nationals. In other words, Japan successfully defended the high seas status of the area beyond the Korean fishery zone. To avoid possible conflict as to the location of violation by Japanese fishing boats, the foreign ministers of the two countries each issued a statement at the signing of the agreement to the effect that each government was prepared to deal fairly and properly with the determination of violations and the disposition of fishing vessels and their crews in case of violations.[35]

Other areas of agreement included a joint resource research zone outside of the joint regulation zone (Article 5), a joint fishery committee (Articles 6 and 7), safe and orderly fishing activities (Article 8), settlement of disputes (Article 9), and the effective duration of the agreement —five years after the exchange of ratifications (Article 10).[36]

As this review of Japan-Korea fishery negotiations shows, by 1962–

1963 Japan was ready to accept a coastal state's 12-mile fishery zone. Not only was Japan prepared to accept Korea's 12-mile fishery zone; in December 1965, it set up its own vis-à-vis Korean fishermen on the basis of the Japan-Korea fishery agreement. This step was taken in order to place Japan on an equal footing with Korea and to protect Japanese coastal fishing against future intrusion by Korean fishermen. The new fishery zone enclosed the high seas area extending twelve miles from the coasts of the western and southwestern prefectures of Shimane, Yamaguchi, Fukuoka, Saga, and Nagasaki and from the islands lying within these prefectures' administrative limits.

In its bilateral fishery negotiations with other coastal states during the 1960s, however, Japan maintained its formal legal stand against recognition of the coastal state's exclusive fishery jurisdiction beyond the 3-mile territorial sea limit.

Negotiations with the United States

The establishment in 1966 of the United States 12-mile fishery zone also demanded that Japan adjust its policy. When the U.S. Senate was about to begin a public hearing on the establishment of a 9-mile exclusive fishery zone beyond the 3-mile territorial sea, the Japanese government, through its embassy in Washington, presented a verbal note to the State Department saying,

> because a substantial amount of Japanese fishing is historically conducted in the high seas within twelve miles from the United States coast, the Japanese government is deeply concerned with the bills now before the United States Congress to establish a twelve-mile fishing zone. The Japanese government wishes to make clear that the right of Japan as regards the freedom of the high seas fishing will be in no way affected by the enactment of such bills.[37]

Despite repeated Japanese protestations, the Senate passed the fishery zone bill (S.221) on October 5, 1966. With the presidential signature, the legislation (Public Law 89–568) went into effect on October 14, 1966. This made it necessary for Japan and the United States to negotiate a new fishing agreement. After preliminary government-level negotiations, substantive discussions began in Washington on February 6, 1967.

The United States stated that it would consider the following factors in deciding the level of Japanese fishing efforts permitted within the newly established fishing zone: the present extent of U.S. fishing in the area; the competitive relationship between the U.S. and foreign fishermen in the area; and whether or not foreign fishing was of real interest to the countries concerned.[38] The Japanese negotiators, judging these factors to be prejudicial in favor of U.S. fishing interests, proposed a different set of factors to be considered in reaching an agreement on Japanese fishing in the new fishery zone: respect for lawful foreign fishing that had been in operation in the past; practical measures to avoid competition between the countries involved; and conservation of fish stocks as separate from the question of fishery zone.[39] Underlying this list of factors was the basic Japanese position that international precedents supported giving priority to long-established fishing over future fishing possibilities of a coastal state. This fundamental approach to the fishery jurisdiction issue became the standard approach that Japan adopted to meet the challenges of expanding coastal state jurisdiction throughout the 1960s and through the first half of the 1970s.

The basic disagreement between Japan and the United States caused the first substantial round of negotiations to be suspended on February 21, just as the fundamental discrepancy between Japan's and Korea's positions with regard to the latter's fishery zone had caused their negotiations to be broken off several times.

At a more concrete level, there were several types of fisheries in which Japan and the United States had conflicting interests. The first was tuna fishery. The basic conflict was between U.S. game fishing and Japanese distant-water fishing within twelve miles of the U.S. coasts, for example, off New York, Florida, Puerto Rico, Hawaii, Guam, and Samoa, and in the Caribbean. The Japanese position was that in some areas such as those around Hawaii and Samoa, Japan was virtually the only country that had invested extensively in tuna fishery development; that in some other areas, such as those off Puerto Rico, U.S. fishing interests were present; but that in yet other areas, such as those off New York and Florida, Japan was willing to curb its tuna fishing because important U.S. game fishing took place in those areas.[40]

As far as the 12-mile limit was concerned, Japan explained that some tuna longlines can extend as far as forty miles and, depending on the direction of ocean currents, some of them would move within twelve miles of the United States coasts. In such cases, Japan pointed out, total exclusion of its tuna fishing from the newly established fishery zone would affect fishing not only inside but also outside the 12-mile limit. Despite these concerns, Japan ultimately agreed to discontinue tuna fishing within twelve miles of the following areas: the continental United States, Puerto Rico, the Virgin Islands, the Panama Canal, and seven of the Hawaiian Islands.[41]

The basic argument of the Japanese negotiating team regarding "international precedents" in favor of established fishing operations was carried over into negotiations in regard to other fisheries, including whaling, king crab fishery, and trawl and long-lining fisheries. In all these fisheries, Japan proposed that its historical fishing and whaling should be allowed to continue, whereas the United States proposed that such activities be limited to designated areas. It was finally decided that Japanese whaling between 150° west longitude and 163° west longitude would be discontinued.[42] As far as king crab fishery was concerned, the two sides agreed that Japan would discontinue fishing within the 12-mile limit except in the area between three and twelve miles off the Pribilof Islands west of Alaska. Furthermore, after arduous negotiations agreement was reached that Japan's trawl and long-lining fisheries would be limited to the areas west of 165° west longitude in the Bering Sea and north of the Aleutian Islands; between three and twelve miles west of 166° longitude in the Bering Sea and south of the Aleutians; between three and twelve miles off the Pribilof Islands; beyond twelve miles south of the Aleutians and east of 166° west longitude; and in the Bay of Alaska, except in nine designated areas outside the 12-mile limit where Japan would voluntarily refrain from fishing during specified periods.[43]

Among other controversial problems was Japanese salmon fishery around the western Aleutians. The formal position of the United States was that given the anadromous nature of salmon, Japan should not catch stocks originating in North America. Japan countered that it could not agree to any limitation on its salmon fishery west of 175° west longitude, which since 1953 had been the established eastern boundary of Japanese salmon fishing.[44] Since the two sides could not reach agreement on this issue, they decided simply to exchange a diplomatic note to the effect that each party would give due consideration to the other party's position concerning the interpretation and application of the agreement.[45] The overall agreement was finally concluded in Tokyo on May 9, 1967, and immediately went into effect.[46]

Negotiations with New Zealand

On September 10, 1965, New Zealand enacted the Territorial Sea and Fishing Zone Act that went into effect on January 1, 1966. The act established a 9-mile fishery zone beyond the 3-mile territorial sea in which New Zealand would apply its domestic laws concerning fisheries in the same manner as in its territorial sea. Although the act did not specify foreign fishing as its target, it was clearly intended as a way to force all foreign fishing out of the new fishery zone, since the domestic laws to be applied there specified that fishing only by New Zealand citizens would be allowed, with government permission.[47] This would eliminate virtually all Japanese sea bream long-lining conducted within twelve miles off New Zealand's coasts.

Beginning on September 21, 1965, Japan repeatedly proposed that the two countries enter into negotiations concerning Japanese fisheries in the coastal waters of New Zealand, but Wellington rejected such a proposal, stating that its establishment of the 12-mile fishery zone was in accordance with international law. With the fishery zone law about to go into effect, in late December 1965 the Japanese government dispatched the director of its Foreign Ministry's Treaties Bureau to Wellington in an effort to get the New Zealand government to enter into negotiations. When the Wellington government would not respond favorably, the Japanese envoy relayed his government's threat that Japan would take the matter to the International Court of Justice. To this New Zealand responded with a request that Japan prepare a draft brief, so that the two governments could jointly submit the issues involved for adjudication by the World Court. At the same time, a kind of "gentlemen's agreement" was reached, according to which New Zealand would not take drastic action against Japanese fishing in its coastal waters even after the new law went into effect and Japan would exercise self-restraint in its fishing activities in the area.[48]

Japan prepared a draft brief and presented it to the New Zealand government in March 1966; the latter, having studied it, replied to Japan about a year later that instead of taking the matter before the International Court of Justice it was prepared to negotiate a fishery agreement. Thus the two governments began substantive negotiations in Wellington on May 22, 1967.[49]

The basic position of the New Zealand government was as follows: Japan would be allowed to continue fishing for two years after the bilateral agreement went into effect; Japan's catch should be limited to the average level recorded since 1965, to be achieved by limitations on the number of vessels and of fishing trips allowed; Japanese fishing would be restricted to the area between six and twelve miles from the coast and only around the North Island; only sea breams should be caught and by long-lining alone; and the management of fishing operations, including the issuing of fishing permits, should be considered in a flexible manner.[50] On the other hand, Japan proposed that the phaseout period should be five rather than two years; that during this period Japanese fishing efforts should be the same as the present level; that the fishing area should be between three and twelve miles from the New Zealand coast and include not only the North Island area only but also the area off the northern coast of the South Island; and, finally, that both long-lining and trawl fisheries should be allowed.[51]

By June 7 these disagreements had been resolved and a draft agreement signed. According to the agreement, Japan would be allowed to continue fishing in the outer six miles of the fishery zone until December 31, 1970 (Article 2). The only fishing allowed would be bottom longlines (Article 2). The fishing area would be limited to the area around the North Island and its surrounding islands and the area off the northern part of the South Island north of 41° 30′ south latitude and east of 172° 30′ east longitude (Article 2). As far as the level of fishing efforts was concerned, the number of fishing boats was not to exceed seventeen at any time and the size of mother boats was limited to 500 tons except for one 700-ton boat initially permitted (according to a note exchanged between the two governments). Fishing permits were to be issued by Japan (Article 2). With regard to the enforcement of these provisions, Article 3 of the agreement simply stipulated that either Japan or New Zealand should be in charge of dealing with violations of the agreement by Japanese fishermen, and according to a note exchanged between the two governments, Japan had the primary responsibility for handling violations. Thus, on observing a violation of the agreement, New Zealand authorities would report it to Japanese authorities with evidence, and the latter would simply report back to the former on any punitive action it had taken upon the offender. New Zealand authorities would not seize, arrest, or detain Japanese fishermen or fishing vessels even when they were found in an act of violation of the agreement.[52]

Thus the content of the agreement was quite lenient toward Japan. However, the generous arrangements thus established were to continue only for the duration of the two-year grace period, and by the end of 1970 all Japanese fishing within twelve miles of New Zealand coasts would be terminated.

An Agreement with Mexico

On January 20, 1967, the Mexican government promulgated a law establishing a 3-mile fishery zone beyond its 9-mile territorial sea. As soon as legislation passed both houses of the Mexican Congress in December 1966, the Japanese government expressed though diplomatic channels its rejection of the unilateral establishment of an exclusive fishery zone beyond what it believed to be the internationally established breadth of the territorial sea—three miles. Mexico responded that under current international law a coastal state could set up an exclusive fishery zone extending between three and twelve miles from its coast. At the same time, it showed its readiness to enter into negotiations with Japan if the latter could show it had historically been engaged in fishing within the newly enclosed area. Thus, negotiations began in Mexico City on November 27, 1967.[53]

The preamble to the Mexican-proposed draft agreement stated that nationals of a foreign country who had been historically developing living resources of the sea outside of nine miles and inside of twelve miles from the Mexican coast would be allowed to continue fishing in that area for a period not exceeding five years from Janurary 1, 1968.[54] The Mexican government maintained it had the right to "permit" Japanese fishing within the 3-mile belt of waters outside of its 9-mile territorial sea. The Japanese negotiating team argued, on the other hand, that the agreement should simply stipulate practical and concrete conditions under which Japanese fishermen would conduct fishing in specified areas of the sea without statements that would affect either party's position on the breadth of the territorial sea or on the fishery jurisdiction of a coastal state. The two sides agreed to avoid expressions that might cause a dispute over their legal positions on these issues.[55]

As a result, the final agreement simply provided for conditions under which Japanese tuna longline fishery was to operate in the area between nine and twelve miles from the Mexican coast.[56] Conditions included areas and the period in which Japanese tuna fishermen could operate (until the end of 1972); species that Japan could catch (big-eyed tuna, yellowfin tuna, banana sailfish, striped marlin, swordfish, and other incidental catches); the Japanese catch level (not to exceed 15,500 tons in the five-year grace period); and reporting by Japan on its scheduled and actual fishing activities. Furthermore, the agreement provided for an annual meeting between the representatives of the two governments to discuss enforcement of the provisions. Other provisions related to measures to be taken against violations of the agreement, consultation for scientific research on the stocks of fish Japan was allowed to catch, the effective date of the agreement, incidental catches, and surcharges (which Mexico decided not to levy at this time). Additionally, as proposed by Japan, the treaty provided that it would not affect either party's position on the breadth of the territorial sea or fishery jurisdiction.[57]

Negotiations with Australia

Shortly before the Japanese-Mexican negotiations began, the Australian Parliament passed on November 8, 1967 an amendment to the Fisheries Act of 1962–1966 to establish a 12-mile fishery zone. The new law, Fisheries Act 1967, went into effect on January 30, 1968. Earlier, the Australian government had publicly declared that its decision to extend its fishery jurisdiction to twelve miles while retaining its 3-mile territorial sea limit was in accord with current international law and practice. The government also expressed its intention to review the status of foreign nationals who had been engaged in fishing between three and twelve miles off the Australian coast to decide whether a short phaseout period might be appropriate.[58]

The Japanese government expressed regret over Australia's decision but stated that it was prepared to negotiate a fishery agreement so that Japanese fishery interests in the affected area would be protected. Canberra agreed and negotiations started in the Australian capital on January 30, 1968.[59] With the negotiations underway, Japan realized that it had a fundamental conflict with Australia similar to those it had encountered vis-à-vis Korea, the United States, New Zealand, and Mexico with regard to exclusive fishery jurisdiction for coastal states. Japan basically proposed that its fishing in the area between three and twelve miles from the Australian coast be limited to tuna longline and shrimp trawl fishing, that there be no limitation on the area in which Japanese fishing would be allowed, and that Japan exercise enforcement rights to enable it to regulate its fishing according to conditions to be agreed upon between the two governments.[60] The Australian government flatly rejected the proposal, for in its view what Japan was demanding was in effect that Australia ignore its own domestic fishing laws. The talks were broken off on February 9 after an understanding was reached on provisional self-restraining measures to be taken until the two governments could conclude a formal fishery agreement.[61]

On the last day of the first unsuccessful round of negotiations, the Australian negotiating team presented its basic proposal for a long-term agreement. According to the proposal, Australia was ready to offer a phaseout arrangement that would be applied only to tuna longline fishing off the Australian coast; Japan could operate a shrimp fishery only through the joint venture enterprise, for which an application was currently being processed; and the proposed phaseout program for tuna longline fishing would follow the conditions prescribed by the Australian government. The conditions related to the areas in which Japanese fishing would be permitted; the scale of fishing operation (not to exceed the 1967 level); the phaseout period (five years starting January 30, 1968); the licensing and inspection procedures; and the ports in which Japanese tuna fishing boats could call.[62]

Other than the basic disagreement concerning the status of fishery jurisdiction in international law, there were disagreements in a number of more specific areas. One such disagreement was whether Japan should be allowed to fish in the area around Papua New Guinea. Australia argued that Japan should not because the economic development of the trust territory was the responsibility of all United Nations member states and not just of Australia.[63] At the end of the negotiations it was agreed that Japan would submit a proposal for a joint venture for fishery development in Papua New Guinea and that Australia would give it favorable consideration. In connection with this, it was also agreed that Japanese fishermen would continue their operation in the area between three and twelve miles off Papua New Guinea, except in two specified areas, for three years from the day the bilateral agreement was signed or until some future date to be negotiated.[64] Another agreement was that Japanese fishing would continue in five areas off New Zealand and in other specified areas of the Tasman Sea, the Coral Sea, and the Indian Ocean, all between three and twelve miles from the Australian coast.[65]

The second area of major disagreement related to Canberra's demand that Japanese fishing be licensed and registered by Australia. Tokyo insisted that it should be required simply to submit a report to Australian authorities on the characteristics and the number of Japanese tuna fishing boats that were scheduled to operate within twelve miles of the Australian coast.[66] The two sides eventually agreed that Japan would submit an annual report to Australia at least fourteen days prior to the beginning of its fishing operations giving the names and registration numbers of the Japanese boats scheduled to operate in the specified areas and the identification and the number of fishermen. Upon receipt of the report, Australia would make "necessary administrative arrangements to facilitate the operation of those vessels in the Designated Waters in accordance with the provisions of this Agreement" (Article 3). In return, it was agreed, Japanese fishing boats would make reasonable payments not to exceed 100 Australian dollars per annum.[67]

As far as enforcement of the agreement was concerned, Japan proposed to use its own inspection service to ensure that the treaty provisions were observed. The Australians proposed that Australian authorities had the right to visit Japanese fishing vessels operating in the declared fishing zone. The final agreement included a compromise stipulation that gave the primary inspection role to Japanese authorities within the new 12-mile fishery zone but that allowed Australian authorities to visit Japanese vessels.[68]

With regard to the size of the Japanese catch, it was agreed that the annual catch of tuna longline fishery would not exceed the average recorded between 1963 and 1967.[69] As to the duration of Japanese fishing, the initial Australian proposal would have allowed Japanese fishing to continue for five years after the effective date of the agreement. The Japanese negotiating team proposed a ten-year period. The two sides agreed on seven years, that is, until November 27, 1975.[70] Finally, the agreement stated it would be in effect for an indefinite period starting on the thirtieth day after the exchange of ratifications.[71]

Again in this agreement, the Japanese government was successful in securing an arrangement that would allow the continuation of Japanese fishing in the 12-mile fishing zone of a foreign country during a grace period. It was also successful in avoiding an agreement that would have compromised its legal position on the fishery jurisdiction of coastal states. In other words, instead of accepting exclusive fishery jurisdiction, which would have given Australia total power to control and regulate Japanese fishing in the 12-mile zone, the Japanese government was able to retain the primary enforcement role vis-à-vis its nationals.

Japan's Strategy

As we have seen in this chapter, Japan reacted to the growing tide of ocean enclosure with a strategy designed to delay, if not eliminate, the practical impact of other states' unilateral actions on its fishing interests and to preserve its legal position against national enclosure. The strategy was directed against those coastal states whose unilateral expansionist actions had not only legal implications for the international ocean regime but also real and practical consequences for Japanese fishing interests. The 12-mile legislation of the United States, New Zealand, Mexico, and Australia, and Korea's more expansionist Rhee Line all strengthened the mounting argument in favor of the decentralized management of ocean resources. These laws demanded that Japan accept regulatory controls of its distant-water fishing by the coastal states—a real challenge to Japanese supremacy in global fisheries. Tokyo's strategy was to oppose but, gradually and reluctantly, to accept increased fishing conservation and management measures—including bans on some fisheries, limits to catch levels, and prohibition of certain fisheries in specified areas or periods—without recognizing the legitimacy of coastal states' claims to exclusive fishery jurisdiction beyond three miles, or six miles in the Mexican case.

This strategy was not sufficient for Japan to maintain its position in favor of the freedom of the seas in dealing with Korea. Japan was forced not only to explicitly accept Korean jurisdiction in its 12-mile fishery zone but also to establish its own 12-mile fishery zone targeted solely against Korean fishing in the western and southwestern coastal waters of the country. What accounts for the important difference between Japan's concession to Korea and its attitude toward the other Pacific-rim states was mainly Tokyo's desire not to let fishing problems stand in the way of the important task of normalizing diplomatic relations with Seoul. Hostile incidents involving Korean authorities and Japanese fishermen certainly did not contribute to a hospitable diplomatic climate. In fact, it was feared that anti-Korean sentiment that already existed among many Japanese in the 1950s and 1960s would hamper the diplomatic efforts to put bilateral relations on a peaceful footing.

Humanitarian considerations were another reason Korean jurisdiction within the 12-mile zone was accepted. Japanese lives had been lost in the troubled waters, but in the absence of normal diplomatic ties, the Japanese government could not pursue the matter legally or diplomatically with the Korean government. At a minimum, Tokyo certainly wanted to prevent further troublesome incidents.

Finally, economic calculations indicated that reconciliation of differences between the two countries would bring more benefits to Japanese fishermen than the continuation of the stalemate in the negotiations. Without an agreement, including Japanese recognition of Korean exclusive fishery jurisdiction, there was no assurance whatsover that Japanese fishing could continue safely in Korean coastal waters. In contrast, in the other bilateral cases, the problem was essentially an economic one, and Japan's refusal to formally recognize the other states' exclusive jurisdictions neither jeopardized its fishery interests nor caused major diplomatic problems.

In coming to terms with the practical consequences of the expansion of coastal state jurisdiction, Japan came to accept in essence one part of the 6 + 6 formula that had been proposed but defeated at the First and Second UNCLOS. Without explicitly abandoning its opposition to the territorial sea or fishery jurisdictional expansion beyond three miles, Japan in effect accepted the phaseout approach of the Canada–United States compromise proposal.

Most importantly, regardless of Japan's formal legal argument concerning coastal states' jurisdiction, its action represented de facto acceptance of exclusive fishery jurisdiction beyond three miles. When in the painful bilateral negotiations Japan begin to search for ways to mitigate its losses, it became clear that there was no alternative but to accept the beginning of the demise of the freedom of the seas.

While Japan could continue to insist in bilateral negotiations that there was no global agreement on the exclusive jurisdiction of the coastal state and maintain its formal legal opposition, when the demise of the traditional ocean regime began to take place within a multilateral framework in the 1970s, Japan could no longer justify its unconditional opposition to jurisdictional expansion without the risk of losing its real interests. And it is to these multilateral challenges that I will turn in the following chapter.

4

The United Nations
Seabed Committee

The Maltese Proposal

ON August 17, 1967, Arvid Pardo, Maltese ambassador to the United Nations, called the attention of the delegates to the General Assembly's twenty-second session to the rapidly developing technology that might make it possible for some advanced states to explore, occupy, and exploit the world's seabeds and ocean floor. He warned that the national appropriation of the seabeds and ocean floor would inevitably produce incalculable consequences. Specifically, he referred to the acceleration of the exploration for offshore petroleum and natural gas in nearly all parts of the world, to the growing interest in the exploration and exploitation of phosphorite and manganese dioxide concretions on the ocean floor, and to the growing threat of expanding military uses of the deep seas and of the ocean floor. Pardo pointed out that the present international legal framework, which recognized cession, subjugation, accretion, prescription, and occupation as legitimate modes of acquiring land territory, encouraged national appropriation of the seabed beyond the geographical continental shelf. His warning continued: The process of jurisdictional extension over selected areas of the ocean had already started and would lead to a worldwide scramble for sovereign rights over the land underlying the world's seas and occean. The consequences would be escalation of the arms race and a sharp increase in world tension.[1] Given this predicament, Ambassador Pardo called for the creation of a new international regime for the seabed beyond the limits of national jurisdiction. In particular, he proposed the establishment of a special agency to serve as a trustee for all countries over the oceans and the ocean floor. The proposed agency would have the power to effectively regulate, supervise, and control all activities on or under the oceans and the ocean floor.[2] Pardo envisioned that the agency would be founded on the basis of an international treaty establishing a set of generally acceptable principles with regard to the use of the deep seas and of the ocean floor.[3] The principles to be incorporated according to the Maltese proposal were: (1) the seabed and the ocean floor beyond national jurisdiction are not subject to national appropriation in any manner whatsoever; (2) the seabed and the ocean floor beyond national jurisdiction shall be used exclusively for peaceful purposes; (3) scientific research with regard to the deep seas and ocean floor shall be free and its results available to all; and (4) the exploration and exploitation of the seabed and ocean floor beyond national jurisdiction shall be conducted in a manner consistent with the principles and purposes of the United Nations' Charter and in a manner not causing unnecessary obstruction of the high seas or serious impairment of the marine environment.[4]

Pardo further asked that the General Assembly agree that the seabed and the ocean floor were "a common heritage of mankind" to be used and exploited exclusively for peaceful purposes and for the benefit of mankind as a whole and that claims to sovereignty over the seabed and ocean floor be frozen at the presently claimed national limits until a clear definition of the continental shelf was found. To this end, the Maltese ambassador proposed the establishment of an international body to consider the security, economic, and other implications of the establishment of the international agency that would ensure that national activities in the deep seas and on the ocean floor would conform to the proposed treaty.[5]

Japanese Ambassador to the United Nations Senjin Tsuruoka welcomed the Maltese appeal. Recognizing the political implications of the seabed and ocean floor use and exploitation—such as military activities and the possible monopoly of the ocean's resources by a few developed countries—and stressing the importance of shipping and fishing, the Japanese delegate expressed his country's interest in participating in the proposed body to study the legal, economic, technical, and other problems related to the peaceful uses of the seabed and the ocean floor. While calling premature an attempt at that time to create an international agency or international legal regime for the seabed and the ocean floor, Tsuruoka emphasized the inadequacy of the 1958 Geneva Convention on the Continental Shelf in limiting the present and future expansionist claims of coastal states. He stated: "In view of the principle of freedom of the seas in general international law, our country cannot accept such claims in any manner whatsoever. In this sense, we fully appreciate the implications of the Maltese proposal as the brake against such possible claims in the future."[6]

In this enthusiastic support for the Maltese initiative, Japan's fundamental position in favor of freedom of the seas was clearly demonstrated. Japan saw in the Maltese proposal an opportunity to strike back against the coastal states' encroachment on this traditional principle. What Japan failed to see, however, was the growing tide of resource nationalism in the developing parts of the world that would turn the Maltese proposal into an opportunity to press their demands for reorganizing the international ocean regime and correct what they considered the inequities inherent in the traditional regime.

The Maltese proposal was supported by the General Assembly resolution (Resolution 2340 [XXII]) to establish an Ad Hoc Seabed Committee to discuss the status of the seabed beyond the limits of national jurisdiction. The committee's thirty-five member states representing all regions of the world met three times in 1968 and submitted their report to the General Assembly during its twenty-third session in the same year.[7] Four resolutions were adopted by the General Assembly on December 21.[8]

The first resolution, adopted by a 112 to 0 vote with 7 abstentions and supported by Japan, established a Committee on the Peaceful Uses of the Seabed and the Ocean Floor beyond the Limits of National Jurisdiction. According to the resolution (GA Resolution 2467A [XXIII]), the new Seabed Committee would study an international regime on the exploration and use of the deep seabed for the benefit of all mankind; study the ways and means of promoting the exploitation and use of the deep seabed resources; review studies in this area for international cooperation; examine cooperative measures for prevention of marine pollution; and study the reservation of the seabed and the ocean floor exclusively for peaceful purposes. Finally, the committee was requested to cooperate with the UN and other intergovernmental organizations, to make recommendations to the General Assembly, and to submit reports on its activities to each session of the General Assembly.

The second resolution (GA Resolution 2467B [XXIII]), adopted by a vote of 119 to 0 with no abstentions, called upon the secretary-general of the UN to conduct a study to clarify all aspects of the protection against pollution and other harmful effects of seabed exploration and exploitation of living and nonliving resources of the seabed, the superjacent water columns, and the adjacent coasts. Japan supported the adoption of the resolution just as every voting member of the General Assembly did. The third resolution (GA Resolution 2467C [XXIII]), sponsored by thirty-eight Asian, African, and Latin American countries called upon the secretary-general to study the question of establishing international machinery for the promotion of exploration and exploitation of the resources of the seabed and the ocean floor and the use of these resources for all of mankind, taking into consideration the interests and needs of the developing countries. Japan, the United States, and Western European countries abstained from voting on this resolution, while the Soviet Union and other Eastern European countries voted against it.[9] Japan supported the idea of creating international machinery and an international legal regime in this area as a long-range objective of the international community but agreed with the United States and others that the idea was yet premature. The resolution was adopted by a vote of 85 to 9 with 25 abstentions. The fourth resolution (GA Resolution 2467D [XXIII]) was adopted at the plenary meeting without voting. With the adoption of this resolution, the General Assembly welcomed the concept of an international decade of ocean exploration—the idea first publicly announced by U.S. President Lyndon Johnson in 1968 in order to call upon all nations to make a concerted long-term, and cooperative effort in ocean exploration in the 1970s.[10]

The Ad Hoc Seabed Committee had received several proposals concerning principles governing deep-seabed mining, and some of them were submitted as resolutions to the General Assembly. But the global body decided not to vote on these resolutions but, upon Pardo's suggestion, to refer them to the new permanent Seabed Committee.[11]

The Seabed Committee

The Seabed Committee, composed of forty-two member states, met for the first time February 6–7, 1969, elected H. Shirley Amerasinghe of Ceylon chairman of the committee, and established the Legal Subcommittee and the Economic and Technical Subcommittee. During its formal and informal discussions in March, the Seabed Committee was able to adopt a report on principles affecting the legal status of the seabed area beyond the limits of national jurisdiction; the applicability of international law in the area; the exclusive reservation of the area for peaceful purposes; the use of the resources of the seabed for the benefit of mankind as a whole; the freedom of scientific research and exploration; the interests of other states in the exercise of the freedom of the high seas; and the prevention of marine pollution. The report also covered the discussions held by the Economic and Technical Subcommittee concerning the exploration and exploitation of seabed resources, international cooperation in the field, and the question of the establishment of international machinery.

The report of the Seabed Committee was then discussed by the First (Political and Security) Committee of the General Assembly during its twenty-fourth session in 1969. On December 2, a vote was taken on relevant draft resolutions and those that passed the First Committee were put to a vote on December 15 in the plenary meeting. As a result, four resolutions were adopted by the General Assembly.

The first resolution (GA Resolution 2547A [XXIV]) called upon the secretary-general to obtain the views of the UN members on whether or not to convene a conference on the law of the sea to review the regimes of the high seas, the continental shelf, the territorial sea and contiguous zone, and fishing and conservation of the living resources of the high seas. The fundamental purpose of such a conference would be to clarify the definition of the area of the seabed and ocean floor beyond the limits of national jurisdiction.[12] The original sponsor of the bill calling for a law of the sea conference was Malta. The United States, Japan, and Western European countries supported the Maltese proposal, which would have restricted the scope of the proposed conference to the discussion of the outer limits of the continental shelf. East European countries also wished to limit the agenda so as to avoid a discussion of comprehensive law of the sea issues. However, a group consisting of Asian and African nations supported the Trinidad–Tobago–Jamaica proposal, which called for the convening of a third conference on the law of the sea to discuss not only the continental shelf question but all of the major issues of the law of the sea. This proposal became a set of amendments to the Maltese proposal. Finally, the plenary meeting adopted the Maltese proposal as amended by a vote of 65 to 12 with 30 abstentions, preparing the way for what was to become the most comprehensive and largest UN conference ever held.[13]

The second resolution (GA Resolution 2547B [XXIV]), adopted by a vote of 109 to 0 with 1 abstention, requested the Seabed Committee to continue in an expeditious manner the work it had thus far undertaken concerning two general questions: preparation of a list of legal principles regarding the area of the seabed and ocean floor beyond the limits of national jurisdiction and formulation of recommendations concerning the economic and technical conditions and rules for exploitation of resources.[14] Japan supported the resolution, as it did the third resolution (GA Resolution 2547C [XXIV]) requesting the secretary-general to prepare a study on various types of international machinery covering their status, structure, functions, and power regarding the peaceful uses of the deep seabed.[15]

The fourth resolution (GA Resolution 2547D [XXIV]) was adopted by a substantially smaller margin, 62 to 28 with 28 abstaining. It declared that pending the establishment of an international regime of the seabed and ocean floor states and persons were bound to refrain from all exploitations of deep seabed resources and that they could lay no claims over any part of the area concerned or resources therein. Japan opposed the resolution, fearing that the language employed in it would have the effect of legitimizing the existing claims of some countries over a wide expanse of the sea and its subjacent seabed.[16] For similar reasons, the United States, the United Kingdom, Canada, Belgium, Norway, Malta, and other Western European countries and Eastern European countries voted against it. Most of the countries that supported the resolution were developing countries of Asia, Africa, and Latin America.[17]

In summary, Japan welcomed the Maltese initiative in placing the question of the status of the seabed and ocean floor on the agenda for discussion at the multilateral level. On the other hand, it did not want to rush into supporting the immediate creation of an international regime of the seabed and ocean floor, nor was it prepared to accept the establishment of international machinery to manage the exploitation and use of the area concerned and resources therein. Before such crucial arrangements could be made, Japan firmly believed, the definition of the area beyond the limits of national jurisdiction had to be established, so that expansionist moves on the part of coastal states could be checked and Japan's high seas fishing interests protected.

The Seabed Committee held two sessions in 1970. The Legal Subcommittee could not produce agreement on legal principles governing the deep seabed and the ocean floor. The Economic and Technical Subcommittee, however, successfully dealt with the economic and technical conditions and rules for the exploitation of resources of the deep sea in the area beyond the limits of national jurisdiction and during the second session prepared a "List of Topics Suggested by Some Members to be Studied in Preparing Economic and Technical Rules and Conditions for the Exploration of the Resources of the Seabed and Subsoil Thereof beyond the Limits of National Jurisdiction within the Context of the Regime to be Set Up."[18]

Japanese delegates' statements in the two subcommittees and in the plenary meeting of the Seabed Committee reflected on the one hand Japan's generally accommodating attitude toward the effort to establish a seabed regime but on the other hand showed its concern that the new regime might hurt its existing interests by legitimizing expansionist coastal claims. Japan's immediate concern was with the limits of coastal state jurisdiction and not with a new international seabed regime. For example, Ambassador Tsuruoka warned that the question of the boundary of national jurisdiction would be difficult to solve and an immediate agreement on the proposed seabed regime was highly unlikely.[19] Another immediate concern of the Japanese government was that a new regime might impinge upon Japanese high seas fishing, including exploitation of sedentary species, which was the issue most crucially linked to the question of the definition of resources of the seabed and ocean floor. Thus the statement by Shigeru Oda, one of the Japanese delegates, to the Seabed Committee's plenary meeting on August 10 to the effect that his government believed only the mineral resources of the area should be included in the natural resources to be governed by the proposed international seabed regime. The Japanese government's view was that all biological resources should be excluded from the category of resources of the seabed and that such resources, including sedentary species, should be governed not by the new seabed regime to be set up or by unilateral national measures but rather by regional and international fishery regimes.[20]

The Seabed Committee's discussions were incorporated into a report submitted to the twenty-fifth session of the General Assembly in 1970. The General Assembly adopted two resolutions, Resolutions 2749 (XXV) and 2750 (XXV). The first concerned the Declaration of Principles governing the deep seabed and ocean floor. Adopted by a vote of 108 to 0 with 14 abstentions, it was largely a compromise between developed and developing countries. Among the principles incorporated were (1) that the deep seabed and ocean floor and the resources in the area are the common heritage of mankind and that no part of the area should be claimed or appropriated by any state; and (2) that no state or person should claim or exercise rights incompatible with the international regime, which would govern all activities regarding resource exploration and exploitation in the area. According to the resolution, such activities should be exclusively for peaceful purposes and for the benefit of mankind as a whole. The international regime to be established, the resolution declared, should provide for orderly and safe development and rational management of the area and its resources, with particular consideration to be given to the interests and needs of the developing countries. Furthermore, it asserted that nothing in the adopted principles should affect the legal status of the waters superjacent to the area or the air space above the waters or the rights of coastal states with respect to measures to keep their coastlines or related interests free from pollution or other hazards. In addition, the resolution included general principles concerning international agreements to prevent an arms race on the seabed; international cooperation in scientific research exclusively for peaceful purposes; implementation of international rules at the national level; standards and procedures for pollution prevention and environmental and resource protection and conservation; states' and international organizations' responsibilities to conform to the international regime; and dispute settlement.[21]

Japan's attitude toward the Declaration of Principles was favorable. On December 7, 1970, Tsuruoka stated that although the proposed declaration was a product of compromise not fully satisfactory to all the delegations, its prompt adoption would be "a definite step forward which will have a significant bearing on future development in the whole field of the law of the sea."[22] He pointed out the principles would provide basic guidelines for the conclusion of an international agreement that would regulate activities with respect to the deep seabed areas. He concluded that his delegation would "look with favor" on the adoption of the proposed Declaration of Principles.[23]

The second resolution, Resolution 2750 (XXV), was composed of three sections. The first, adopted by a vote of 104 to 0 with 16 abstentions, called upon the secretary-general to cooperate with the United Nations Conference on Trade and Development (UNCTAD) and specialized agencies of the UN system to identify, study, and propose effective solutions for problems arising from the production of certain minerals from the ocean floor. It was a response to the concern among mineral exporting countries, particularly those in the developing parts of the world, about the adverse impact of seabed mineral exploitation on the world mineral market.[24] The second part of the resolution called upon the secretary-general to prepare an up-to-date study on the question of landlocked states' access to the sea and on special problems of landlocked states in the exploration and exploitation of deep ocean floor resources and to submit a report on these issues to the Seabed Committee in 1971.[25] This resolution was adopted by the plenary session of the General Assembly by a vote of 111 to 0 with 11 abstentions. The last section, adopted by a vote of 108 to 7 with 6 abstentions, was a decision to convene in 1973 a conference on the law of the sea that would deal with the establishment of an equitable international regime, including international machinery for the deep ocean floor and its resources; a precise definition of the area; and a broad range of other issues, including those concerning the regimes of the high seas, the continental shelf, the territorial sea and the contiguous zone, fishing and the conservation of living resources, the preservation of the marine environment, and scientific research. Resolution 2750 (XXV) also contained a provision that increased the number of the Seabed Committee members by forty-four and charged the committee with preparing a draft treaty on the basis of the Declaration of Principles and a comprehensive list of issues to be discussed by the Third UNCLOS.

What was the attitude of the Japanese delegation toward the decision to convene the Third UNCLOS? The head of the delegation, Ambassador Tsuruoka, stated his government's main concerns:

As far as my delegation is concerned, the principal questions of the law of the sea which remain so far unsettled and which need our urgent treatment and final settlement are two: one is the question of the breadth of the territorial sea and such directly related matters as the question of international straits and the question of fisheries by coastal states on the high seas; the other is the question of the international regime to regulate activities for exploration and exploitation of the resources of the seabed, with its clearly defined boundary.[26]

Tsuruoka reiterated his country's dependence on and interest in the seas and pointed out that the opportunities offered by the seas had "been made possible because, unlike the land mass which is now divided between sovereign nations with fixed boundaries, the sea has been kept free to all peoples for all kinds of constructive activities under a stable regime consecrated by the international law of the sea." He declared furthermore, "It is important that it should remain so, if this common asset of mankind is to contribute to serve the interest of humanity as a whole rather than that of a particular State or a group of States whose claim to exclusive domination over part of this *res communis* might jeopardize this situation.[27]

Lamenting the trends toward national enclosure, Tsuruoka opposed unilateral national enclosure and urged multilateral efforts to produce international agreement to ensure stability and order in the regime of the sea. In summary, Japan's attitude toward the law of the sea conference reflected its status quo–oriented concern that as much of the high seas and freedom thereof as possible should be maintained by putting a stop to or, if possible, rolling back the trend to enclose the ocean by "creeping national jurisdiction."

Parenthetically, we note that Japan's unwavering commitment to the freedom of the seas, so routinely emphasized and defended by its representatives, had convinced many of them as well as policymakers at home of the virtue of the regime. What John Steinbruner calls "grooved thinking" or "theoretical thinking" may very well have been in operation.[28]

Unilateral National Enclosure

Just as the enlarged Seabed Committee was beginning to set the agenda for the Third UNCLOS, unilateral national enclosure was gathering global momentum; it was supported by one regional organization after another. Nine Latin American countries met in Montevideo, Uruguay, from May 4 to 8, 1970, and adopted a declaration affirming the coastal states' rights to avail themselves of their coastal waters and soil and subsoil thereof in order to promote economic development and to raise their standards of living. The document endorsed the littoral states' right

> to establish the limits of their maritime sovereignty and jurisdiction in accordance with their geographical and geological characteristics and with the factors governing the existence of marine resources and the need for their rational utilization; . . . to explore and conserve their coastal living resources and to establish regulations for fishing and aquatic hunting; . . . to explore, conserve, and exploit the natural resources of their continental shelves to where the depth of the superjacent waters admits of the exploitation of such resources; . . . [to explore, conserve, and exploit] their resources of the soil and subsoil of the seabed and ocean floor up to the limit within which the State exercises its jurisdiction over the sea; . . . [and] to adopt regulatory measures applicable in areas under their maritime sovereignty and jurisdiction, without prejudice to freedom of navigation by ships and overflying by aircraft of any flag.[29]

As to the extent to which the coastal states were entitled to lay sovereign and jurisdictional claims, the declaration acknowledged in its preamble that the nine Latin American countries had extended their sovereignty or exclusive jurisdiction over the area of the sea adjacent to their coasts, the seabed, and the subsoil thereof up to two hundred miles from the baseline from which their territorial seas were measured.

Following the Montevideo Declaration, twenty Latin American countries met in Lima, Peru, from August 4 to 8, 1970, and adopted, over some objections, a declaration supporting the same rights of coastal states.[30] As to the extent of coastal state sovereignty and jurisdiction, the Lima Declaration failed to specify a limit, largely because about half of the participants in the conference strongly supported the 200-mile limit, but the other half were not ready to accept it or were opposed to it.

The support for expanded coastal claims was not limited to these Latin American countries. The twelfth session of the Asian–African Legal Consultative Committee met in Colombo, Ceylon, from January 18 to 27, 1971, and the majority of delegations indicated that "a state had the right to claim certain exclusive rights to economic exploitation of the resources in the waters adjacent to the territorial sea in a zone the maximum breadth of which should be subject to negotiation."[31] Most delegations also supported "in principle, the right of a coastal state to claim exclusive jurisdiction" over a zone adjacent to its territorial sea, for economic purposes.[32] At the fourteenth session of the Asian–African Legal Consultative Committee, the representative of Kenya introduced the concept of an "exclusive economic zone," according to which coastal states would have the right to establish an extensive jurisdictional zone outside their territorial sea in which they would have exclusive enjoyment of all resources, both living and nonliving. The Kenyan proposal was endorsed by the African States Regional Seminar on the Law of the Sea, held in Yaounde, Cameroon, from June 20 to 30, 1972.[33] The seminar's general report went further and recommended that African states "extend their sovereignty over all the resources of the high seas adjacent to their Territorial Sea within an economic zone to be established and which will include at least the continental shelf," and called upon them "to uphold the principle of this extension at the next International Conference on the Law of the Sea."[34] Later, in June 1974, the Council of Ministers of the Organization of African Unity, meeting in Mogadiscio, Somalia, issued a declaration endorsing the seminar's recommendation, this time specifying two hundred miles as the maximum distance of the exclusive economic zone.[35]

Earlier that same year, on June 7, the Conference of the Caribbean Countries on Problems of the Sea met in Santo Domingo and adopted a declaration known as the Santo Domingo Declaration. In it, the participating Caribbean countries adopted the concept of "patrimonial sea," or the waters, the seabed, and the subsoil of an area adjacent to the territorial sea in which coastal states would have sovereign rights over the renewable and nonrenewable natural resources.[36] According to the declaration, in the patrimonial sea, not exceeding two hundred nautical miles, coastal states would have the duty and the right to regulate the conduct of scientific research, to adopt the necessary measures to prevent marine pollution, and to ensure their sovereignty over the resources of the sea.[37] The declaration recognized all other traditional freedoms in this zone—freedom of navigation, overflight, and the laying of submarine cables and pipelines.[38]

Support for extended coastal state jurisdiction was also found among some developed coastal states. For example, Australia and New Zealand submitted a joint fishery proposal to the enlarged Seabed Committee in its 1972 summer session, according to which littoral states would have exclusive jurisdiction over the living resources in the broad areas of the waters adjacent to their territorial seas—superjacent to the continental shelf according to Australia and a 200-mile zone according to New Zealand.[39] In the spring of 1972, France had explicitly supported two hundred miles as the limit of national jurisdiction over the seabed and resources thereof.[40] Furthermore, by 1972, the United States began to show an accommodating posture toward the 200-mile economic zone.[41] One important observer in Japan wrote: "Before long the United States might abandon the concept of the freedom of fisheries in offshore waters, if it can receive in compensation the freedom of navigation through straits."[42] With the overwhelming support of the developing nations and some developed countries, Kenya formally submitted its proposal on the 200-mile economic zone to the enlarged Seabed Committee in the summer of 1972.[43]

Japan's Position

How did Japan respond to these challenges? Its head delegate, Motoo Ogiso, stated to the Second Subcommittee of the enlarged Seabed Committee during its sixtieth meeting on April 4, 1973, that his delegation had studied the patrimonial sea and exclusive economic zone proposals but decided it could not accept them, "mainly because to extend national sovereignty into the high seas would increase rather than diminish existing inequities and would prevent effective international control and management." He charged that "freedom of the high seas should be limited and rectified where necessary rather than entirely replaced by a poor substitute."[44]

Japan was not necessarily the only country that was categorically opposed to the proposals for a 200-mile economic zone. The other maritime powers with extensive distant-water fishery interests, namely the Soviet Union and other Eastern European countries, shared the Japanese concern. For example, in their 1972 "Declaration of Principles of Rational Exploitation of the Living Resources of the Seas and Oceans in the Common Interests of All Peoples of the World," the Soviet Union, Bulgaria, Hungary, East Germany, Poland, and Czechoslovakia set forth their opposition to exclusive economic zones beyond the 12-mile limit.[45] As regional and interregional support for the concept of 200-mile exclusive economic zones found its way into the enlarged Seabed Committee and not only developing coastal states but some developed coastal states began to take the concept under serious consideration, it became increasingly clear that the views of Japan and Eastern Europe were in the minority.

On the question of high seas fishing, Japan's position had shown no significant change. As a point of departure, Japanese delegates continually referred to the Geneva High Seas Convention of 1958 as establishing the right of all states to engage in fishing on the high seas as a principle of international law. Ambassador Shinichi Sugihara stated: "Any proposal which, in protecting the rights and interests of the coastal states, disregarded the rights and interests of other states under a long-established principle of international law would not be a real solution to the problem."[46] From this conservative perspective, Japanese delegates attempted to persuade other delegations of the benefits of the traditional regime of high seas fisheries and the unfairness of the coastal states' proposals to chip away at that regime.

First, on the question of coastal state jurisdiction, Japan maintained that the establishment of exclusive coastal fishery zones would not necessarily serve the interests of coastal, particularly developing, states. Japanese delegates gave two reasons for their contention. The exploitation of living resources did not necessarily result in the reduction of the size of stocks of fish if appropriate conservation measures were taken. On the other hand, the Japanese delegates' reasoning went, unharvested living resources would simply go to waste. Moreover, due to the uneven distribution of marine living resources and the productive capacity of oceans, only a very limited number of coastal states enjoyed large and lucrative fishing in their coastal areas, and their moves to close off such fishing grounds would limit the resources available to the other countries, including many developing countries that were just beginning to develop their distant-water fishing.[47]

Second, Japan was adamantly opposed to a U.S. proposal regarding coastal states' jurisdiction over anadromous species of fish. The proposal, originally submitted to the Second Committee in 1971 and revised in 1972, provided for coastal states' regulatory authority and preferential rights to anadromous fish, such as salmon, which spawn in their fresh or estuarine waters, throughout the migratory range of the fish on the high seas.[48] Salmon fisheries in the North Pacific region had been one of the most important and lucrative fisheries that Japan had developed since the end of World War II, and the inclusion of the U.S. proposal in the new regime would have extensive impact on Japanese salmon fisheries. Japan's professed rationale for its opposition was that salmon was the only truly anadromous species and, therefore, it would be inappropriate to include a principle governing only one species in the general regime of the law of the sea.[49] Japan further maintained that since the question of anadromous fish affected only a small number of countries, the matter should be left for them to work out among themselves or through regional or international bodies that had already been dealing with the issue.[50]

Third, with regard to conservation of fishery resources, Japan was of the opinion that existing regional and international fishery organizations rather than individual coastal states should play the central role because coastal states would be inclined to establish unilateral conservation measures discriminating against other fishing countries. Japan's professed reason for this position was that scientific, biological, and ecological factors could be best dealt with at the regional or international rather than the national level. In particular, Japanese delegates contended, regional fishery commissions could adopt flexible approaches suitable to the specific conditions of stocks of fish requiring conservation.[51] In response to the Canadian criticism that existing international fishery commissions had been grossly ineffective in conservation and management of marine resources, the Japanese delegation stated that while there were some shortcomings and weaknesses with the existing organizations, any arrangements for fish conservation and management should take into consideration the special interests of not only the coastal state but also other fishing countries. Instead of replacing the established international commissions, a Japanese delegate maintained, they should be strengthened and supplemented.[52]

Fourth, regarding the fishery jurisdiction of coastal states, Japan made a distinction between its approach toward developing coastal states and toward developed coastal states. Recognizing the desire of the former to develop their coastal fisheries and aware of the disadvantageous position they found themselves in vis-à-vis advanced distant-water fishing countries, the Japanese delegation demonstrated a readiness to accept the concept of "preferential fishing rights" for developing coastal states. However, Japan maintained such rights should be recognized only to the extent that these countries were actually able to harvest a major proportion of the allowable catch. On the other hand, Japanese delegates were of the view that developed coastal states had the necessary financial and technological means to make internal adjustments, including modernization of their fishing fleets, and that protection of their "preferential fishing rights" would encourage overinvestment in inefficient fishing industries and would impose unfair sacrifices on the distant-water fishing interests of other countries. The Japanese delegation did acknowledge that small-scale coastal fisheries of developed countries were vulnerable to foreign competition and required special consideration. For these reasons Japan proposed that preferential fishing rights of developed countries be recognized in terms of the minimum annual catch required for the continuation of clearly and precisely defined small-scale coastal fisheries.[53]

On August 14, 1972, the Japanese delegation submitted to the Second Subcommittee its government's proposals for a regime of fisheries on the high seas that incorporated all the interests, concerns, and views discussed above.[54] To summarize, Japan's proposals were as follows:

1. The rules concerning the preferential rights of coastal states should ensure sufficient protection for coastal fisheries, particularly of the developing countries, in areas adjacent to the 12-mile limit.[55]

2. Developing coastal states should be entitled to an annual allocation of fishery resources corresponding to their harvesting capacity.

3. The general rules for the protection of coastal states should be flexible enough to take individual cases into account and should be the subject of negotiations between the coastal and other states concerned.

4. Should negotiations fail, disputes should be referred to a body of

experts for a binding decision, unless they were settled by some other means as agreed upon by the parties.

5. International cooperation should be established between the developing coastal states and other fishing states to protect the former's interests.

6. No preferential rights of catch for coastal states should be recognized with regard to highly migratory and anadromous species of fish. The conservation and management of such stocks should be the subject of international or regional consultation or agreement or should be entrusted to existing regional fishery commissions.

7. Enforcement jurisdiction should be retained by flag states, though coastal states would have the right to inspect foreign vessels and to inform the flag state of any violations.[56]

The Japanese strategy thus reviewed can be seen as a set of three components:

1. Stop the expansionist claims of coastal states, represented by the demand for 200-mile exclusive economic zones, and impress upon other countries, both developed fishing countries and developing coastal states interested in starting their own distant-water fisheries, their "common interest" in preserving the freedom to fish the high seas.

2. Keep the fishery conservation and management control under international or regional arrangements.

3. Show some understanding of the concerns of developing coastal states while resisting proposals that would impinge upon Japan's distant-water fisheries.[57]

With regard to the question of the seabed regime, Japan maintained its fundamental interest in keeping broad high seas and narrow coastal jurisdiction. Japanese delegates continued to emphasize the importance of clearly defining the boundary of the seabed to be governed by the proposed international regime. Beyond that, Japan had not developed any more specific proposal.[58] It simply stated that the definition of the area of the regime should be such that significant hydrocarbon and hard mineral deposits would fall beyond national jurisdiction, so that the international community could benefit from the revenue to be derived from the exploitation of these resources.[59]

Even while debating the question of the international seabed regime,

Japan's utmost concern had to do with the high seas fishing that would be affected by the delimitation of the seabed to be placed under international management. In a working paper, "Outline of a Convention of the International Seabed Regime and Machinery," Japan contended that freedom of navigation and fishing and the right to lay submarine cables and pipelines were guaranteed under the existing regime of the high seas and should not be affected by the new regime.[60] In the same document Japan maintained that the new regime should govern what it called the "seabed resources," which included the mineral resources of the seabed and the ocean floor and the subsoil thereof, excluding the living resources.[61] On August 15, 1973, Japan submitted to the Second Subcommittee a paper entitled "Principles on the Delimitation of Coastal Seabed Area," which stated that "coastal states exercise sovereign rights for the purpose of exploring the coastal seabed area and exploiting its *mineral* resources [emphasis added]."[62] In short, Japan wanted the living resources both on and superjacent to the seabed subject to the proposed regime to be excluded from the definition of "resources." This position was consistent with Japan's basic approach to the question of resource jurisdiction, both national and international.

On the now perennial question of the breadth of the territorial sea, in July 1971 Japanese delegate Okawa presented a statement that marked a major departure from Japan's earlier position on this question: "My delegation is of the view that the figure of *twelve miles* presently claimed by more than forty-five States, represents the *best possible compromise as the maximum breadth of the territorial sea* [emphasis added]."[63] As we noted, Japan's formal position at the end of the Second UNCLOS was that three miles was the established territorial sea limit under international law. However, by early 1970s there had emerged, in the words of a Mexican delegate, "a sufficient international consensus of opinion for the twelve-mile limit of the territorial sea to be regarded as a customary rule."[64]

Support for the 12-mile limit for the territorial sea came from outside the framework of the Seabed Committee as well. For example, in the Declaration of Santo Domingo cited earlier, the Caribbean countries asserted that although the breadth of the territorial sea and the manner of its delimitation should be the subject of an international agreement, in the meantime "each state has the right to establish the breadth of its territorial sea up to a limit of 12 nautical miles to be measured from the applicable baseline."[65] In 1972, the African States Regional Seminar on the Law of the Sea (cited earlier) supported the view that coastal states had the right to determine their territorial sea limits not to exceed twelve nautical miles.[66] Moreover, in January 1971, the Asian–African Legal Consultative Committee adopted a report which recorded that its Sub-committee on the Law of the Sea, with the exception of very few delega-tions, "considered that at the present time any state would be entitled under international law to claim a territorial sea of twelve miles from the appropriate baseline."[67]

Furthermore, by 1971 the United States had come to accept the maxi-mum of twelve miles, albeit with one important condition. In its "Draft Articles on the Breadth of the Territorial Sea, Straits, and Fisheries," sub-mitted to the Second Subcommittee of the enlarged Seabed Committee on August 3, 1971, the United States stipulated: "Each State shall have the right, subject to the provisions of Article II, to establish the breadth of its territorial sea within limits of no more than 12 nautical miles, measured in accordance with the provisions of the 1958 Geneva Conven-tion on the Territorial Sea and Contiguous Zone."[68] The provisions of Article II set the condition that in straits used for international naviga-tion, all ships and aircraft in transit should enjoy the same freedom of navigation and overflight as they did on the high seas.[69] This major deci-sion by the United States government to conditionally accept the 12-mile territorial sea was one of the most important background factors in Japan's decision to speak of its readiness to accept the 12-mile limit. The Japanese delegation did not forget, however, to emphasize its pro–status quo position. As Okawa maintained,

> It is widely held that the interests of coastal States, such as the protection of coastal fisheries and the marine environment, could best be served by the extension of their territorial seas or by the establishment of other forms of jurisdictional zone. This argument cannot be entirely denied. But what is often overlooked is the fact that *the widening of the territorial seas means the corresponding shrinking of the high seas,* which are open to all na-tions. . . .
>
> [I]t seems clear to my delegation that for the international community to derive the maximum benefit from the oceans, our objective must be to rein-force the law of the sea on the basis of the *widest possible high seas* and *the narrowest possible territorial sea.*[70] (Emphasis added.)

On the issues affecting international navigation, Japan's defense of the status quo was not nearly as vocal and vigorous as on the questions of fisheries, territorial sea limits, coastal states' resource jurisdiction, and the seabed beyond national jurisdiction, but the basic attitude of the delegation was exactly the same. Okawa stressed, "The growth of world trade, so important for all nations, depends on efficient maritime transport, which can only be secured under the freedom of navigation."[71]

One issue that united Japan with the United States, the United Kingdom, France, and the Soviet Union was that of the status of straits used for international navigation. These maritime powers all supported free transit and opposed the establishment of a regime of innocent passage in international straits. They feared that the application of the concept of innocent passage would give straits states excessive and prejudicial discretion as to the determination of what constituted "innocent passage." Spain, with Gibraltar in mind, indicated in the enlarged Seabed Committee in 1972 that it was strongly opposed to the concept of free transit through straits, emphasizing that such a concept was justified only by the political, military, and strategic interests of a few states.[72] The pro-free transit states called for the establishment of a special status for international straits distinct from that of the territorial sea and attacked the draft articles submitted by Cyprus, Greece, Indonesia, Malaysia, Morocco, the Philippines, Spain, and Yemen, which demanded that navigation through the territorial sea and through straits used for international navigation be dealt with as one issue, since the straits in question were or formed part of territorial seas.[73]

The second issue on which Japan was in basic agreement with the other maritime powers had to do with the status of "archipelagic waters." In 1973, Fiji, Indonesia, Mauritius, and the Philippines proposed the concept of "archipelagos" as deserving of special status in international law.[74] According to the proposal, "archipelagic states" could enclose all waters lying within their outermost islands as "archipelagic waters" in which only innocent passage would be permitted. Accordingly, overflight would also be subject to exclusive jurisdiction of the island states claiming the status of archipelagic states. To counter this move, the United Kingdom submitted a proposal to limit the application of the archipelago principle. According to this proposal, no baseline connecting the outermost points on the outermost islands could exceed forty-eight nautical miles, and the ratio of the area of the sea to the area of land territory within the archipelagic perimeter could not be greater than five to one. The U.K. proposal also stipulated that the same regime that would apply to straits used for international navigation should also apply to those parts of archipelagic waters used as routes for international navigation between one part of the high seas and another or the territorial sea of another state.[75] The Japanese delegation supported this proposal, believing a clear definition of the archipelago would keep island states from enclosing too large a part of the high seas as archipelagic waters.[76] With regard to the nature of archipelagic jurisdiction, the Japanese delegation also supported the British proposal that attempted to secure free passage of ships through those parts of the archipelagic waters that had been used as routes for international navigation.[77] Furthermore, concerned that the establishment of a regime of the archipelagic waters might limit Japan's fishing, the Japanese delegation proposed that discussion on this question should consider not only the interests of the archipelagic states but also those of other states that had legtimately engaged in fishing in what would become archipelagic waters.[78]

On another issue of concern to Japan—measures to prevent and control marine pollution in the territorial sea and in the straits used for international navigation—Japanese head delegate Ogiso appealed to the Second Subcommittee on April 4, 1973, for agreement on a set of draft articles providing for internationally acceptable antipollution measures to be applied by the coastal states to ships passing through those areas. Ogiso emphasized that such measures should be adopted not unilaterally but on the basis of generally recognized international standards relating to the prevention of accidents, to the prevention of discharge of harmful substances into the marine environment, and to civil liability in case of pollution damage.[79]

Yet another controversial issue concerned the definition of the continental shelf. In accordance with Japan's position that seabed resources beyond the limits of national jurisdiction should refer only to mineral resources, its delegates maintained that "coastal seabed resources"—an expression they proposed to replace the more conventional term "continental shelf resources"—should include only mineral resources and exclude biological resources of the continental shelf such as sedentary species. They also proposed that the question of living resources in the water column should be examined separately from the issue of seabed resource exploration and exploitation.[80]

Japan also proposed that a new definition of the continental shelf be established to replace the one adopted by the Geneva Convention on the Continental Shelf. The Japanese delegation contended that the 1958 definition based on the criteria of depth and exploitability lacked precision and was inappropriate in view of technological progress. Japan's proposal defined the outer limit of the continental shelf strictly on the basis of a single and uniform criterion of distance.[81] The Japanese delegation hoped such a definition would help to hold back the coastal states' expanding resource and jurisdictional claims and settle the boundaries of the continental shelf between opposite or adjacent states on the basis of the equidistance principle.[82] Japan formally submitted these criteria for continental shelf delimitation to the Second Subcommittee in 1973.[83]

Marine pollution and coastal states jurisdiction over the formulation and implementation of measures to protect the marine environment were discussed by the Third Subcommittee of the Seabed Committee. In this area, Japan emphasized the universal nature of ocean environmental problems and the fact that marine pollution, once it has occurred, quickly spreads or moves from the coastal area of one country to that of another, thus rendering unilateral remedial approaches ineffective and requiring cooperative efforts among all the coastal states concerned. Japan found support for its position in the Declaration on the Human Environment and the General Guidelines and Principles for the Preservation of the Marine Environment. Adopted by the Conference on the Human Environment held in Stockholm in 1972, it embodied the concept of joint responsibility.

Japanese head delegate Ogiso pointed out that close cooperation between states was essential for the prevention and control of marine pollution and that action to prevent and control marine pollution should not be merely to transfer damage or hazards from one part of the marine environment to another. As a fundamental rule, he argued, the world's oceans should be treated as an integrated whole, and the partitioning of the oceans by coastal states with a view to protecting their own environment, while ignoring the environment of other states, could not be a solution to the global problem of pollution.[84] He further appealed to the international community to adopt a global framework in which international rather than national rules and standards would be observed by all states in every part of the ocean. More specifically, he rejected the assertion by a number of delegates that coastal states should be allowed to establish a pollution zone beyond their territorial waters in which they could exercise special authority for the prevention of pollution.[85] He noted three considerations that led the Japanese delegation to object to the zonal approach. First, the approach would create inconsistent modes of control inside and outside a given zone, while marine pollution knew

no boundaries. Second, with each coastal state setting up its own pollution control zone according to its policy and standards, the enforcement
of individual national legislation would create a state of confusion on the
high seas. Third, coastal states would be tempted to extend their coastal
zones as far as possible into the high seas, presumably to secure more
effective control of marine pollution.[86] For these reasons, Japan spoke in
favor of a coordinated regional and global approach in which states in
each region would cooperate in the formulation and implementation of
antipollution measures in accordance with the standards and principles
established by the international community as a whole, as well as in data
acquisition, exchange of information, and monitoring.[87]

With regard to the right of coastal states to regulate the movement of
vessels in their coastal area, Ogiso proposed that a set of common rules
and standards be developed and applied universally to all vessels. He
maintained that freedom of navigation might be endangered if national
pollution zones were established and coastal states inspected and arrested
foreign ships arbitrarily.[88]

These proposals stemmed from the Japanese desire to keep international navigation as free as possible from arbitrary interference by coastal
states. This basic approach was applied also to the question of enforcement of antipollution measures and the question of liability. On the first
question, Japan preferred the principle of flag-state jurisdiction until
detailed enforcement regulations concerning judicial procedures and
punitive measures could be worked out on the basis of internationally
established standards.[89] On the question of liability, Ogiso stated that his
government would cooperate with other governments in the development of internationally acceptable rules of law relating to liability and
compensation for environmental damages.[90]

In the area of scientific research, as in all other law of the sea areas, the
Japanese delegation maintained its basic approach in favor of international agreement and against unilateral action by coastal states. One of
the Japanese delegates, a prominent professor of international law and
World Court judge, Shigeru Oda, spoke on this question at the Third
Subcommittee in its twenty-eighth meeting on August 8, 1972, and out-
lined Japan's position on several specific issues. First, Oda stated that the
subcommittee's task was to establish a legal framework within which freedom of oceanographic research could be safeguarded to the fullest extent
possible and the exchange and dissemination of the results of scientific
research facilitated most effectively. He pointed out that freedom of

oceanographic research should be protected and that it should be restricted only when it was exercised without reasonable regard for the activities
of other states.[91]

Second, Oda spoke on the question of freedom of scientific research on
the high seas and stated that it should be added to the list of freedoms
established by the 1958 Convention on the High Seas—the freedoms of
navigation, fishing, laying of submarine cables and pipelines, and flying
over the high seas.[92] He pointed out that the new regime of the sea
should not result in any interference with fundamental oceanographic or
other scientific research conducted with the intention of open publication
for the benefit of the international community, although open publication should not be a condition for the right to freedom of scientific
research. He added that his country would do everything it could to promote the transfer of marine technology and experience in ocean research
to the developing countries.[93]

Third, on the question of scientific research relating to the seabed
under the high seas, Oda stated that the spirit of the provision in the
1958 Convention of the Continental Shelf regarding scientific research on
the continental shelf should apply equally beyond the continental shelf.
The provision he referred to stipulated that exploration of the continental
shelf and exploitation of its natural resources must not result in any interference with basic oceanographic or other scientific research carried out
with the intention of open publication.[94] In applying the spirit of this
provision to scientific research concerning the seabed beyond the limits of
national jurisdiction, Oda stated, Japan was of the view that the new seabed regime should not in principle jeopardize freedom of research on the
international seabed, or more specifically, that scientific research in the
area should not be subject to regulation by the international machinery.
Japan did recognize, however, as Oda added, that such research including
drilling, dredging, and excavation should be conducted with due consideration for the protection of the marine environment.[95]

Fourth, with regard to scientific research within the jurisdictions of
coastal states, Oda stated that fears that research by foreigners would lead
to the worsening of resource conditions were probably groundless and
that restrictive measures stemming from such unfounded fears could not
be accepted. Japan could not support the trends of unilateral and creeping jurisdiction, which, according to proponents of the trends, would be
applied to scientific research as well as to other activities by foreign
nationals.[96] The Japanese spokesman further maintained that his delega-

tion understood coastal states' interest in closely following any scientific research conducted in their territorial sea or on their continental shelf; that it supported the view that adequate information concerning research programs should be supplied in advance to the coastal states concerned; and that it believed that coastal states' participation in the research and access to its results should be assured. However, said Oda, his delegation did not agree that coastal states had any right to withhold their consent to such research.[97]

Preparations for the Third UNCLOS

Throughout the debate in the Ad Hoc Seabed Committee (1968), the permanent Seabed Committee (1969–1970), and the enlarged Seabed Committee (1971–1973) participating countries had begun to define their interests in all aspects of the international ocean regime and formulate their positions on issues of central concern to themselves. Developing countries, dissatsified with the traditional regime, wanted sweeping changes in all aspects of the regime. An increasing number of developed countries also saw greater benefits in new international legal arrangements and realized that they shared a number of interests with the developing coastal states. On the other hand, traditional maritime powers generally attempted to limit the expansionist demands of the other coastal states. Even among them, however, largely due to a different emphasis on various ocean interests, substantial differences appeared in their approach to the law of the sea debate, and these differences resulted in the weakening of the cohesion among the status quo states. This was an ominous sign of what was awaiting Japan as it prepared for the Third UNCLOS.

The Seabed Committee presented its reports to the General Assembly in the fall of 1973; thereupon the latter began setting up procedures for the Third UNCLOS. The preparatory work in the General Assembly was marred by difficulties arising from disagreements, largely between the developing and developed maritime countries, regarding procedural matters, particularly with regard to the manner in which UNCLOS was to make decisions on the law of the sea questions. The developing nations were convined that the majority vote system would help them achieve an international ocean regime favorable to their interests. The developed nations demanded that the conference make decisions by consensus according to which procedure a few developed states would be able to veto any majority vote they considered to be against their important interests. A related question was whether or not a vote would be necessary, and if so, at what point it would be taken. Eventually, they agreed that voting should be postponed until all possible attempts at consensus formation had been exhausted. With the procedural question out of the way, the General Assembly adopted Resolution 3067 (XXVIII) scheduling a two-week opening session for substantive discussions to take place in Caracas, Venezuela, in June 1974, following a preparatory session in New York in December 1973.

The New York session decided to set up a General Committee to be responsible for all aspects of conference progress composed of forty-eight nations—twelve each from Asia and Africa, nine each from Latin America and "Western Europe and others," and six from Eastern Europe. It also established three committees to deal with three distinct sets of issues. The First Committee would discuss matters relating to the seabed and ocean floor. The Second Committee would deal with general issues of the law of the sea, including the questions of the territorial sea, contiguous zone, straits used for international navigation, continental shelf, exclusive economic zone, coastal states' preferential rights, high seas, landlocked states, shelf-locked countries and states with narrow shelves or short coastlines, states with broad shelves, archipelagos, enclosed and semienclosed seas, artificial islands and installations, regime of islands, and transmission from the high seas. The Third Committee was to address the issues of marine environment and scientific research. These organizational decisions took up so much time that the first session was unable to formalize the important rules of procedure, including voting and consensus, and the session concluded on December 14. Nor were these questions resolved during the two informal sessions held in February and June 1974.

The second session opened in Caracas on June 20, 1974. The first week was devoted to the settlement of the outstanding procedural questions. Some participants proposed a majority vote, others preferred consensus, and the Soviet Union proposed a nine-tenths affirmative vote to adopt any decision. Finally, 115 participating nations agreed on the rules of procedure.[98] The rules stated, that voting would take place only on those substantive issues on which there was no prospect of consensus and that an affirmative vote equal to or greater than a number representing two-thirds of the participating states would be required for adoption of a decision on any issue. The rules also stipulated that the number of affirmative votes would have to be more than one-half of the states registered at the conference. Thus, a major hurdle was cleared for the beginning of substantive negotiations on the new law of the sea.

We have documented Japan's attitude toward and arguments against the mounting unilateral and multilateral pressures for a radical transformation of the international ocean regime during the 1960s and through the early part of the 1970s. Conservative, status quo–oriented, and even recalcitrant would be the most appropriate characterization of Japan's position during this period. But how long could Japan maintain its stubborn posture? However persistent its adherence to the principle of freedom of the seas and however consistent its application of this attitude to all the specific issues, Japan could not totally ignore the global push toward national ocean enclosure. Indeed, as its reluctant but unmistakable de facto acceptance of the 12-mile fishery zones of a number of coastal states on the Pacific rim made clear, Japan does not live in a vacuum. It is an "open system" capable of internal adjustments in response to external changes.[99] The question then is how effective was the Japanese policy-making system in making the necessary adjustments? Was Japan's seeming inflexibility and obstinacy simply a product of the country's economic dependence on the ocean? In other words, was it the outcome of careful, rational calculations of the costs and benefits of accepting demise of freedom of the seas? Or was it also a result of the way Japan's political system operated in reponse to the need for internal adjustments? It is to these questions that we now turn.

5

The Caracas–to–Geneva Session of the Third UNCLOS

As the first substantive round of negotiations at Caracas approached, domestic discussion in Japan began to gather momentum. As we saw in earlier chapters, unilateral, regional, and multilateral support for extended coastal state sovereignty and jurisdiction was clearly on the rise in the early 1970s. Domestic actors, both governmental and nongovernmental, began to respond to it, some with greater anxiety than others. Their concerns were focused on the two questions that had both symbolic and real implications for Japan's fishing and shipping interests—the 12-mile territorial sea and the 200-mile economic zone. In fact, the domestic debate during this period almost totally concentrated on these two questions.

Japan's Domestic Debate

The Ministry of Foreign Affairs (MFA) showed an accommodating attitude toward the question of the 12-mile territorial sea. At the House of Representatives Committee on Foreign Affairs on April 24, 1970, Foreign Minister Kiichi Aichi stated that Japan would accept twelve miles as the uniform breadth of the territorial sea provided that the majority of nations agreed on it. He warned, however, that Japan would not recognize a coastal state's special rights beyond that limit.[1] A year later, in explaining his government's general approach to the Caracas session, he reiterated Japan's willingness to accept the 12-mile limit.[2] On the other hand, the Ministry of Agriculture, Forestry, and Fisheries (MAFF) and the Fisheries Agency (FA) remained conspicuously quiet on this question. Rather, it was some fishery industry representatives who in the early 1970s began making public statements that indicated an increasing readiness, although by no means a consensus in the private sector, to accept the 12-mile limit. For example, Takeshi Nakamura, an executive of the Japan Fisheries Association, said, "The three-mile limit to which Japan adheres is not realistic in light of the world trend toward twelve-mile territorial waters."[3] Another accommodating statement was made by the president of Japan's largest fishing company, Taiyō Fisheries. Tojiro Chubu was quoted as saying, "The twelve-mile principle is the dominant trend of the world and it is desirable for Japan to act in accordance with the international trend."[4] Mass media also reported there was a consensus at the government level that Japan should accept the 12-mile limit.[5]

On the question of the 200-mile economic zone, however, there was little sign of accommodation. The fishery industry was as adamantly opposed to it as it was when the demand for it began in the 1960s. Opposition was particularly strong among fishery groups on the northernmost island of Hokkaidō, which stood to lose the most if 200-mile zones were established universally. On June 12, 1974, the prefectural government of Hokkaidō and Hokkaidō Fisheries Association submitted to the Fisheries Agency and the MFA their unanimous demand that Japan oppose the economic zone claims of coastal states at the upcoming Caracas session.[6] The industry's opposition grew even stronger when the MFA began hinting that perhaps the government should consider acceptance of the 200-mile economic zone. On May 17, 1974, Foreign Minister Masayoshi Ohira stated at the House of Representatives Committee on Foreign Affairs that the international situation was such that Japan could no longer block the coastal states' claims for economic zones.[7] Apparently, one of the key factors that prompted the MFA to take an accommodating posture was the decisions by the United States and the Soviet Union to accept the position of the developing coastal states. For at the same session of the Foreign Affairs Committee, Director-General Shinichi Sugihara of the Foreign Ministry's Office for the Law of the Sea Conference referred to the U.S. and Soviet decisions while he repeated the foreign minister's statement. Sugihara also gave a talk at the Japan Press Club in Tokyo on May 28 and stated, "The stage has passed for Japan to maintain its absolute opposition [to the 200-mile zones]." Instead, he suggested, the nation should engage in a discussion of how to utilize what could become Japan's own economic zone, which would be the seventh largest in the world.[8]

These signs of accommodation met stiff resistance from the fishery industry, which put pressure on the Fisheries Agency not to give in to the MFA.[9] As a result, the MAFF minister recommended with the Cabinet's formal support to oppose the concept of 200-mile economic zone at the coming UNCLOS session.[10] There were fishery policymakers who were convinced that the 200-mile economic or fishery zone would eventually become part of the international ocean regime, but they expected it would still take some time before it became a reality.[11] The Cabinet decision placed the MFA in an awkward position because it contradicted the foreign minister's earlier public statement. In an effort to explain the apparent inconsistency, Ambassador Motoo Ogiso, heading the Japanese delegation to the Caracas session, held a press conference in Caracas on June 19 and stated that Foreign Minister Ohira's statement at the House of Representatives Foreign Affairs Committee "simply explained that Japan's position had become difficult because a large number of states came to accept [200-mile economic zone]. Japan will maintain its opposition, but, depending on the progress of the conference, it may become difficult to maintain the opposition."[12] The Cabinet decision meant that the fishery policymakers achieved one of their immediate goals, that is, to get the government committed to the policy it favored. Another objective, to get other countries to accept this position, was to be tested at the Caracas session. On the other hand, the makers of foreign policy failed to convince the Cabinet to adopt their preferred approach. However, given the extremely uncertain and fluid situation at UNCLOS, the defeat of that goal did not necessarily constitute the defeat of the MFA's other central role, to balance Japan's policy with the international recognition of the 200-mile exclusive economic zone.

The Caracas Session

The Caracas session began on June 20 with 138 nations and the United Nations Council for Namibia attending.[13] On July 15, Japanese head delegate Ogiso made a general statement in the plenary session, reiterating what the Japanese delegates had argued throughout the discussions in the Seabed Committee. It was largely reactive, defensive, and status quo–oriented. Ogiso stated that the survival of an island country like Japan was inexorably linked to the seas and that, with limited potential for raising livestock, the Japanese depended on fish and fish products for about half of the total animal protein in their diet. Ogiso pointed out that Japan's basic interest lay in increasing international cooperation in the ocean area, and he demanded that the conference seek to accommodate the interests of all participating countries—developed and developing, coastal and landlocked or otherwise geographically disadvantaged as well as those traditionally dependent on the sea and its resources.[14] He then briefly addressed each major issue of the law of the sea. He indicated that Japan was prepared to support the 12-mile limit if the conference could agree upon a comprehensive arrangement for a regime of the sea that would be fair and reasonable to all states.[15] He asked that freedom of international navigation, particularly through straits used for international navigation, be ensured to the maximum extent but added that the legitimate interests of the coastal states with regard to pollution, the safety of navigation, and security should be given due regard.[16] On the question of exploration and exploitation of deep-seabed minerals, Ogiso stated that the extent of the coastal states' sovereign rights over the mineral resources of the seabed should be clearly defined in accordance with a distance criterion, which should not exceed two hundred miles.[17]

As for the question of conservation and management of the living resources of the sea, Ambassador Ogiso expressed Japan's support for any proposal aimed at increasing the role of international or regional bodies and its opposition to any claims to exclusive rights over fishery resources in a zone extending beyond the limits of the territorial sea.[18] His government was concerned, the ambassador continued, that the regime of the economic zone would cause underutilization of fishery resources and discrimination against landlocked or otherwise geographically disadvantaged states and distant-water fishing states.[19] Finally, Ogiso maintained that the management and exploitation of anadromous fish should not be exclusively in the hands of the coastal states in whose waters they spawned and emphasized that existing regional fishery commissions had dealt with this question for many years; its resolution should be left to the small number of countries directly involved.[20]

As we can readily see, these general positions were exactly the same as those the Japanese delegations presented to the Seabed Committee. That is, the outward expression of Japan's basic views and positions showed no discernible change during this period. But what about Japan's precise position on the questions of the breadth of the territorial sea and the 200-mile economic zone?

On July 30, Japanese head delegate Ogiso explained his government's position on these two questions at the Second Committee. He stated that Japan believed a coastal state should have the right to establish beyond its territorial sea—which in its view should be established at twelve miles—a coastal seabed area up to a maximum distance of two hundred miles, in which it exercised sovereign rights for the purpose of exploring and exploiting nonliving resources.[21] Japan's acceptance of the 12-mile limit was consistent with the overwhelming support that emerged in the Second Committee.[22] With regard to the delimitation of the territorial sea between two states opposite or adjacent to each other, Japan referred to and supported the provision in the 1958 Geneva Convention on the Territorial Sea and the Contiguous Zone setting out the principle of the median line.[23]

As far as the question of the 200-mile economic zone was concerned, Japan proposed that the coastal state's sovereign rights within the area beyond the 12-mile territorial sea, up to two hundred miles, be limited to only the mineral resources on the seabed. Japan called this area the "coastal seabed area" to replace what it considered an ambiguously defined concept of "continental shelf." It was opposed to claims of sovereign rights over resources beyond the 200-mile limit up to the end of the whole continental margin.[24] Where the coasts of two or more states are opposite or adjacent to each other, Japan proposed that the delimitation of the coastal seabed area be determined by agreement between the states involved on the basis of the principle of equidistance. Should such agreement fail, the proposal further stipulated that no state was entitled to extend its sovereign rights over the coastal seabed area beyond the median line.[25]

Throughout the Japanese presentation at the Second Committee, the central concern was to protect Japan's high-seas fisheries. In response to economic zone proposals that would grant coastal states sovereign rights over both seabed mineral resources and living resources in the zone, Japan adamantly charged that freedom of access limited to fishery resources beyond two hundred miles would be practically meaningless. Except for highly migratory ocean species, the Japanese maintained, fish live close to the shore, mostly within areas that would be covered by a 200-mile zone, and they were also unevenly distributed, tending to gather in great abundance off the coasts of a few countries. Should the proposed 200-mile economic zone be adopted, Japan warned, the major fertile fishing grounds of the world would come under the exclusive jurisdiction of a limited number of coastal states.[26] Therefore, Japan proposed, the areas beyond the territorial sea should retain basically the character of the high seas.[27] However, this proposal received little or no support.

With respect to the question of conservation of living resources, Japan reiterated its earlier position: the central role of regional and international organizations should be maintained and national-level conservation measures should be closely linked with international cooperation through regional and international organizations. Moreover, the Japanese delegation insisted that the new convention lay down certain basic principles relating to conservation measures on the basis of the best scientific evidence available, in consultation with appropriate regional or international organizations, and without discrimination among fishermen on the basis of nationality.[28]

There was no agreement on this issue in the Second Committee, but three alternative approaches emerged. One would have given coastal states complete exclusivity with regard to fisheries in the economic zone. Another—supported by the United States—would have combined exclusive coastal state regulation with conservation and full utilization duties and special treatment for anadromous and highly migratory species. The third approach—proposed by eight European Economic Community (EEC) states and Japan—emphasized the role of regional international organizations.[29]

On the issue of highly migratory species, the United States presented a proposal providing for coastal state regulation in the economic zone in accordance with international and regional conservation and allocation regulations—including fees, special allocations, enforcement rights, and other protections for coastal states. With regard to anadromous species such as salmon, the United States proposed a ban on fishing beyond the territorial sea, except as authorized by the state of origin, which Japan opposed, saying it would not be fair for coastal states in whose rivers salmon spawned to claim proprietary rights over the stock throughout their migration when they spent more than three-quarters of their life cycle in the middle of the ocean, thousands of miles away from their spawning grounds. Japan proposed instead that the problem be resolved through consultations among the limited number of countries directly affected.[30]

The trend with regard to the international straits question was in the direction of unimpeded passage on, over, and under straits used for international navigation.[31] In response to the concerns of straits states with respect to security, safety, and pollution, the United States and others suggested limiting the right of unimpeded passage to continuous and expeditious passage; prohibiting any threat or use of force against the territorial integrity or political independence of straits states; providing for adherence to international pollution and safety standards; stipulating strict liability in case of damage; and so forth.[32] Japan was silent on this particular issue.

Japan's navigation-related concerns and views were expressed in conjunction with the question of the regime of archipelagos. The main focus of discussion on this question in the Second Committee was the definition and limitation of the areas that could be enclosed as archipelagic waters and the rights of navigation and overflight in and over these areas. On both of these issues, the Japanese delegation spoke from the perspective of a major user of international navigation routes. Although Japanese head delegate Ogiso showed his government's understanding of the concerns of archipelagic states by pointing out that Japan itself was composed of a number of islands, his statement was designed to impress upon the participating countries the need to maintain as much freedom of navigation as possible. He maintained that the interests of the archipelagic states should be brought into harmony with those of other states and of the international community. In this regard, Ogiso suggested that an objective and reasonable definition of an archipelagic state should be provided, freedom of navigation for international maritime traffic safeguarded, and the existing navigational and other interests of the countries in the region protected.[33] The Japanese delegation supported the British proposal that the ratio of the area of the sea to that of land territory inside the perimeter of the area claimed to be archipelagic waters should not exceed five to one and that the length of archipelagic baselines should not exceed forty-eight miles.[34]

As far as archipelagic states' jurisdiction in such areas was concerned, Japan spoke in favor of the preservation of freedom of navigation. More specifically, the Japanese head delegate stated that the right of passage through archipelagic waters should not be as restricted as innocent passage. Accordingly, his delegation supported the right of transit passage by foreign vessels through archipelagic waters used as routes for international navigation on the one hand and on the other the right of innocent passage by foreign vessels, including fishing vessels, in other parts of archipelagic waters.[35] Japan was also concerned with the effect of an archipelagic regime on fishing and on the laying of submarine cables and pipelines. To ensure protection of these interests, Ogiso made a general statement that the future convention should protect the rights and interests of states relating to the existing uses of the areas enclosed by archipelagic baselines, including these two sets of rights and interests.[36]

Although substantive discussions on these and other key issues of the law of the sea had just begun in the Third UNCLOS and their resolution was hard to predict at the time, at least two things had become clear. First, the future convention would provide for a coastal state's right to establish a 12-mile territorial sea and a 200-mile economic zone even though the nature of the zone remained yet unclear. Second, Japan was by and large close to the main trend on the territorial sea question but in the extreme minority as far as the question of the 200-mile economic zone was concerned.

A Reassessment of Japanese Policy

Japanese government officials, particularly the fishery policymakers, were shocked that Japan was the only country among the UNCLOS participants to speak actively against the concept of the 200-mile economic zone. Table 2 testifies to this fact. Both the foreign policy and fishery policy sectors recognized that Japan was isolated in the international debate on the law of the sea.[37] In the area of fisheries, major changes in the Japanese strategy were clearly in order. On December 24, 1974, Prime Minister Takeo Miki, MAFF Minister Shintaro Abe, Chief Cabinet Secretary Ichitaro Ide, and other fishery-related government officials met with influential leaders of the fishery industry to assess the situation. There was a general consensus among those who gathered that the time had come for Japan to drop its unreserved opposition to the establishment of 200-mile economic zones.[38]

The industry began to reassess its own position following the Caracas session. On January 7, 1975 the Japan Fisheries Association set up its Law of the Sea Headquarters, with association president Iwao Fujita as its director. Four vice-directorships were allocated among other top leaders of the industry: Kohei Oikawa, president of the National Federation of Fisheries Cooperatives; Masao Okai, president of the Japan Deep-Sea Trawlers Association; Shoichi Masuda, president of the Federation of Japan Tuna Fisheries Cooperatives; and Tojiro Chubu, president of Taiyō Fisheries.[39] The Law of the Sea Headquarters coordinated the opinions of the fishery industry and submitted its position on law of the sea questions to the FA, the MAFF, and the MFA. The industry's new position was as follows:

1. The breadth of the territorial sea should be twelve miles.
2. Economic zones should be kept as limited as possible and the man-

TABLE 2
Positions of UNCLOS Member States on the 200-Mile Economic
Zone Issue at the 1974 Caracas Session

	No. of States	%	Selected States
Unconditional support	85	69	South Korea, India, Philippines, Malaysia, Indonesia, Egypt, Ghana, Kenya, Tanzania, Nigeria, Algeria, Zaire, Brazil, Chile,* Argentina, Canada, Iceland, Norway, Greece, China, Ecuador,* Peru
Conditional support	24	19	United States, Poland, Singapore, Soviet Union, Afghanistan
Passive opposition	15	11	8 EEC member states, Vatican
Active opposition	1	1	Japan
Total	125	100%	

SOURCE: Gaimushō Jōhōbunka Kyoku, *Dai Sanji Kaiyōhō Kaigi* [The Third Law of the Sea Conference] 2 (1975): 58.
*Countries supporting the 200-mile territorial sea.

agement of resources within the zones should be kept in accordance with standards to be established through international agreement rather than by unilateral decisions by coastal states.

3. Judicial power in economic zones should rest with the flag state rather than with coastal states.

4. Fishing fees within economic zones should be recognized only for those developing coastal states in dire financial need of resource conservation and fisheries development programs, and the amount of the fees should be decided by agreement between the coastal states and fishing countries concerned.

5. The status of anadromous species of fish should be determined by international fishery commissions in accordance with the fisheries development needs of the world, with due regard for the resource conservation and utilization needs of the world and the past records of traditional fishing countries.

6. The rule of free passage through international straits should be established with respect to nonmilitary ships and fishing boats.[40]

The industry clearly abandoned its earlier absolute opposition to coastal states' extended jurisdiction in favor of what can be called a "conditional acceptance." The condition was that the traditional fishing interests of Japan and other fishing nations should receive due regard in establishing a new fisheries regime.

The position adopted by the MAFF/FA was virtually identical to the industry's. On the other hand, the MFA emphasized the "package approach" to the law of the sea questions—that is, the position that all law of the sea questions should be resolved as a package through international agreement. Unlike the Fisheries Agency, which saw the protection of Japan's traditional fishing interests as its foremost objective, the MFA was concerned not only with fisheries but also with other law of the sea questions, including the status of straits used for international navigation; coastal states' jurisdiction over pollution control measures and scientific research activities in their economic zones; the definition of "archipelagic waters"; the regime for deep-seabed resources development; the regime for scientific research beyond economic zones; and so forth.[41] The MFA was well aware of the intricate trade-offs among these issues, particularly after it saw the importance of the relationship between the security-centered concerns of the United States and the Soviet Union with regard to the straits question and their position on the issue of economic zones. Furthermore, one of the MFA's central objectives was balancing Japan's own decisions with those most likely to be reached by the international community. Therefore, the ministry's approach was by necessity more complex than that of the single-issue–oriented strategy of the Fisheries Agency or MAFF. The existing uncertainty surrounding the direction of the UNCLOS debate also contributed to the foreign policymakers' difficulties. They found it particularly problematic to coordinate the government's decision on whether or when Japan should extend its territorial sea limit with the UNCLOS debate on the status of straits used for international navigation.

At the same time government policymakers were reassessing their UNCLOS strategies after the Caracas session, domestic pressure for the extension of Japan's territorial sea limit was mounting. The pressure was largely due to the extensive fishery damage being caused by Soviet fishing operations in the northern and eastern coastal areas of the country.

Soviet fishing began on an experimental basis off Hokkaidō coasts in the early 1960s and gradually grew both in scale and in the area it covered. Free of Japanese domestic fishery regulations, Soviet fishermen could operate large-sized boats just outside the 3-mile territorial limit, out-competing Japanese coastal fishermen who were subject to various strict restrictions for purposes of resource conservation. Fishing gear losses, direct physical interference, and dumping of empty cans and garbage resulted in extensive damage. As Table 3 indicates, the number and size of hazardous incidents increased drastically around 1974–1975.

Damage was most extensive off the coasts of Hokkaidō, accounting for as much as 90 percent of the total number of reported cases and 80 percent of the total value of damage. After repeated Japanese protests, the Soviet Union agreed to enter into negotiations on ways to curb future problems. After seventy days of hard negotiations, the two sides signed a three-year agreement on June 7, 1975.[42] The accord included the establishment of preventive measures, procedures for dispute settlement, and a bilateral committee for damage compensation settlement, but the system did not operate as effectively and smoothly as the coastal fishermen had hoped. For example, of the 752 compensation requests that Japanese fishermen had filed with the committee by April 11, 1976, only two of them had been forwarded to Moscow for settlement. The total compensation requested by Japanese fishermen amounted to as much as ¥600 million.

Fishery damage did decline in the months immediately following the signing of the Japan-Soviet fishing operation agreement. But soon after the MiG incident of September 1976, involving the defection of a Soviet pilot, the damage again increased.[43] Dissatisfied with the continuing Soviet fishing and resulting trouble, coastal fishermen pressed their demand for an early extension of Japan's territorial sea from three to twelve miles. They hoped that the action would effectively force Soviet fishermen out of their traditional fishing grounds. President of the National Federation of Fisheries Cooperatives Kohei Oikawa and other representatives of the fishing industry visited Prime Minister Miki on July 1, 1975, and requested that the government decide to extend Japan's territorial sea limit, but the prime minister gave no clear-cut answer.[44] On September 17, all fishery groups in the northern prefectures gathered in Sapporo, Hokkaidō, for an annual East Japan Fisheries Promotion Conference and demanded that the government immediately extend the country's territorial sea limit to twelve miles. Fishermen in the

TABLE 3
Damage to Japanese Fisheries Caused by Soviet Fishing Off the Coasts of Japan

		Apr.	May	June	July	Aug.	Sept.	Oct.	Nov.	Dec.	Jan.	Feb.	Mar.	Total
1973–1974	Number of incidents	—	—	—	—	—	—	9	4	8	42	38	22	123
	Value of damage (¥)	—	—	—	—	—	—	502	567	127	3,575	1,086	576	6,433
1974–1975	Number of incidents	—	—	—	—	—	—	86	68	139	301	410	38	1,042
	Value of damage (¥)	—	—	—	—	—	—	2,783	6,327	4,873	5,885	13,203	947	34,018
1975–1976	Number of incidents	—	3	5	2	2	1	91	85	56	11	40	31	327
	Value of damage (¥)	—	105	73	23	53	13	2,686	1,170	1,474	170	1,294	1,877	8,938
1976–1977	Number of incidents	—	—	11	9	1	12	100	99	69				301
	Value of damage (¥)	—	—	326	814	22	1,259	1,897	1,673	1,039				7,030

SOURCE: Shūgiin Nōrin Suisan Iinkai Chōsashitsu, *Ryōkai-hōan ni tsuite* [On the Bill for the Law on the Territorial Sea], April 7, 1977, pp. 6–7.

NOTES: The statistics are based on reports submitted by prefectures to the Fisheries Agency. The 1976–1977 statistics include those reports submitted by telephone and are not final. Damage includes cutting of nets, obstruction of fishing operations, dumping of empty cans and other waste materials, and so on.

western prefectures of Japan, who held their annual West Japan Fisheries Promotion Conference on November 7 in Yamaguchi Prefecture, made the same demand. On October 30, representatives of fishery groups and the prefectural government of Hokkaidō visited the Fisheries Agency and submitted a written request for immediate declaration of territorial sea extension. Furthermore, on December 9, the fishery industry sponsored a "National Fishermen's Conference" in Tokyo and adopted a resolution calling for the same action.

The government's response was slow. On February 26, 1975, Foreign Minister Kiichi Miyazawa stated in the House of Representatives Foreign Affairs Committee that Japan would eventually have to extend its territorial sea limit from three to twelve miles but that such action would have to wait until it became clear that the UNCLOS could not reach an agreement on the question of the breadth of the territorial sea.[45] Behind the foreign minister's cautious statement was the MFA's basic stand that the law of the sea questions should be solved as a package. In particular, the ministry was concerned with the question of the international legal status of straits used for international navigation and Japan's policy regarding its own straits areas.

At the time, "free passage" was the rule for Japanese straits, including the Straits of Tsugaru, Tsushima, and Sōya (Figure 1), through which foreign warships—namely those of the United States and the Soviet Union —passed in considerable numbers. Should Japan decide to extend its territorial sea limit to twelve miles, the Straits of Tsugaru and Tsushima would be enclosed by Japan's national sovereignty. If the status of these straits were to be the same as that of the other areas of Japan's territorial sea, then the same domestic laws and policies should apply there as to the other areas. This would create a difficult problem because the so-called "three nonnuclear principles," which had become one of the main components of Japan's nuclear policy, would have to be applied as well.[46]

The three nonnuclear principles were, stated simply, that nuclear weapons were not to be possessed, manufactured, or introduced into Japanese territory. The principles in this form dated back to the 1960s. On December 11, 1967, Prime Minister Eisaku Sato had presented them to the House of Representatives, and they had since become a national consensus. All political parties, both conservative and progressive, strongly supported the principles, as demonstrated by the fact that in November 1971 the House of Representatives unanimously adopted a resolution endorsing the government's policy. Public support for the policy is

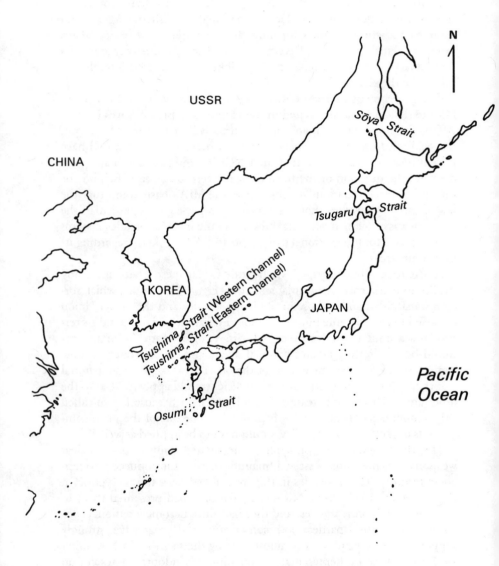

N

USSR

CHINA

Sōya Strait

Tsugaru Strait

KOREA

Tsushima Strait (Western Channel)

Tsushima Strait (Eastern Channel)

JAPAN

Osumi Strait

Pacific Ocean

FIGURE 1: Japanese Straits

strong, and the slightest sign of departure from it on the part of the government is subject to highly emotional, politicized criticism. As I will discuss in the next chapter, in the 1970s the government was in no position to abandon any one of these three principles.

The nonnuclear principle that had the most immediate relevance to the territorial sea and straits questions was that Japan would not allow the introduction of nuclear weapons into its territory, presumably both its land and sea territory. If Japan were a party to some international treaty that provided for the rule of free passage or "innocent passage" allowing passage of warships, nuclear-armed or otherwise, through straits used for international navigation, then the provision would take precedence over the domestic policy. That would mean that the government would permit foreign warships carrying nuclear weapons to pass through the Japanese straits in question. However, the status of the so-called international straits was at the time being debated in UNCLOS and a final agreement was not yet in sight. In the absence of an international agreement on this question, the MFA was not ready to acquiesce in the domestic pressure for territorial expansion that would enclose most of the straits areas in question.

In contrast, the response of fishery policymakers was more accommodating toward the wishes of the coastal fishermen. On February 28, the MAFF minister stated in the Budget Committee of the lower house that Japan should extend its territorial sea limit irrespective of the result of the Geneva session in the spring.[47] The statement was strongly supported by the fishery industry and opposition political parties as well as by the fishery-oriented members of the Liberal Democratic Party (LDP).

As the Geneva session approached, the government had to formalize its position on the upcoming round of negotiations. It also had to show its response to the coastal fishermen's demand for an early extension of the territorial sea limit. The MFA wanted to "wait and see," while the MAFF/FA wanted to set up Japan's 12-mile territorial sea regardless of the outcome of the Geneva session. When the competing proposals were presented to the Cabinet, it decided on March 14, 1975 to adopt the "wait and see" approach. Its formal position may be summarized as follows:

1. Japan would support an international agreement on twelve miles as the uniform breadth of the territorial seas of all nations.

2. Japan would agree to coastal states' establishment of 200-mile eco-

nomic zones, provided that the traditional fishing interests of Japan and other fishing countries were protected.

3. Japan would support the rule of free passage through straits used for international navigation.

4. Japan would support the solving of these and all other law of the sea issues as a package.[48]

In arriving at this official government position, there was a conspicuous absence of any significant attempt to resolve the important differences between the policy responses recommended by the MFA and by the MAFF. The Cabinet simply adopted the noncontroversial position—to wait and observe the Geneva session before making a final decision—on the territorial sea issue. On the other hand, there was a general consensus within the government that Japan would recognize the establishment of 200-mile economic zones. Although there was a condition attached to the position, it marked an important departure from the government's stand on this issue prior to and during the Caracas session a year earlier.

Now that categorical opposition to the 200-mile economic zone was abandoned, the fishery policymakers' goal changed to that of protecting within foreign economic zones as much of Japan's fishing rights as possible. Operationally, this meant the protection of what distant-water fishermen termed *jisseki,* literally "established record," or the catch level that they had thus far enjoyed within foreign coastal waters. From the perspective of the Cabinet, the task of unifying the government's position on the 200-mile economic zone question had become slightly easier than prior to the Caracas session, since both foreign and fishery policymakers had come to agree that there was now an international consensus on the 200-mile economic zone. The question of the 12-mile territorial sea, however, became a formidable issue for the Cabinet.

The Geneva Session

The third session of the Third UNCLOS took place in Geneva from March 17 to May 10, 1975, with 140 nations and a number of observers attending. The session produced two important documents: the Informal Single Negotiating Text (ISNT) prepared by the chairmen of the three committees and an informal text on the economic zone prepared at the initiative of Jens Evensen of the Norwegian delegation and reflecting the views of many moderate states.⁴⁹ Together the two documents indicated areas in which some compromises had been made and more could be expected, as well as other areas in which substantial intraregional and interregional conflicts over specific issues remained.

The ISNT reflected the general consensus on the 12-mile breadth of the territorial sea.⁵⁰ An attempt had been made with regard to the concept of "innocent passage" to provide objective criteria for the determination of "innocence." As a result, Article 16 of the ISNT elaborated a dozen activities that would render passage not innocent, or "prejudicial to the peace, good order, or security of the coastal State."⁵¹ None of the stipulated activities presented any significant problem to Japanese fishing interests since Japan was willing to abide by the rule that no foreign fishing would be allowed in the territorial sea; nor did they pose any serious problem for Japan's shipping interests. By comparison, however, the status of straits used for international navigation was far from settled at the close of the Geneva session. There were four primary coalitions involved in negotiations on this issue: (1) the United States and the Soviet Union; (2) the archipelagic states of Indonesia, the Philippines, Fiji, Malaysia, and Mauritius; (3) about seventeen moderate states known as the United Kingdom/Fiji coalition; and (4) Spain and five Arab countries.⁵² The superpowers insisted on unimpeded transit through straits used for international navigation, so that their naval and air mobility through and over strategically located straits around the world would be protected. The archipelagic group insisted that the superpowers accept the concept of "transit passage," which would at the same time give the straits state control over navigation and establish an obligation against straits states' arbitrary action and some objective measures by linking that obligation with dispute settlement procedures proposed elsewhere for the new regime.⁵³ The Spain/Arab group demanded that straits states maintain full authority to regulate passage and that prior notification be required for tankers, warships, aircraft, nuclear-powered vessels, and other ships of "special characteristics." It was this extremist position that made it difficult for the other groups to produce a compromise solution to the straits issue. However, the United Kingdom/Fiji group of moderate states did manage to produce a compromise that was eventually included in the ISNT, Part II.⁵⁴

According to the ISNT, a right of transit passage would be recognized for straits used for international navigation.⁵⁵ "Transit passage" was defined as "the exercise in accordance with the provisions of this Part of

the freedom of navigation and overflight solely for the purpose of continuous and expeditious transit of the strait between one area of the high
seas or an exclusive economic zone and another area of the high seas or an
exclusive economic zone."[56] Article 40 stated that straits states would be
able to designate sea-lanes and prescribe traffic separation schemes for
navigation in the straits for safety purposes. While such sea-lanes or traffic separation schemes were to conform with generally accepted international regulations and straits states were required to refer proposals for
sea-lanes or traffic separation schemes to the competent international
organization, the Intergovernmental Maritime Consultative Organization
(IMCO), the organization's adoption of sea-lanes and separation schemes
was contingent upon the straits state's agreement. According to Article
41, straits states would have the right to make laws and regulations relating to transit passage through straits, with respect to their safety, environmental, fishing, and other concerns. Foreign ships would be required to
comply with such laws and regulations, but such laws and regulations
should "not discriminate in form or fact among foreign ships" nor
should their application "have the practical effect of denying, hampering
or impairing the right of transit passage."[57] Article 43 prohibited suspension of transit passage.

These provisions indicate that the ISNT was clearly a product of compromise: on one side were the security, safety, environmental, and economic concerns of straits states; on the other, the user-oriented interests
of states that wanted to keep international navigation through straits as
free as possible. The compromise nature of the document may also be
seen in the absence in the negotiating text of any provisions, as proposed
by the Spain/Arab group, concerning prior notification for passage of
warships, airplanes, tankers, nuclear-powered vessels, or other ships of
"special characteristics." All in all, the right of transit passage through
straits used for international navigation would be subject to much less
coastal state discretion than the right of innocent passage through other
straits and in the ordinary territorial sea. However, these ISNT provisions
were not a final agreement of the UNCLOS participants, and uncertainty
regarding the straits issue continued after the Geneva session.

Uncertainty also persisted with regard to the exclusive economic zone.
One of the basic difficulties was that the concept was relatively recent and
subject to the different and inconsistent requirements that various nations attached to it. This was clearly demonstrated by the multiplicity of
approaches to its definition that were proposed during the Geneva ses

sion.[58] First, on the question of the legal character of the economic zone, some delegates argued that the economic zone was neither territorial sea nor high seas but *sui generis*. Others, including Japan, argued that the economic zone was high seas and that high seas freedoms should be preserved in the zone.[59] Japan, of course, wanted to retain as many of the high seas freedoms as possible, including the freedom of fishing in the economic zone. Therefore, the Japanese delegates paid close attention to the set of disagreements that emerged in the Second Committee regarding fishery jurisdiction within the economic zone. The Soviet Union and the EEC wanted to empower regional fishery commissions to determine the allowable fish catch in the economic zone, whereas a large number of developing coastal states demanded that they have the full power to determine the allowable catch. The ISNT adopted a compromise position on this question by providing, in Article 51, that "the coastal State shall determine the allowable catch of the living resources in its exclusive economic zone" but that conservation and management measures to be developed by the coastal state should "be designed to maintain or restore populations of harvested species at levels which can produce the maximum sustainable yield," subject to qualifications for environmental, economic, and biological reasons.[60] The informal text further stipulated that "the coastal State shall promote the objective of optimum utilization of the living resources in the exclusive economic zone without prejudice to Article 51."[61] However, the ISNT specified that "the coastal State shall determine its capacity to harvest the living resources of the exclusive economic zone," thus giving the coastal state near-monopoly over the allocation of the living resources in the economic zone.[62]

According to the ISNT, other states would have access only to the surplus of the allowable catch, to be determined by agreements or other arrangements between the coastal state and the fishing countries concerned.[63] Furthermore, nationals of other fishing states would have to comply with the conservation measures and other requirements established by the coastal state, including licensing, specification of required information concerning fishing activities, and enforcement procedures.[64] Thus, in the opinion of some legal scholars and participants in the conference, Articles 50 and 51 together left virtually nothing that the coastal state could not do with respect to resources in the exclusive economic zone.[65] Should almost exclusive resource jurisdiction such as this be adopted as part of the new law of the sea, Japan's efforts to reject exclusive claims by coastal states, as we saw in its bilateral negotiations with other Pacific-rim countries in the 1960s, would be of no avail. Coastal states would be able to substantially reduce Japan's fish catch and significantly increase the cost of its fishing efforts in foreign economic zones.

There were other issues equally threatening to Japan. One concerned the status of highly migratory species. Japan wanted to provide regional and international fishery organizations with the maximim authority over the conservation and management of these stocks of fish and vehemently opposed the attempt by other coastal states to obtain exclusive jurisdiction over these species. Since the basic disagreement could not be solved at this time, the ISNT simply stipulated that "the coastal State and other States whose nationals fish highly migratory species in the region shall cooperate directly or through appropriate international organizations" to ensure conservation and to promote optimum utilization of such species both within and beyond the exclusive economic zone. It added that where no such international organizations existed, the states concerned should cooperate to establish one and participate in its work.[66]

The status of anadromous species of fish was another issue over which there were major disagreements, although a consensus was beginning to appear in favor of the state of origin over conservation, management, and allocation decisions concerning these species. Japan found itself in a minority position in support of regional rather than national conservation and management schemes. The ISNT finally adopted provisions that recognized for the state of origin "the primary interest in and responsibility for such stocks."[67] The state of origin could establish the maximum allowable catch and regulate fishing for anadromous species within its own economic zone and on the high seas beyond the jurisdiction of other states.[68] On the other hand, the state of origin would have the obligation to cooperate in minimizing economic dislocation in other states fishing these stocks.[69] Only economic dislocation would be a sufficient reason for the state of origin to give special consideration to the states fishing the anadromous species that spawned in its rivers and estuaries. Otherwise, fisheries for anadromous stocks would be allowed only in the exclusive economic zone.[70] Special rights of coastal states were also recognized with respect to catadromous species.[71]

These provisions in the ISNT were highly objectionable to Japanese fishery concerns. For example, the director of the FA's Oceanic Fisheries Bureau, Akira Matsuura, had four major objections.

1. Japan could not accept a coastal state's right to determine the allowable catch within its exclusive economic zone.[72]

2. The ISNT failed to protect traditional fishing interests because, according to the document, the traditional fishing interests of fishery-dependent economies were but one among several factors to be considered in a coastal state's decision to grant other states access to its exclusive economic zone.[73]

3. According to the ISNT, sedentary species on the continental shelf would be considered to belong within coastal state jurisdiction.[74]

4. For the continuation of distant-water fishing of highly migratory species, more specific arrangements would be necessary than were provided for in the ISNT, which simply referred to cooperation between the coastal and fishing states through international organizatons with regard to these stocks.[75]

The question of passage through archipelagic waters was yet another controversial issue at the Geneva session. According to the compromise provisions in the ISNT, the archipelagic state would have the right to design archipelagic sea-lanes and air routes "suitable for the safe, continuous, and expeditious passage of foreign ships and aircraft through its archipelagic waters."[76] Within the sea-lanes, the right of archipelagic sea-lanes passage would be established. This right was defined as "the exercise of the rights of navigation and overflight in the normal mode for the purpose of continuous and expeditious transit through an archipelago between one part of the high seas or an exclusive economic zone and another part of the high seas or an exclusive economic zone."[77] The ISNT also provided for the duties of the archipelagic state in exercising its right to create archipelagic sea-lanes, the designation and international review of sea-lanes and traffic separation schemes, and the regulatory rights of the island state with regard to archipelagic sea-lanes passage, all of which were similar to the provisions concerning transit passage of straits.[78] In archipelagic waters outside sea-lanes and airspace, the ISNT established a right of innocent passage. Unlike the right of transit passage through international straits, however, the right of innocent passage through archipelagic waters would be subject to suspension by the archipelagic state where such suspension was "essential for the protection of its security."[79]

While the navigation- and fishing-related concerns of a number of states were not satisfactorily answered by the debate among the Second Committee participants, there appeared to be agreement on the 1:9 land-to-sea area ratio as a criterion for the maximum area of the sea that could be enclosed as archipelagic waters.[80] Second, agreement appeared to be emerging on the use of straight baselines connecting the outermost points of the outermost islands, seaward of which the territorial sea, the contiguous zone, the economic zone, and the continental shelf were to be measured.[81]

Despite such important progress, the debate in the Second Committee was also characterized by increased conflict among and within caucusing groups and numerous regional and issue-specific groups of states, and the debate by no means produced a stable consensus on the key issues addressed by the committee.[82] Add to that the extremely difficult negotiations regarding the regime of the seabed and international seabed machinery that were taking place in the First Committee and one would have to conclude that as of the spring of 1975 the international community had a long road ahead before it could agree on a universally acceptable law of the sea.

Japan Moves Toward Territorial Sea Expansion

After the Geneva session, the MFA was still committed to its earlier position that the law of the sea questions should be resolved as a package. Therefore, it was opposed to unilateral actions by coastal states, including Japan. It did recognize, however, that the government needed to respond to the growing domestic demand for territorial sea expansion. Support for the 12-mile limit had been expressed not only by the fishery industry and the fishery policymakers but also by all the opposition parties and the fishery-oriented members of the ruling LDP, not to mention the general public. The ministry's response came in the form of a proposal for the establishment of a 12-mile fishery zone instead of a 12-mile territorial sea. The proposal was based on the precedent Japan had set for itself in its dealings with Korea in 1965. All Japan had to do now was to set up the fishery zone uniformly throughout its coastal waters. The practice had also clearly been followed by many other coastal states, and Japan's 12-mile fishery zone at the time certainly would not have posed serious domestic or international problems.[83]

Domestically, the MFA proposal was supported by those LDP members who were concerned with the intricate relationship between the question of Japan's territorial sea and Japan's other interests, particularly marine transportation and defense concerns. On July 8, the LDP's Special Committee on the Law of the Sea adopted a position supporting the establishment of a 12-mile fishery zone to deal with the problem of Soviet fishing in Japanese coastal waters. The Special Committee listed three reasons why the extension of the territorial sea limit to twelve miles was not appropriate. First, Japan should not take up the question of the territorial sea apart from the closely related and unresolved questions of the 200-mile economic zone and of the status of straits used for international navigation. Second, the government had to make some decision on the question of passage of ships through Japan's international straits, since such passage might affect the three nonnuclear principles. Third, it was not clear whether territorial sea expansion was necessarily advantageous to Japan, particularly because it would have implications for the country's defense capabilities.[84]

In contrast, fishery policymakers were still committed to their earlier pledge that they would promote an early territorial extension. MAFF minister Shintaro Abe reaffirmed this pledge on May 7, when he stated after a Cabinet meeting that the developments in the UNCLOS debate led him to believe "there [was] no longer any external obstacle to [Japan's] declaration of a twelve-mile territorial sea."[85] His position was supported by the fishery-oriented LDP members who composed the Fishery Division of the LDP's Policy Affairs Research Council. Additional support came from within the Parliament. For example, on July 3, the House of Councillors Committee on Agriculture, Forestry, and Fisheries adopted a resolution calling for the prompt declaration of the extension of Japan's territorial sea to twelve miles.[86] Further support came from all opposition political parties. In response to a questionnaire sent by the National Federation of Fisheries Cooperatives, the Socialist Party, Kōmeitō (the Clean Government Party), the Communist Party, and the Democratic Socialist Party unanimously expressed support for early establishment of a 12-mile territorial sea. They also voiced opposition to the MFA's proposal for a 12-mile exclusive fishery zone.[87]

In the meantime, demands by coastal fishermen for a 12-mile territorial sea had developed into a nationwide campaign. On July 15, 1975, President Oikawa of the National Federation of Fisheries Cooperatives met with Prime Minister Takeo Miki and Chief Cabinet Secretary Ichitaro Ide and requested that the government promptly declare the extension of Japan's territorial sea to twelve miles. He submitted the same request to the chairman of the LDP Policy Affairs Research Council, Raizo Matsuno, the following day.[88] On September 17, fishery groups in the northern prefectures gathered in Sapporo for an annual East Japan Fisheries Promotion Conference and demanded that the government move immediately to adopt the 12-mile territorial sea.[89] The same appeal was made by fishery groups in the western parts of Japan, which held a similar promotional conference in Yamaguchi Prefecture on November 7.[90] Furthermore, on October 30, thirty representatives of the fishery groups and the prefectural government of Hokkaidō visited the Fisheries Agency and submitted a written request for immediate declaration of territorial sea extension.

By late 1975 it had become evident that interministerial coordination was in order; the MFA and MAFF/FA were supporting inconsistent policies. A new office was set up in the Councillor's Office of the Prime Minister's Office to deal with this problem. Although the new office was far from a genuine coordinative body in the sense of having policy coordinative authority—because it did not—it provided a channel of communication among the ministries concerned.[91]

On January 30, 1976, the Cabinet decided that Japan would indeed extend its territorial sea limit from three to twelve miles but that the timing of the action would be determined after the New York session in the spring.[92] The decision was a step forward compared with the Cabinet's previous decision to "wait and see." While the January decision did not fully accommodate the MAFF/FA proposal for prompt territorial sea extension, it did mark an incremental change. However, it fell far short of satisfying the wishes and desires of the coastal fishermen in the northern and northeastern parts of Japan who wanted more immediate measures to ban foreign fishing in their fishing grounds.

What added to the frustration of these fishermen were the South Korean fishing boats that had begun large-scale fishing operations in the northern coastal areas of the country. Along with the Soviet fishing that had become a cause of great anxiety and frustration among the coastal fishermen, the South Korean fishing caused them to push even more vigorously their campaign for early establishment of a 12-mile territorial sea. As Table 4 indicates, the South Korean fishing caused serious damage to the fishing operations of small-scale fishermen on the northern coasts of Japan. The damage was most extensive from 1975 to 1976.

To solve this problem, private-level discussions began between representatives of the Japanese and South Korean fishery industries in June 1975. It was not until the end of 1976, however, that an agreement was reached on measures for preventing future trouble between the fishermen of the two countries. When the private-level agreement proved ineffective, discussion was moved up to government level but was equally ineffective in

TABLE 4
Damage to Japanese Fisheries Caused by South Korean Fishing
Off the Coasts of Japan

	1973–1974	1974–1975	1975–1976	1976–1977
Number of incidents	9	6	270	57
Value of damage (in thousands of yen)	2,730	1,580	86,651	18,660

SOURCE: Shūgiin Nōrin Suisan Iinaki Chōsashitsu, *Ryōkai-hōan ni tsuite* [On the Bill for the Law on the Territorial Sea], April 7, 1977, pp. 6–7.
NOTE: Each period is from April of the beginning year to March of the following year, except for 1976–1977, which is April 1976 to December 1976 only. Damages are mostly gear losses.

alleviating the problem. To the coastal fishermen's great dismay, further-more, the government could not break the interministerial deadlock over the question of the territorial sea expansion and, as the 1976 New York session of the Third UNCLOS approached, the government adopted vir-tually the same strategy on this question that it had adopted earlier in January.

6

Japan's 12-Mile Territorial Sea Decision

WHILE the government was suffering from the inability to solve the disagreement between the MFA and MAFF/FA on the question of Japan's territorial sea limit, a number of other coastal states were resorting to unilateral decisions. On October 15, 1975, Iceland extended its fishery zone from fifty to two hundred miles; on November 5, Mexico established a 200-mile economic zone; and in December, the EEC member nations were preparing for the establishment of a joint 200-mile fishery zone. Among the unilateral actions by coastal states, that of the United States attracted the most attention in Japan.

When Japanese decision makers learned around 1974 that there was a legislative effort in the United States to establish a 200-mile fishery zone, they were hoping that the move would not materialize. The reports received were ambivalent and contradictory. On the one hand, they were aware of growing domestic pressure in favor of protecting U.S. coastal fisheries by extending its fishery jurisdiction, and at the same time they knew that the administration was opposed to such a move.[1] Indeed, as late as October 1975 Secretary of State Henry Kissinger stated that the United States should refrain from unilateral actions.[2]

To clarify the U.S. administration's position and to express Japan's concern, the Japanese government contacted the U.S. government through diplomatic channels. The Japanese ambassador submitted a formal request that the United States refrain from the proposed unilateral action.[3] Foreign Minister Kiichi Miyazawa met with the U.S. secretary of state in late October and asked that the United States consider the matter with caution.[4] Domestic groups in Japan also expressed anxiety about the prospect of a U.S. 200-mile fishery zone. For example, on November 11, 1975, the members of the LDP Maritime Dietmen's League asked Prime Minister Miki to make a personal appeal to the U.S. president to use his veto power to block the 200-mile bill.[5]

By the end of 1975, however, it became clear that the administration would not be able to override congressional pressure. Finally, the 200-mile zone bill was passed by Congress in March and signed by President Gerald Ford on April 7, 1976. As a result, the Fishery Conservation and Management Act of 1976 was scheduled to go into effect on March 1, 1977.

The first Japanese reaction was a strong protest. The day after the president signed the bill, the director of the Public Information and Cultural Affairs Bureau of the MFA issued a statement expressing the government's regret over the U.S. action.[6] The government's formal protest was conveyed to the U.S. government when MAFF Minister Shintaro Abe met with U.S. Commerce Secretary Elliot Richardson in Tokyo on May 28. Abe expressed regret over the U.S. action in the absence of a final UNCLOS agreement, to which Richardson replied by saying that 200-mile zones had already become the central trend in the world and that the recognition of the U.S. fishery zone was a prerequisite for future foreign fishing in the area.[7]

Japan's concern over the new U.S. fishery zone was conveyed to the United States through nondiplomatic channels as well. For example, between July 19 and 22, 1976, the LDP Maritime Dietmen's League sent a delegation to Washington headed by Takeo Okubo, chairman of the LDP Special Committee on the Law of the Sea. Members of the Japanese Parliament visited Commerce Secretary Richardson, other high government officials, and influential members of Congress and proposed that Japan and the United States conclude a provisional fisheries agreement without recognition of the U.S. 200-mile jurisdiction until the conclusion of the Third UNCLOS. The proposal was flatly rejected.[8] Japanese fishery industry management and workers also joined the protest. The All-Japan Seamen's Union sent its representatives to the United States during the summer to carry out a public relations campaign to apprise U.S. labor organizations of the serious consequences that the new 200-mile fishery zone would have for the Japanese fishery labor force.[9] A group of fishery management leaders toured the western United States and met with regional fishery groups to emphasize the importance of fisheries to Japan.[10]

Before the close of the spring UNCLOS session in New York, however, it became evident that the U.S. fishery zone would go into effect on March 1, 1977, as planned. The Japanese government, while maintaining its opposition to the United States and others' unilateral actions, hoped that UNCLOS would produce a final agreement that would include an internationally acceptable and clear definition of the 200-mile economic zone. However, the spring session came to an end without a final agreement. In the hopes that another session in 1976 might bring the whole debate closer to a conclusion, Japan cooperated with other countries in scheduling a second New York session that summer. The effort was successful, and some 140 countries agreed to meet again from August 2 to September 17.

On March 19, the Cabinet adopted its formal position for the summer New York session, the same one that had been adopted for the spring session. To the disappointment of the Japanese government, the summer UNCLOS debate was no more conclusive than the spring session had been. What became clear during both sessions in New York, however, was that most of the issues concerning the substantive content of the 200-mile economic zone had been settled, but in a manner detrimental to Japan's high seas fisheries.[11]

With regard to the determination of the allowable catch in the exclusive economic zone, the language of the provisions in the Revised Single Negotiating Text (RSNT), produced by the chairmen of the three committees and the president of the conference at the close of the spring session, was virtually identical to that used in the ISNT.[12] Furthermore, the provisions in the ISNT regarding the access by foreign nationals to the surplus of allowable catch were retained almost word for word in the revised negotiating text.[13] In brief, they reaffirmed the coastal state's right to determine the allowable catch, harvest to capacity, and allocate the surplus to foreign nationals whose governments had concluded agreements or made other arrangements for that purpose. Furthermore, in the surplus allocation decision by the coastal state, economic dislocation of foreign fishermen who traditionally fished in the economic zone was listed as but one of several factors to be taken into consideration. These provisions gave Japanese fishery policymakers no reason to feel less pessimistic about the prospect of protecting Japan's traditional distant-water fishing than after the Geneva session in 1975.

The situation was no better with regard to the status of highly migratory species, anadromous fish, or sedentary fishery resources. The RSNT simply provided, in rather general terms, for international cooperation in conservation and management of such stocks between the coastal and other states engaged in the fishing of those stocks.[14] The status of anadromous species also remained virtually unchanged in the new negotiating text.[15] The provisions gave the state of origin the primary interest in and responsibility for anadromous species. They further stipulated that harvesting such stocks should be limited to the exclusive economic zone, except in cases where this provision would result in the economic dislocation of a fishing state other than the state of origin. In these exceptional cases, the RSNT and the ISNT both provided, the adversely affected state would be given special consideration by the state of origin as long as the former would participate in the latter's effort to renew anadromous stocks. Beyond the exclusive economic zone, furthermore, enforcement of regulations regarding anadromous species would be by agreement between the countries concerned. Finally, with respect to the status of sedentary species, Article 65 of the RSNT relating to the rights of the coastal state over the continental shelf recognized, just as the ISNT had in its Article 63, the exclusive sovereign rights of the coastal state over the continental shelf, including sedentary species.

Left unanswered were a number of important questions, including the status of the continental shelf beyond the exclusive economic zone and the rights of landlocked states and certain developing coastal states in the exploitation of the resources of the exclusive economic zone.[16] The provisions of the ISNT relevant to the regime of archipelagos were retained in the RSNT without major changes, indicating the existence of broad consensus on the regime. Neither did the RSNT indicate any major changes on the question of the territorial sea. For example, with regard to the rule of innocent passage through the territorial sea, there were no major differences between the relevant provisions in the ISNT and the RSNT, with the exception that the revised text explicitly listed fishing activities in the territorial sea of a foreign country as prejudicial to the peace, good order, or security of that state, and therefore not "innocent."[17]

On the critical question of the straits used for international navigation, the ISNT articles were incorporated into the RSNT with only minor changes, mostly required to make the legal language more precise and complete. Most importantly, "transit passage" was defined identically, except for a minor difference in wording.[18] No significant changes were made with respect to the duties of ships and aircraft during their unimpeded transit passage through straits used for international navigation;[19]

the sea-lanes and traffic separation schemes in international straits;[20] the right of straits states to establish laws and regulations in their straits for safety, environmental, fishing, customs, fiscal, immigration or sanitary purposes;[21] or nondiscrimination of foreign ships and prohibition of the denial, hampering, or impairment of the right of transit passage.[22] On the important question of the duties of straits states, the two texts adopted identical language in stipulating that the straits state should not hamper or suspend transit passage of foreign ships or aircraft.[23]

There appeared to be a rather stable consensus on or at least no sufficiently powerful dissension from the regime of the straits used for international navigation as embodied in the texts. As far as Japanese government decision making on the territorial sea question was concerned, the stabilization of the debate on the straits issue at the New York sessions was helpful but not enough to bring about a final decision on its own straits in relation to the territorial sea expansion. As late as January 1977, the MFA was still reluctant to commit itself to the MAFF/FA proposal.

In the absence of a final agreement on the 200-mile economic zone issue in UNCLOS, one coastal state after another resorted to unilateral decisions.[24] Guatemala, Mozambique, India, and Sri Lanka all set up 200-mile economic zones in the summer and fall of 1976. On October 1, the Canadian 200-mile economic zone went into effect. About the same time, Australia was also considering the establishment of a 200-mile fishery zone. On October 30, the EEC member states adopted a resolution calling for the establishment of their joint 200-mile fishery zone; on December 10, the British Parliament passed a 200-mile fishery zone bill to go into force on January 1, 1977; and Norway, Pakistan, and West Germany all followed suit in December. Then what Japan had feared the most happened. On December 10, the Soviet Union announced that it would set up a 200-mile fishery zone in the near future. As I will discuss in the following chapter, the Soviet action was the major impetus for Japan's decision to establish its own 200-mile fishery zone.

It became clear that Japan's opposition to unilateral actions had lost whatever effect it may have had. It also became unmistakably evident that by rigidly adhering to that position, Japan failed to provide a necessary response to its own domestic needs, but before the government decision makers could search for a new response, they found themselves faced with the immediate task of dealing with the direct consequences of 200-mile decisions of foreign governments—negotiations for new fisheries agreements.

Treaties with the United States and Canada

The first task after the United States announced its 200-mile fishery zone was to negotiate a new treaty concerning Japanese fishing in the expanded fishery zone. During preliminary talks in June 1976 and during the first round of formal negotiations in August, the Japanese rejected the U.S. insistence that Japan recognize the new fishery zone. The reasons given by the Japanese negotiators were (1) the U.S. establishment of its 200-mile fishery zone was invalid because there was no international customary law or international convention supporting such a unilateral decision, (2) a new fishery agreement between the two countries would require ratification by the Japanese Diet but it would be difficult to secure ratification by March 1, 1977, when the new U.S. legislation was to go into effect, and (3) the regional fishery councils to be set up under the new U.S. system to participate in determining foreign fish allocations were excessively protective of their regional fishery interests to the neglect of the overall diplomatic relations between the two countries.[25]

Fishery management and labor leaders in Japan persistently put pressure on the government not to recognize the U.S. position. On November 4, fishery groups throughout the country gathered in Tokyo and held a massive rally. About four hundred representatives of the industry demonstrated their resolve against the U.S. fishery zone. Keynote speakers from the industry included president of the Japan Fisheries Association Tomoyoshi Kamenaga; president of Taiyō Fisheries Tojiro Nakabe; and president of the Hokkaidō Fisheries Association Junkichi Kanehira. From the LDP came chairman of the Policy Affairs Research Council Yoshio Sakurauchi and chairman of the Dietmen's League for Fisheries Promotion Zenko Suzuki. Representing the government were MAFF Minister Sempachi Oishi and Foreign Minister Zentaro Kosaka. Party leaders and government representatives pledged that the government would do everything it could to secure Japan's fishery interests in the negotiations with the United States, Canada, and the Soviet Union. On the same day, fishery labor unions held their own national conference in Tokyo. Participating organizations included the All-Japan Seamen's Union, the Federation of Food Industry Unions, and the Federation of Fishing Boat Unions. Furthermore, the fishery industry made a public appeal through the mass media about the impending crisis should Japan accept the U.S. jurisdiction in the new 200-mile fishery zone. In view of these pressures, it was only natural that the government could not offer any important concessions in the bilateral negotiations. Even if it knew its opposition to the U.S. proposal was futile, the government had to demonstrate to domestic groups and the public that it was doing its best in opposing U.S. demands.

When the first round of negotiations was broken off because of disagreement, it became clear that the United States was not about to retract its fundamental proposal that Japan recognize U.S. jurisdiction in the newly established fishery zone, but the Japanese could not come up with a new position before the second round of negotiations took place between November 8 and 12. In that round the United States reiterated that it could determine foreign catch quotas, issue fishing permits, charge fishing fees, and exercise U.S. judicial powers in the zone. The positions of the two governments were so far apart that no agreement could be expected unless the parameters of the situation were somehow changed. This happened on November 26 when the United States and the Soviet Union signed a new fishery agreement recognizing the U.S. Fishery Conservation and Management Act of 1976. This event deprived the Japanese government of the rationale for maintaining its unqualified opposition to the U.S. 200-mile decision. The U.S.-Soviet agreement would put Japan at a disadvantage, for the Soviets would be allowed to continue fishing within the U.S. fishery zone, while the Japanese would not. As a direct result of the U.S.-Soviet agreement, the Japanese government decided to make important concessions.[26] A Cabinet-level meeting on December 11 produced Japanese recognition of the U.S. jurisdiction over the fishery zone. Japan's effort was now to gain as large a fish quota as possible.[27] The fishery industry also changed its position along the same line.[28]

Japanese concessions paved the way for an agreement. On December 13, U.S. and Japanese negotiators agreed to conclude a provisional agreement and a five-year agreement for Japanese fishing, the former to serve until the latter went into effect following ratifications. The provisional agreement was signed on February 10, 1977, and the long-term agreement was initialled on the same day. As a result, Japan's quota was set at 1,191,000 tons for 1977, a drop of about 11 percent from its estimated 1976 catch of 1,334,000 tons.[29] Japan also agreed to pay fishing fees ranging from US $45 per ton for some demersal species to US $614 per ton for pelagic armorhead, substantially less than the United States had originally demanded but slightly more than Japan was prepared to pay at first.[30] Despite the increased cost of Japanese fishing, the result of the agreement was generally received favorably by the Japanese fishery industry.

Japan's fishery talks with Canada began on October 27, 1976. In contrast to the Japan-U.S. negotiations, they went fairly smoothly, mainly because Canada decided to allow Japanese fishing in its 200-mile zone without a new agreement past January 1, 1977, when the new fishery zone was to go into force. Canada also decided not to charge fees for the 1977 fishing season. Japan's quota was set as follows: on the Pacific side, 3,000 tons of sablefish, 3,000 tons of ocean perch, and 5,000 tons of hake; on the Atlantic side, 14,000 tons of *shishamo (Osmerus lanceolatus),* 4,250 tons of deep-sea smelt, and 3,000 tons of *matsuika* (a type of squid).[31]

The Shelving Formula: Japan's Decision to Expand Its Territorial Sea

The U.S. 200-mile decision, its recognition by the Soviets, and the reluctant Japanese acquiescence had direct consequences for the Japanese government's position on the 200-mile economic zone. The government had up to this point maintained that it would not recognize the 200-mile fishery zone decisions of other countries, and it had continued emphasizing the package approach to law of the sea questions. However, this approach had become obsolete by the end of 1976. Unilateral actions had become so widespread that it became difficult to even consider them "unilateral." They represented national decisions that were by and large in consonance with the UNCLOS negotiating text provisions on the economic zone question. If Japan chose to, it could simply follow suit and set up its own 200-mile fishery zone. But it chose not to for various reasons, which are discussed in chapter 7.

Meanwhile, the question of the 12-mile territorial sea continued to present serious problems for the Japanese government. As I briefly pointed out in chapter 5, the most difficult to solve was the potential conflict between Japan's three nonnuclear principles and the status of Japanese straits used for international navigation. The MFA preferred a "wait and see" strategy. By the end of 1976, however, the MFA had come to the view that Japan's 12-mile territorial sea per se would not be a problem insofar as international law was concerned, but it was greatly concerned with the lack of international consensus on the question of the status of international straits.[32] For the MFA, which clearly preferred an international over a unilateral approach to the handling of this question, it was important that there be an international consensus or, better yet, a global agreement. At the end of 1976 there was no such consensus, much less agreement.[33]

In the absence of an international agreement, there were theoretically three options for the Japanese government:

1. Move ahead of the UNCLOS debate and extend the territorial sea limit from three to twelve miles, while adopting a rule of relatively free passage and flight through and over the straits.

2. Extend the territorial sea to twelve miles and prohibit the passage of warships through the Japanese straits.

3. Refrain from territorial sea extension at this time and wait for the multilateral debate to produce a final agreement on the question of the status of straits used for international navigation.

The first option offered one major advantage: Japan would be able to protect its coastal fisheries from foreign intrusion. However, there were two serious drawbacks. First, a unilateral decision would run counter to Japan's own external pronouncements in support of the package approach to law of the sea questions. If Japan should isolate the question of the breadth of the territorial sea from all the other issues, how could it criticize other coastal states for making unilateral decisions? Second, to permit foreign warships carrying nuclear weapons to pass through Japanese straits would be considered by many tantamount to the abrogation of the three nonnuclear principles. Since the principles were supported by a strong national consensus, the government would be taking political risks if it should decide to permit the passage of nuclear-armed warships. In fact, most opposition political parties demanded that the government apply the principles in the straits areas as well as in all the other territorial waters of the country.[34] The government was already having difficulty convincing domestic critics that the three nonnuclear principles were intact and that no U.S. warships calling in Japanese ports carried nuclear weapons. If nuclear-armed ships should be openly permitted to pass through the straits areas, domestic opposition would be certain to create a political crisis.

The second option would have the same advantage as the first in excluding foreign fishermen from the new territorial sea, but it would mean serious implications for Japan's defense policy. In accordance with the Japan–U.S. Mutual Security Treaty, Japan placed itself under the "nuclear umbrella" of the United States. The exclusive reliance on the

United States for nuclear deterrence became Japan's international commitment when it ratified the Nuclear Nonproliferation Treaty in June 1976, thus binding itself to the obligation of nonnuclear-weapons states not to possess or manufacture nuclear arms. The ratification took place over some domestic opposition that it would deprive the country of the "nuclear option." To prohibit nuclear-armed U.S. warships from passing through such strategically important straits as Tsugaru and Tsushima would cause serious problems for the bilateral security arrangements. The second option would also cause problems in terms of Japan's strategic position vis-à-vis its adversaries. What could Japan do if a submarine belonging to an adversary passed through Japanese straits on the ground that there was no international agreement prohibiting the passage of foreign warships through those waterways? Technicalities aside, the Japanese government would certainly wish to avoid such difficult situations.

The third option, on the other hand, would clearly add to the frustration of the coastal fishermen over the inability of their government to take effective measures to protect their interests. It would have a definite advantage, however, in that it was in line with the government's "wait and see" approach. By refraining from a unilateral action, Japan would be able to continue emphasizing that it would not recognize unilateral decisions. Moreover, the government would not have to decide on the question of how to balance the three nonnuclear principles with its interest in maintaining relatively free international movement of ships. If the international community later agreed on passage through international straits that was freer than what would be allowed in the ordinary territorial sea under the principle of innocent passage, as the Japanese government hoped, it would not be necessary for the government to abandon the three nonnuclear principles, for the international agreement would take precedence over the domestic policy.

There was another domestic policy problem that the MFA seemed unwilling to touch at this time but hoped the international community would solve for Japan. At least since 1968, Japan had not recognized as innocent the passage in its territorial sea of nuclear submarines and other foreign warships carrying nuclear weapons. In that year Japan acceded to the Geneva Convention on the Territorial Sea and Contiguous Zone and announced domestically that it would ban nuclear-armed warships from its territorial waters. The Geneva Convention on the Territorial Sea and Contiguous Zone stated that ships of all states shall enjoy "the right of innocent passage through the territorial sea," which passage means "navigation through the territorial sea for the purpose either of traversing that sea without entering internal waters, or of proceeding to internal waters, or of making for the high seas from internal waters," and that passage is innocent "so long as it is not prejudicial to the peace, good order or security of the coastal State" (Article 14). The same article further stipulated that submarines are required to navigate on the surface and to show their flags. Article 15 stated that the coastal state must not hamper innocent passage through the territorial sea. On the other hand, Article 16 gave the coastal state the right to "take the necessary steps in its territorial sea to prevent passage which is not innocent"; in the case of ships proceeding to internal waters, the right to "take the necessary steps to prevent any breach of the conditions to which admission of those ships to those waters is subject"; and, subject to the provisions of paragraph 4, the right to "suspend temporarily in specified areas of its territorial sea the innocent passage of foreign ships if such suspension is essential for the protection of its security." Paragraph 4 provided that there shall be no suspension of the innocent passage of foreign ships through straits used for international navigation. Finally, Article 17 provided that foreign ships exercising the right of innocent passage "shall comply with the laws and regulations enacted by the coastal State in conformity with these articles and other rules of international law and, in particular, with such laws and regulations relating to transport and navigation."[35]

By accepting the Geneva Convention, Japan had to recognize the right of ships of all nations to innocent passage through Japanese territorial waters but was allowed to take "the necessary steps" to prevent passage that is not innocent. Such steps might, in the Japanese government's judgment, include the prohibition of passage of nuclear-armed ships. Since the government had banned nuclear-armed warships from its territorial waters in 1968, the only way Japan could allow foreign warships carrying nuclear weapons unhampered passage through its straits would be to make an exception for the straits areas after its territorial sea limit was extended to twelve miles—again a politically vulnerable option—or to wait for the international community to agree on the special status of straits used for international navigation, allowing warships, including those carrying nuclear weapons, unhampered passage in those areas. The Foreign Ministry wanted UNCLOS to agree on a regime that would establish transit passage of nuclear-armed and other warships through international straits. Japan could not effectively influence, much less control, the

UNCLOS debate on the straits question. Consequently, "wait and see" was the preferred approach of the MFA.

The distance between MFA and MAFF/FA policy remained substantial, as the former continued to warn against unilateral action and the latter pressed for taking effective measures to protect the coastal fishermen now being challenged by both Soviet and South Korean fishing vessels. There had been little effort by the two to coordinate their positions on the territorial question, and no clear solution was in sight as long as each insisted on its preferred alternative. Interministerial coordination was clearly in order, but there was no effective mechanism in the government to provide it. The government was rigidly structured along hierarchical lines of authority and communication. If the deadlock was to be broken, something bordering on a crisis had to take place. The U.S. and Soviet 200-mile fishery zone decisions helped create a crisislike atmosphere in the domestic political system, but they did not offer a way out of the dilemma caused by the incompatibility between the straits issue and the nonnuclear policy. With no external solution in sight in the immediate future, domestic change was the only answer. Fortunately, developments on the domestic front began to unfold toward the end of 1976. Namely, a new Cabinet was formed under the premiership of Takeo Fukuda, and the new prime minister appointed Zenko Suzuki, an influential pro-fishery Dietman, as the new MAFF minister.

Suzuki was well trained in fisheries affairs and, through his career as a member of the LDP and the Diet, had earned a reputation as a statesman sympathetic to the country's fishery industry. Himself a son of a fishing family, Suzuki had studied at a fishery technical school of the MAFF. Upon graduation he joined the Japan Fisheries Association and worked as a fishery technocrat. After World War II, he was active in promoting labor movements in the fishery industry as chairman of the Workers' Union of the National Federation of Fisheries Cooperatives. He was first elected to the Diet in 1947 as a member of the Socialist Party. Two years later he ran as a Liberal and was elected to the House of Representatives for the second time. Since then, he had occupied several Cabinet-level posts, including minister of postal services, minister of welfare, and chief cabinet secretary. In the LDP he had served numerous terms as chairman of the Executive Board.[36]

As soon as he was appointed to the new post, Suzuki began actively promoting efforts to break the interministerial deadlock that stood in the

way of the government's response to domestic pressure for a 12-mile territorial sea. On December 26, two days after the new Cabinet was formed,
the new MAFF minister stated,

> It is necessary to realize the extension of the territorial sea to twelve miles as
> soon as possible. Unlike the 200-mile fishery zone, [the 12-mile territorial
> sea of Japan] does not pose much difficulty for [Japan's] coordination of its
> relations with foreign countries. The question of [territorial sea] is a domes-
> tic one—how to harmonize it with the three nonnuclear principles. I will
> develop a dialogue with the opposition parties in order to realize the twelve-
> mile territorial sea.[37]

With interministerial coordination thus about to take a new turn, a
crucial event took place. The Soviet Union on December 10 announced
its decision to establish a 200-mile fishery zone.[38] The decision—set forth
in the Decree of the Presidium of the Supreme Soviet for the Provisional
Measures Concerning the Conservation of Living Resources and Fishery
Regulation in the Areas of the Ocean Contiguous to the Coasts of the
Soviet Union—prompted the Japanese government to implement its
usual strategy—diplomatic protest. On December 15, the Japanese
ambassador to the Soviet Union conveyed an official protest to Soviet
Fisheries Minister Aleksandr Ishkov.[39] However, the Japanese government
quickly learned that such a protest had no real effect.

Amid these external disturbances and the near-crisis situation at home,
fishery policymakers under Suzuki's leadership came up with an extraordinary new proposal. Simply put, it recommended that Japan extend its
territorial sea limit from three to twelve miles except in controversial
straits areas, where the 3-mile limit then current would be maintained.
The proposal was known as the "shelving formula" and was based on the
following considerations.

1. Japan should extend its territorial sea from three to twelve miles as
soon as possible to protect its coastal fishermen from Soviet and South
Korean fishing boats.

2. The measures to be adopted by the government would have to be
effective in forcing foreign fishing boats out of the 12-mile limit because
it was within that limit that the fishery damage was the most extensive.[40]

3. At the same time, the new policy should be such that it would not
force the government to make a controversial decision on the relationship

between the three nonnuclear principles and the status of the so-called international straits.[41]

4. Other theoretically possible measures, such as a 12-mile fishery zone or a 200-mile fishery zone, were not acceptable under the current situation. For one thing, such alternatives would not be effective in excluding foreign fishermen from Japan's immediate coastal waters.[42]

On January 7, 1977, Suzuki invited vice-minister of Foreign Affairs Shoji Sato and working-level MFA officials to his ministry to explain the rationale and content of the shelving formula. The Foreign Ministry representatives agreed that some measure should be taken to protect Japanese costal fishermen. They pointed out, however, that the shelving formula would be met by strong opposition from domestic critics, that there was no international precedent for more than one breadth of territorial waters in one country, and that the proposed territorial sea extension would give states adjacent to the Straits of Malacca and Singapore an excuse to enclose those strategic straits as part of their territorial waters. They proposed instead that Japan extend its fishery jurisdiction to two hundred miles and argued that this option would pose no serious problems because, for one thing, the 200-mile economic zone was already an accepted part of international practice.[43] The same exchange of views took place the following day when Foreign Minister Ichiro Hatoyama invited to his ministry permanent vice-minister of the MAFF Yoshihide Uchimura, Fisheries Agency director-general Makoto Okayasu, and high-ranking MAFF bureaucrats. The two sides could not reach agreement on which action to take.

When the shelving formula was made public, all the opposition parties objected to it, just as the MFA had anticipated. The Japan Communist Party demanded that the government extend the territorial sea limit uniformly to twelve miles and that the three nonnuclear principles be applied throughout the territorial sea.[44] The other opposition parties with the exception of the Democratic Socialist Party held the same position as the Communists. The Democratic Socialists proposed that a uniform 12-mile territorial sea be adopted in which foreign warships would be allowed to pass through the so-called international straits of Japan.[45] Despite Suzuki's efforts to win their support for the shelving formula, opposition continued.

On the other hand, interministerial discussions showed an important development in early 1977. On January 25, an informal meeting was held among the MAFF minister, the foreign minister, the transport minister, the chief cabinet secretary, and the director of the Cabinet Legislation Bureau. Their discussion was carried over to the next day, when the MAFF minister and the foreign minister came up with new proposals from their respective ministries.

The foreign minister proposed that Japan set up a 12-mile "fishery-territorial sea," in which, as a provisional measure, only fishery jurisdiction would be enforced.[46] According to the scheme, the fishery-territorial sea would be turned into an ordinary territorial sea when the international community reached a final agreement on the law of the sea. The obvious advantage of this strategy would be that it would have no political implications for the three nonnuclear principles because the exercise of fishery jurisdiction would not alter the high seas status of the area beyond three miles and, as such, within that area foreign warships carrying nuclear weapons would be able to navigate just as they had in the past. In short, the proposal was designed to "buy time" until UNCLOS solved the problem for Japan.

The MAFF minister countered that the fishery-territorial sea was in effect a fishery zone and would not be able to keep foreign fishing boats out of the 12-mile limit.[47] According to the principle of reciprocity, if Japan wanted to continue its fishing operations within the 12-mile or 200-mile fishery zone of another country, then Japan would have to allow the nationals of that country to fish in Japan's fishery zone. Therefore, the MAFF/FA counterproposed that Japan promptly extend its territorial sea limit from three to twelve miles but that until a final UNCLOS agreement only fishery jurisdiction be exercised.[48] Although provisionally only fishery jurisdiction would be enforced in the area, it would nonetheless be a territorial sea and, as such, it would enable Japan to exclude all foreign fishing within twelve miles of its coast. This proposal was also a kind of "buy-time" approach, for it would allow the government to postpone its final decision on the status of the controversial straits areas.

The two ministers could not come to an agreement on either proposal, but since there was a strong need to expedite a government decision, the chief cabinet secretary suggested that they agree to the shelving formula, which they did. The agreement was adopted by the Cabinet on January 28 as the government's formal decision. The Cabinet also decided to charge Suzuki, as state minister, with the responsibility of preparing legislation for Japan's 12-mile territorial sea.[49] The decision was welcomed by the fishery industry. Representing northern and northeastern coastal fishermen, President Oikawa of the National Federation of Fisheries Cooperatives stated that the 12-mile territorial sea would not solve all the problems caused by the Soviet fishing but it was a big step forward.[50] Thus, the long and painstaking process of decision-making finally produced a consensus among those whose policy or economic interests would be directly affected by government decision in this issue-area.[51]

The opposition political parties were still opposed to the shelving formula. While supporting the territorial sea extension per se, they expressed from moderate to strong opposition to the provisional measure of retaining the 3-mile limit in the controversial straits. The director of the Japan Socialist Party International Bureau, Kanji Kawasaki, stated that his party wanted to extend the territorial sea to twelve miles in order to protect the livelihood of coastal fishermen. Since the party believed that the three nonnuclear principles should be strictly maintained, Kawasaki stated, "the setting up of the exception of a three-mile limit in the international strait areas leads to the emasculation of the principles. If the United Nations Conference on the Law of the Sea reaches an international treaty including free passage through international straits, then [our party] will accept it." Even then, however, the Socialists would not accept the passage of warships carrying nuclear weapons because, as Kawasaki put it, "the three nonnuclear principles are an acknowledged line of the national policy of Japan."[52] Chairman of the Kōmeitō Foreign Relations Committee Ichiro Watabe said, "The government's decision came too late." He criticized the preservation of the 3-mile territorial sea limit in the international straits areas, saying it had the effect of "stripping the three nonnuclear principles of their essence." "The setting up of the two territorial sea limits of three and twelve miles in one country," Watabe exhorted, "is an extraordinary situation for which there is no international precedent."[53]

The director of the Democratic Socialist Party International Bureau, Katsu Kawamura, was less critical. "Although the government's decision came belatedly," he stated, "it is nonetheless an appropriate measure. But the plan to maintain a three-mile limit in the handling of the Tsugaru and other straits is a makeshift measure."[54] Deputy-director of the Communist Party Secretariat Mitsuhiro Kaneko was quoted as saying, "The government's plan is an improvement over the present [situation], but it is a complete avoidance of the question of international straits. [The government] should enforce a twelve-mile territorial sea throughout the coastal areas and apply the three nonnuclear principles in all areas."[55]

Finally, the chief secretary of the New Liberal Club, Takeo Nishioka, stated, "The twelve-mile territorial sea should be [enforced] promptly. [We] cannot agree to the government's carefree approach of setting up straits where the territorial limit is frozen at three miles." Instead he proposed that the government "should provisionally establish a free navigation zone and permit the passage of all foreign ships until UNCLOS produced a final decision." Nishioka stated his party believed "the passage of warships carrying nuclear weapons through the zone is not a violation of the three nonnuclear principles."[56]

Despite this criticism from the opposition parties, the government decided to proceed with the implementation of the shelving formula as a means to protect coastal fisheries from Soviet and South Korean fishing. The strong leadership of the MAFF minister vis-à-vis the fishery industry and among the fishery-oriented members of the Diet had helped the Cabinet to overcome the concerns expressed by the Foreign Ministry concerning the straits issue and bring an end to the protracted deadlock in government discussion.[57]

Once the Cabinet decided to prepare legislation for the 12-mile sea, the ministries concerned agreed to work through ad hoc coordinative arrangements at three levels. At the Cabinet level, informal talks were held among the MAFF minister, the transport minister, the chief cabinet secretary, and the director-general of the Defense Agency.[58] At the bureau level, an executive committee was formed among the bureau directors of the agencies concerned, and within the Cabinet Secretariat a "Territorial Sea Law Preparation Office" was established, composed of two working-level bureaucrats each from the MFA, the MAFF, the Cabinet Secretariat, and the Ministry of Transport, and one from the Defense Agency.[59] The work went fairly smoothly, and by March 5, a formal draft had been drawn up. The drafting was relatively easy because the ministries and the Cabinet Secretariat had decided that the territorial sea law itself would be formulated as a simple declaration of Japan's decision to extend its territorial sea limit and to leave the technical details relating to the delimitation of the territorial boundary and the 3-mile status quo in the straits areas to be prescribed in a Cabinet order separate from the main legislation.[60]

On February 14, 1977, Suzuki revealed for the first time the names of the straits in which the government was planning to maintain the 3-mile limit. Of the sixty-nine straits whose maximum width was less than twenty-four miles, five were chosen for special status.[61] They were the

Sōya Strait between the northern end of Hokkaidō and Soviet Sakhalin Island; the Tsugaru Strait between Hokkaidō and Honshu; the Osumi Strait off the southern coast of Kyushu; and the western channel and the eastern channel of the Tsushima Strait between Kyushu and the Korean Peninsula.[62] (Figure 1 in chapter 5 shows the location of these straits.) The government explained the move as follows:

> [With] regard to the passage of ships through the so-called international straits . . . , currently the discussion at UNCLOS is moving in the direction of accepting a rule of transit which is freer than the rule of innocent passage through general territorial sea. . . . From the comprehensive viewpoint of the national interest of Japan, which imports the majority of its resources from overseas and depends heavily on trade and maritime shipping in particular, it is necessary to ensure free passage of merchant ships and large-size tankers through the Straits of Malacca and elsewhere. . . . Therefore, as a provisional measure, for the time being, we shall not alter the present situation with respect to the so-called international straits of Japan.
>
> Furthermore, the decision to maintain the present territorial sea limit in the so-called international straits will not affect the passage of ships through them. Therefore, it does not alter our position to maintain the three nonnuclear principles as far as our country's authority reaches. This measure is taken for these reasons and is not related to the question of the three nonnuclear principles.[63]

From this explanation, it is clear that the government was indeed concerned about the possible implications of its decision with regard to the territorial sea question for international shipping. It would have preferred an international agreement on this issue over unilateral action. To monitor the reactions of other countries to this territorial sea expansion, in May and June 1977 the MFA sent an English translation of the territorial sea law to all major countries. The Soviet Union did not indicate any opposition, the United States expressed appreciation for the decision to maintain the 3-mile limit in the straits areas, and neither China nor South Korea showed any apprehension.[64] It is equally evident that despite the government's insistence that the shelving formula was unrelated to the three nonnuclear principles, the government wanted to minimize the impact of the decision on this controversial policy.

During the debate on the shelving formula, another interagency disagreement emerged. It related to Japan's ability to effectively enforce the law in the enlarged territorial sea. More specifically, the question was whether it would be necessary to revise the Law on the Self-Defense Forces to provide those forces with the authority to participate in the enforcement of territorial sea and fishery zone regulations against foreign violators.

Under the law as current, the Maritime Self-Defense Force (MSDF) would not have authority to control foreign ships violating domestic legislation concerning the territorial sea and the economic zone. MSDF authorities could report violations to the Maritime Safety Agency but they could neither force an offending vessel to leave the area nor inspect it. Teiji Nakamura, chief of the Defense Agency Maritime Staff, complained, "MSDF cannot accomplish what it hopes to accomplish unless it is given a power similar to the scramble mission of the Air Self-Defense Force vis-à-vis aircraft violating Japan's airspace."[65] To remedy the situation, the Defense Agency indicated in January 1977 that it was considering a revision of the Law on the Self-Defense Forces to expand the role of the maritime branch.[66]

The Transport Ministry, which supervises the director-general of the Maritime Safety Agency responsible for the territorial sea control mission, was understandably opposed to such a move. Given the sensitive and highly emotional public opinion concerning defense-related issues, it is generally feared that any hint at a broadening of the authority of the Self-Defense Forces or a revision of its legal basis will lead to public speculation that the government is contemplating a major expansion of Japan's military capabilities. In order to forestall such a possibility, the ministers concerned quickly put an end to the dispute by deciding not to take up the proposal by the Defense Agency to revise the Law on the Self-Defense Forces. On February 17, Prime Minister Fukuda stated at a meeting of the Budget Committee of the House of Representatives that the government did not intend to revise the current law. At the same committee session, the director-general of the Defense Agency also stated that the current law was "fine."[67] It was also affirmed that the Maritime Safety Agency would continue to be the sole enforcer of the domestic laws in the territorial sea of Japan and that the primary role of the MSDF in this regard was to provide information to the Maritime Safety Agency on possible violations of Japan's territorial sovereignty.[68]

Furthermore, in response to the concern that the capabilities of the Maritime Safety Agency might be wanting with respect to the expanded territorial sea, the agency decided to identify a few coastal areas in which its enforcement effort would be concentrated. Proposed areas included the northern seas facing Hokkaidō, where trouble with the Soviet and South Korean fishing boats was expected; the Strait of Tsushima, where Korean and Japanese fishing boats were operating side by side; and the area around the Senkaku Islands to the southwest of Japan where mainland Chinese and Taiwanese fishing boats were spotted from time to time and where territorial disputes involving the People's Republic of China, Taiwan, and Japan had erupted. In these areas, the Maritime Safety Agency made sixteen arrests involving Korean nationals and twenty-two arrests of Taiwanese fishermen between July 1977 and June 1979 for violating the territorial sea law. Similarly, the maritime authorities made thirty-eight arrests of Soviet fishermen and fourteen arrests of South Koreans for violating the fishery zone law.[69]

7

The Soviet 200-Mile
Fishery Zone and Japan's 200-Mile
Fishery Zone Decision

The Soviet Fishery Zone

AS we noted in chapter 6, on December 10, 1976, the Soviet Union in the decree of the Presidium of the Supreme Soviet declared its intention to extend Soviety fishery jurisdiction out to 200 miles from its coast. The decree stated that the Soviet Union had sovereign rights over the exploration, exploitation, and conservation of the fisheries and other living resources, including anadromous species of Soviet origin; foreign fishing within the fishery zone would be permitted only on the basis of agreement or other arrangements between the Soviet Union and the countries concerned; the optimum utilization of fishery and other living resources within the fishery zone would be ensured on the basis of scientific data and, if necessary, in consideration of the advice of competent international organizations; and the Soviet Union would determine the fish catch quotas for and issue fishing permits to foreign fishermen.[1] The decree further stated that the actual establishment of the fishery zone would be implemented by another law, which would prescribe the specific details of the zone, including its delimitation.

The Soviet decision prompted the usual Japanese reaction—diplomatic and other forms of protest. Despite Japan's outcry that it would not recognize the Soviet move, the MFA had come to realize the inevitability of 200-mile zones as a central feature of the new international ocean regime. In fact, as we have seen, the ministry had begun to propose that Japan extend its own fishery jurisdiction to two hundred miles. The ministry's recommendation was not without some domestic support. As soon as the Soviet announcement came, for instance, the vice-governor of Hokkaidō and chairman of that prefecture's Law of the Sea Committee, Junkichi Kanehira, visited Fisheries Agency director-general Okayasu and asked that the government consider the establishment of a 200-mile fishery zone.[2]

The fishery policymakers cautioned against such a move. The MAFF was particularly concerned that South Korea and China might counter Japan's 200-mile fishery zone with similar jurisdictional claims.[3] Should the two neighboring countries extend their fishery jurisdictions, Japanese fishermen operating in their coastal waters would suffer considerable losses. MAFF minister Suzuki therefore warned that it was premature for Japan to consider extending its fishery jurisdiction to two hundred miles.[4]

The same cautious attitude was shared by the fishery industry leadership. On December 27, Japan Fisheries Association president Tomoyoshi Kamenaga, who had been a member of the Japanese delegation at the third, fourth, and fifth sessions of the Third UNCLOS, and other industry leaders paid a visit to Suzuki and submitted their view that a 200-mile zone was premature and that the government should act so as to promote the interests of the fishery industry as a whole, keeping a watchful eye on the Soviet, Chinese, and South Korean neighbors.[5] The Fisheries Agency's attitude in this regard was much the same.[6]

The situation changed drastically, however, with the Soviet announcement on February 24, 1977, that their fishery zone extension would take effect on March 1. That the Soviet Council of Ministers should make such an important decision only one week before the 200-mile zone was to become operative came as a surprise to Japanese policymakers. More importantly, the parameters of the Soviet fishery zone as indicated by the Council of Ministers had implications of far more significance than simple fishery policy decisions would have had. The area to be enclosed by the Soviet exclusive jurisdiction included that part of the sea around the so-called Northern Territories of Habomai, Shikotan, Etorofu, and Kunashiri islands to the northeast of Japan, over which both Japan and the Soviet Union had maintained territorial claims since the end of World War II.[7] This required immediate attention at the highest level of the government. One day after the Soviet announcement, the Cabinet decided to lodge a formal protest. Chief Cabinet Secretary Sunao Sonoda stated, "The Soviet inclusion of the area around the four northern islands in its fishery regulation zone is a matter of extreme regret and will not be accepted."[8] The Cabinet also decided to have Suzuki personally deliver the protest to Soviet Fisheries Minister Aleksandr Ishkov, whom the Japanese minister was scheduled to visit later that month to discuss fishery relations between the two countries. Before his departure for Moscow, Suzuki stated that the deliberations on Japanese-Soviet fishery problems should not be mixed with any discussion of the territorial dispute. The Japanese government knew from earlier experience in dealing with the Soviets that if the territorial dispute should be interjected into the bilateral fishery talks, no agreement would be possible.[9]

The first round of talks between Suzuki and Ishkov began on February 28 but was soon deadlocked when the territorial issue surfaced in connection with the Soviet demand that Japan recognize the Soviet fishery zone delimitation. Unable to reach an agreement on this fundamental question of the legitmacy of Soviet fishery claims, the ministers simply exchanged notes indicating areas of agreement and Suzuki returned to Tokyo. One point of agreement was that until the two governments concluded a provisional treaty, which they hoped to do between March 15 and 31, Japanese fishing would be allowed in the area to which the decree of the Presidium of the Supreme Soviet was to apply.[10] As far as Japan was concerned, the accord simply indicated Japan's acknowledgment of the Soviet decision to extend its fishery jurisdiction to two hundred miles but not acceptance of the actual delimitation, which was in the Council of Ministers' decision and not in the decree of the Presidium.

The notes also referred to Japan's intention to establish its own 200-mile fishery zone in the near future. This was the first time that the government had pubicly mentioned a plan to set up a 200-mile fishery zone. It is clear in this context that the Japanese decision to set up a 200-mile fishery zone came as a direct consequence of the Soviet decision to include the controversial northern islands in the Soviet fishery zone and that Japanese policymakers viewed the Soviet decision not simply as an economic problem but, more importantly, as a political problem that required a political response.[11]

The deadlock in the Moscow talks had an impact on other aspects of Japanese-Soviet fishery negotiations. For example, the meeting in Tokyo on March 15 of the Japan-Soviet Fisheries Committee on salmon fisheries, one of the long-standing and regular committees established in 1956 as a part of the bilateral fishery arrangements, came to a standstill soon after it started. The impasse resulted from Soviet insistence on and Japanese rejection of a proposal that Japan recognize the Soviet jurisdiction over the resources in its fishery zone and that Japanese salmon fishing in the zone be totally banned. The meeting was broken off on March 31.

The Moscow negotiation on the conclusion of a provisional fishery agreement also began on March 15, but it too came to a halt on March 31. The Soviets insisted that Japan accept Soviet jurisdiction in the fishery zone as delineated by the Council of Ministers' decision; Japan contended that the decree of the Presidium of the Supreme Soviet should be used as the basis of the provisional agreement. The Soviet demand for exclusive jurisdiction in its new fishery zone was met in turn by the Japanese proposal for a joint regulatory arrangement based on international law and the domestic laws of the two countries.

Another point of contention related to the Soviet request that its fishermen be allowed to fish in Japan's territorial sea, soon to be extended to twelve miles. According to Suzuki, this demand was based on the Soviet conception of the relationship between a territorial sea and a fishery zone. In their view, a fishery zone extending out to two hundred miles from the baseline of a coastal state includes its territorial sea out to twelve miles from the same baseline, and it is up to that state to allow or not to allow foreign fishing in any part of the fishery zone, including the area within the territorial sea. This was the case with the Soviet jurisdiction as prescribed by the decree of the Presidium of the Supreme Soviet, and the Soviet side argued that the same principle should apply to the Japanese fishery jurisdiction.[12] Since Japan could not accept Soviet fishing in Japanese territorial waters, the Japanese negotiating team rejected the request.

Back in Japan, the fishery industry, both management and labor, and political parties, the Diet, prefectural governors, and city mayors whose constituencies would be affected by the Soviet fishery zone rallied behind the Japanese negotiators. They held protest rallies and sent their representatives to the Soviet Embassy in Tokyo and to the Japanese government to express their views. The House of Representatives passed a resolution calling on the government to exert its utmost effort to secure the continuation of traditional fishing in the North Pacific, including within the Soviet-claimed 200-mile fishery zone. The resolution stated that the North Pacific was an important fishing area for the Japanese, who had invested many years of effort in the conservation and efficient utilization of the fisheries in the area and that the bilateral negotiations then underway would "determine the future of Japan's North Pacific fisheries" because they would affect not only the fishery community but also the consumers who depended on fishery products for more than one half of their daily animal protein intake.[13] Two days later the House of Councillors passed a similar resolution. Moreover, the House of Representatives decided to send an all-party delegation to present their views to the Soviet leadership.[14]

On March 30, the National Conference of Prefectural Governors, the National Conference of City Mayors, and the National Conference of Town and Village Mayors joined the fishery industry in sponsoring a "People's Conference to Overcome the Crisis of the North Pacific Fisheries." They adopted a resolution stating

> The Soviet position in the Japan-Soviet fisheries talks is one of power diplomacy based on big powerism and disregards international law. We cannot accept it. It will bring about important repercussions for the friendly relations between the two countries and [we request that the Soviet Union] reconsider its position. [The Soviet government] should respect the historical accomplishments of Japan in the North Pacific fisheries and secure safe fishing [for Japanese fishermen].[15]

On that same day, representatives of all six political parties visited Soviet Ambassador Dimitrii Polyansky at the Soviet Embassy in Tokyo and submitted a request from the Agriculture, Forestry, and Fisheries Committee of the House of Representatives that the Soviet government retract its demand for Soviet fishing in what was to become the 12-mile territorial sea of Japan.[16]

Clearly, the strongly negative response of the Japanese government to the Soviet 200-mile zone decision was shared by all major domestic groups. Within this context it is quite understandable that Japan's 200-mile fishery zone, which was supported by only a minority group in the country as late as the end of 1976, should have become a national consensus by the early spring of 1977. In contrast to the domestic debate on the 12-mile territorial sea question, in which the fishery industry took the initiative, it was the government that led the "national campaign" for the 200-mile fishery zone decision.

The Japanese Fishery Zone

With the national consensus secured, the government quickly got on with the task of extending Japan's fishery jurisdiction. On March 29 the Cabinet agreed on the following principles:

1. Japan would establish its own 200-mile fishery zone in response to the 200-mile decisions by other coastal states such as the Soviet Union, the United States, Canada, and EEC member states.
2. Vis-à-vis South Korea and China, the status quo would be maintained so that the present stable fisheries order might continue.
3. In the straits areas excluded from the application of the 12-mile territorial sea limit, a special measure would be devised to protect coastal fisheries.
4. The government would introduce the necessary bill to the Diet so that Japan's new fishery zone would be set up by the fall of 1977.[17]

The second principle was adopted in response to the concern of fishermen in the western parts of Japan that the decision might prompt South Korea and China to set up 200-mile fishery zones. Should this happen, the fishermen would stand to lose more than they would gain. Their traditional fishing operations in the southern Sea of Japan, the East China Sea, and the Yellow Sea were quite extensive compared with foreign fishing in their own coastal areas. The most important type of fishery in the area was *isei sokobikiami* (bull trawl) fishery, which operated in the East China Sea and the Yellow Sea west of 128° 30' east longitude and in the South China Sea north of 10° north latitude. In 1977, this fishery's total catch was 206,000 tons, valued at ¥71.9 billion. Of this, more than 90 percent was caught within two hundred miles of the South Korean and Chinese coasts. Another major fishery in the area, *enyō makiami* (pelagic purse seine) fishery, produced in 1978 a total of 280,000 tons of fish, amounting to ¥34.8 billion in value. Of this about 60 percent came from within two hundred miles of the neighboring countries. In addition otter trawl and squid angling collectively produced in 1977 ¥5.4 billion in the southern part of the Sea of Japan off South Korean coasts and ¥72.8 billion in the East China and the Yellow seas.[18]

Another reason the western and southwestern fishermen were concerned about the impact of Japan's 200-mile fishery zone of their fisheries was that they remembered the long years and difficult efforts required to establish stable fisheries arrangements with their neighbors. They simply did not wish to have the new fishery zone make any waves. The western fishermen's past difficulties cannot be understated. There was a series of seizures of Japanese fishing boats by Taiwanese authorities between May 1948 and October 1954 and starting around December 1950 by mainland Chinese authorities. Due to these and the Korean action discussed in

chapter 3, 72 Japanese lives were lost, 566 boats seized, and 6,835 fishermen detained by foreign authorities. Twelve long years of negotiations
with South Korea and equally long and difficult negotiations with China,
including the so-called 100-day talks in 1955, which finally produced a
government-level fishery agreement in 1975, were still fresh in the
memories of the Japanese fishermen. These concerns were given serious
considerations by the MAFF/FA.[19]

The third principle was adopted to alleviate the concern among some
Japanese fishermen operating in and around the straits areas in which the
3-mile limit was to be retained that foreign fishing boats excluded from
other areas might rush to their fishing grounds.[20] The fourth principle
indicated the government's desire to expedite the establishment of the
200-mile fishery zone, in clear contrast to the slow and time-consuming
decision-making process for the extension of the territorial sea limit.

As soon as the Cabinet reached an agreement on the general principles
listed above, a working-level office was set up to begin drafting the necessary bill. The new office, the 200-mile Fishery Zone Law Preparation
Office, was composed of officials representing the FA, MFA, and the Maritime Safety Agency. Another setting, a bureau chief–level *renraku kaigi,*
or liaison conference, was used for interministerial communications,
involving the MFA, FA, MAFF, the Ministry of Transport (MOT), the Maritime Safety Agency, the Defense Agency, the Finance Ministry, and the
Prime Minister's Office. Additionally, an informal forum among the
heads of these ministries and agencies, as well as the Prime Minister's
Office, was established.[21]

The drafting work proceeded smoothly, since the Cabinet had reached
an agreement that the process should be expedited in view of the difficult
Japan-Soviet fisheries talks. By April 8, the formal draft had been completed and referred to the Cabinet Legislation Bureau for legal examination. By this time the drafting team had already consulted with and
received the general approval of the LDP, particularly the Agriculture,
Forestry, and Fisheries Division and the Foreign Affairs Division of the
party's Policy Affairs Research Council, a necessary procedure for government legislative action.[22] The process was further facilitated by the fact
that only the MAFF and MFA were directly and extensively concerned
with the drafting of the bill. While the Maritime Safety Agency pointed
out some technical difficulties with the drawing of the outer limits of the
fishery zone, this did not become a serious problem.[23]

The single most problematic aspect of the drafting work related to the handling of the areas of the sea between Japan, Korea, and China. First, the government adopted a provisional measure stating it would not apply the proposed law to these areas or to the citizens of South Korea and China. Then, to prevent costly retaliation by those countries, the MFA telegraphed their governments to explain the provisional measure. Receiving no replies, the MFA concluded that the Japanese action would not cause diplomatic problems vis-à-vis South Korea or China.[24] The MAFF/FA also believed that neither South Korea nor China would retaliate by establishing 200-mile fishery zones as long as Japan did not establish its 200-mile zone in the western waters.[25] The extraordinary exemption of specified areas and countries from the new legislation was based on the government's principle of reciprocity. That is, as long as others did not apply their exclusive resource jurisdictions against Japan, Japan would not enforce its jursidiction against them.[26] If they did, as in the case of the Soviet Union, then Japan's new law would apply to their nationals.

Although Japanese fishermen in the western and southwestern parts of the country were reluctant to support Japan's 200-mile fishery zone, northern fishermen were eager to see the new fishery zone established as soon as possible to respond to the Soviet challenge. To dissolve the disagreement between the two regions, representatives from each area jointly met with government officials in Tokyo on April 16. The government representatives successfully persuaded the western and southwestern fishermen of the urgent need to support the effort to legislate the 200-mile fishery zone.[27]

In the meantime, the government had to decide what to do about the bilateral fishery negotiations with the Soviet Union. By the end of March, it had become clear that political decisions at a high level had to be made to break the deadlock. To this end, on March 30, Prime Minister Fukuda invited to his official residence Foreign Minister Hatoyama, MAFF Minister Suzuki, and Chief Cabinet Secretary Sonoda and discussed the problem. The ministers decided to send Sonoda to Moscow with three important concessions: (1) that Japan would take measures to provide the Soviet Union with the fisheries stocks it would lose in Japan's 12-mile limit in return for Soviet retraction of its request for continued fishing in Japan's 12-mile limit, (2) that Japan would agree to upgrading the provisional fisheries agreement to an intergovernmental agreement requiring Diet ratification, and (3) that Japan would agree to include in the provisional agreement its acceptance of Soviet enforcement jurisdiction and Japan's obligations in the Soviet fishery zone on condition that such a provision would not affect Japan's territorial claim over the disputed islands.[28] With these concessions Sonoda flew to Moscow and met with Soviet Prime Minister Aleksei Kosygin on April 7. They agreed that another meeting should be held between Suzuki and Soviet Fisheries Minister Ishkov the following day. Suzuki immediately flew to Moscow and met with Ishkov but the two could not reach an agreement and simply decided to resume talks at a later date.

During this time the drafting of the 12-mile territorial sea bill was underway, and by March 5 the formal draft had been drawn up. It was then circulated among all the ministries and agencies for final review and to the LDP for final approval. This process was relatively smooth because the bill, in its earlier versions, had been presented to and discussed by the concerned government subunits and the ruling party. It had also been presented to the opposition parties.[29] After formal Cabinet approval, the bill was introduced to the Diet on March 29. On April 7, Prime Minister Fukuda described its background and main points to the plenary session of the House of Representatives. The government's explanation of the rationale for the territorial sea expansion was as follows:

> In recent years, the coastal fisheries of our country have been significantly affected by the large-scale fishing operations of large-sized foreign fishing boats, including frequent cases of fishing boat and gear damage and constraints on fishing operations. The government has earnestly considered the issue of the 12-mile territorial sea. At the United Nations Conference on the Law of the Sea, despite disagreements regarding the rule of passage through the so-called international straits, hardly any country speaks against . . . twelve miles as the breadth of the territorial sea. Furthermore, lately one country after another has been establishing 200-mile fishery zones, and international society is moving at a high speed toward a new order of the sea.
>
> Considering these domestic and external situations, with a view to protecting coastal fisheries, [the government] has decided to extend the territorial sea limit of our country and to introduce this bill.[30]

Despite the opposition parties' rejection of the government decision to freeze the territorial sea limit at three miles in the controversial areas, discussion in the Diet on the territorial sea bill moved ahead without difficulty. On April 18, the heads of the six political parties met to discuss the deadlock of Japan-Soviet negotiations and agreed that they would cooperate on early passage of the territorial sea and fishery zone bills through

the Diet. On the following day, the chairmen of the Diet affairs committees of the six parties agreed to try and pass the territorial sea law by a
unanimous vote, to hold intraparty meetings to discuss the fishery zone
bill, to discuss the two bills simultaneously in the two houses, and to pass
a resolution concerning the Japan-Soviet fisheries negotiations and the
problem of North Pacific fisheries.[31]

The fishery zone bill, with the blessings of the ministries and agencies
concerned and the LDP, was formally approved by the Cabinet on April
21 and introduced to the Diet on the following day.[32] The government
explained its purpose as follows:

> Looking at the recent international situation surrounding the fisheries, we
> can see a rapid movement toward a new order of the sea including the estab-
> lishment of 200-mile fishery zones by the United States, the Soviet Union,
> the European Economic Community, and others.
>
> With respect to the establishment of Japan's fishery zone, [Japan], as a
> distant-water fishing country, has hitherto carefully considered [the issue]
> while observing the development of the Third UN Conference on the Law of
> the Sea, taking into consideration the need to continually maintain a
> smooth fishery order with foreign countries, particularly with the neighbor-
> ing countries. But, with the rapid arrival of the age of 200-mile zones, the
> necessity has arisen for Japan to promptly rearrange [Japan's] ocean system
> from the fisheries perspective. From this standpoint, along with the [bill for]
> the extension of the breadth of the territorial sea to twelve miles, [the gov-
> ernment] has submitted this bill with a view to establishing a fishery zone as
> a provisional measure until the Third United Nations Conference on the
> Law of the Sea produces a final conclusion and exercising Japan's jurisdiction
> concerning the fisheries and the taking of marine animals and plants in the
> area [of the fishery zone].[33]

Although the formal government explanation did not refer to the
northern territorial question, it is clear from the context in which the government's 200-mile decision was made that the action was in large part
designed to maintain the *de jure* territorial status quo over the disputed
islands.[34] As MAFF Minister Suzuki stated in the Agriculture, Forestry,
and Fisheries Committee of the House of Representatives on April 19, the
fishery jurisdiction around the disputed territories would be "delimited
with the appropriate result that the delimitation by Japan and by the
Soviet Union will overlap, [signifying the status] of the unsettled problem since the end of the war." Suzuki said Japan recognized and the

Soviet Union should also "recognize this state of affairs."[35] Since the disputed islands were under Soviet occupation, Japan could not realistically expect to be able to enforce its fishery jursidiction in the area around them, but the government hoped to freeze the status quo, at least in terms of international law as it understood it, for as long as it would be necessary to do so.

The House of Representatives and the House of Councillors unanimously passed the two maritime bills on April 28 and May 2, respectively. The Law on the Territorial Sea (Law no. 30) went into force on July 1, 1977.[36] The baselines adopted under the law and defined by the Cabinet order were identical to those under the 3-mile regime, that is, with the low-water line as the normal baseline; closing lines or straight lines of twenty-four miles for bays; straight lines across the mouths of rivers; and the straight lines closing the three entrances to the Seto Inland Sea, which had been established as Japan's internal waters under international customary law.[37] The new law also incorporated the median line principle to be applied if and when Japan's and its neighbors' territorial claims should overlap. The Law on the Territorial Sea designated five straits areas and the Cabinet order defined the territorial limit there as three miles.[38] Foreign fishing in the same areas, out to twelve miles, was prohibited by the 200-mile fishery zone law.[39]

The Law on Provisional Measures Relating to the Fishing Zone (Law no. 31) also went into effect on July 1, 1977.[40] As a result, Japan placed under its jurisdiction about 376 square kilometers of ocean space, or fifty times as large an area as it did when it claimed only a 3-mile territorial sea. One of the main characteristics of the 200-mile fishery zone law is its provisional nature. That is, given the continuing discussion in UNCLOS on the extent of coastal state jurisdiction in the economic zone at the time of the Japanese action and given the different practices of coastal states around the world with regard to the exercise of jurisdiction within their fishery or economic zones, it would not have been appropriate for the Japanese government to establish a permanent law establishing fishery jurisdiction in its 200-mile zone. Therefore, the government decided to make the fishery zone law provisional pending the outcome of UNCLOS.[41] This was in line with the provisional nature of the U.S. and the Soviet laws establishing their respective 200-mile fishery zones.[42]

Another characteristic of the 200-mile fishery zone law, as we noted earlier, is that it exempted areas of the sea to the west of Japan and South Korean and China nationals from the provisions of the law.[43] As Figure 2 indicates, the East China Sea, a part of the Pacific Ocean adjacent to the

East China Sea, the Yellow Sea, and the western part of the Sea of Japan were all excluded from the 200-mile fishery zone law.[44] It should be noted, however, that Japan's 12-mile fishery zone established in 1965 in accordance with the Japan-Korea fishery agreement prohibits Korean nationals from fishing in the eastern and western channels of the Tsushima Straits. In April 1978, the Republic of Korea established a 12-mile territorial sea. As a result, the 1965 fishery agreement upon which the two countries' 12-mile fishery zones had been based has practical effect only in limited areas of the sea surrounding the Tsushima Islands where Japan retained the 3-mile limit.[45]

The third important feature of the 200-mile fishery zone is that it established Japan's "jurisdiction" over living resources within the limits prescribed by the law and not "exclusive fishery management authority" or "sovereign rights."[46] There were two reasons why the Japanese government chose the term "jurisdiction." First, it wanted to maintain the high-seas status of the 200-mile zone.[47] This is in keeping with the government's persistent claim that the 200-mile economic zone should remain basically high seas under the new international regime of the sea. Second, the term "jurisdiction" would suggest a limited function, in this case, pertaining only to fisheries, rather than more generally inclusive authority suggested by such terms as "exclusive fishery management authority," "exclusive jurisdiction," or "sovereign rights."[48] The fishery zone law also stipulated that, in exercising its jurisdiction, Japan would respect the recommendations of international organizations of which the nation was a member concerning conservation and management of fishery resources.[49] This provision is also in line with Japan's basic opposition to coastal states' arbitrary, unilateral conservation and management measures.

Fourth, needless to say, Japan's jurisdiction in the 200-mile zone extends only to living resources and does not apply to nonliving resources. In this sense, it is clearly to be distinguished from exclusive coastal state jursidiction in a 200-mile economic zone. The government's decision to exempt the western waters precluded for the time being Japan's exclusive jurisdiction over mineral as well as living resources in the excluded areas. Since most of the potential petroleum deposits in the oceans adjacent to Japan lie on the continental shelf in those areas, that decision had the clear effect of postponing Japan's exclusive claims to those resources.[50]

Fifth, with respect to the status of anadromous species of fish that originated in Japan's fresh or estuarine waters, the 200-mile fishery zone law provided that "from the standpoint that in areas of the sea beyond the fishing zone . . . [except in areas of the sea under foreign jurisdiction]

FIGURE 2: Areas of the Sea Not Included in Japan's Fishery Zone

Japan has jurisidiction over the anadromous species which spawn in fresh waters of Japan, Japan shall endeavor to achieve, through international cooperation, proper conservation and management of anadromous species in the aforesaid areas of the sea."[51] This provision indicated the Japanese government's acceptance of international recognition of the primary interest of the state of origin in anadromous species and its responsibility for conservation and management of those resources. Acceptance of this rule was clearly an important departure from Japan's earlier position in favor of according regional fishery commissions the primary function in conservation and management decisions regarding anadromous species. Provisions concerning the status of anadromous species in Japan's new legislation closely resembled those found in the RSNT of 1976, as well as those in the Informal Composite Negotiating Text, or ICNT, which was prepared at the close of the sixth session of the UNCLOS in New York in 1977.[52] Japan's continuing interest in deterring arbitrary and prejudicial coastal state measures in this area was reflected, however, in the provision concerning international cooperation.

Sixth, while the Japanese government appeared to make an important adjustment in its position on the anadromous stocks of fish in favor of the international consensus, it maintained its long-standing position on highly migratory species: Japan was opposed to coastal states' exclusive jurisdiction over such stocks of fish in their 200-mile economic zones. At the time the 200-mile zone law went into effect in 1977, the international community had not yet solved the problem of the status of high migratory species. On the one hand, Japan, the United States, France, and other countries whose nationals were engaged in the fishing of highly migratory species wanted to limit coastal states' jurisdiction over such stocks of fish in their economic zones. On the other hand, Ecuador, Mex-

---

The areas of the sea to the west of the line laid down in the Enforcement Order of the Law on Provisional Measures Relating to the Fishing Zone were not included in the fishing zone. In the eastern and western channels of the Tsushima Strait, however, those areas of the sea that were part of the 12-mile fishery zone established under the provisions of the Cabinet Order relating to the Establishment of Fishery Zones provided for in paragraph 1 of Article 1 of the Agreement on Fisheries between Japan and the Republic of Korea are excluded from the areas covered by the first part of this note and are therefore part of the 200-mile fishing zone.

Point A is the point of intersection of the line of 135° east longitude and the line that at every point is twelve nautical miles from the baseline of Japan. The line is drawn, from point A, along "the 12-nautical mile line," which is the outer limit of the territorial sea of Japan, and between such points as lighthouses to connect islands. Off the coast of Yonakunijima Island, the line is drawn at an angle of 131° from the point 24° 17′ 15″ north latitude, 122° 47′ 42″ east longitude.

ico, and other coastal states asserted jurisdiction over all species, highly migratory or otherwise, in their 200-mile economic zones.[53] Article 6 of the Japanese law exempted highly migratory species from those that foreign nationals were prohibited from taking within the newly established fishery zone. Furthermore, Article 9 stipulated that the requirement for foreign nationals to obtain the approval of the MAFF minister for fishing within the fishery zone would not apply to activities pertaining to the highly migratory species, defined by a Cabinet order as skipjack, black skipjack, frigate mackerel, blue mackerel, albacore, yellowfin tuna, bluefin tuna, bigeye tuna, longtail tuna, broadbill swordfish, blue marlin, black marlin, striped marlin, sailfish, and shortbill spearfish.[54]

The seventh characteristic of the Japanese 200-mile law relates to foreign access to the fishery resources within the newly established zone. One of the major difficulties that the drafters of the law faced was how, if at all, to incorporate the internationally accepted, albeit not yet formally agreed upon, principle that the coastal state had the right to determine the maximum catch levels and to allocate the surplus among foreign countries that had concluded agreements or other arrangements with it.[55] The Japanese UNCLOS delegation had strongly opposed the principle that would give the coastal state virtual monopoly over the fishery resources within its economic zone. With regard to foreign access to fishery resources within the newly established fishery zone, the Japanese law stipulated that foreign nationals would have to secure permission from the MAFF minister before they could engage in fishing except in areas, including the five straits areas, where no fishing by foreign nationals would be allowed.[56] Otherwise, no foreign fishing would be permitted, unless it pertained to highly migratory species, was conducted for experimental or research purposes with the approval of the MAFF, or pertained to the catching and taking of insignificant marine animals, for example, small-scale recreational fishing.[57]

Permission for fishing by foreign nationals would be granted on the basis of three criteria. First, compliance with Japanese regulations in the fishery zone should be ensured through a treaty or other arrangements between their government and Japan prior to application for fishing permission.[58] Second, the catch by foreign fishermen should not exceed the levels prescribed by the MAFF minister for different species of marine animals and plants, areas of the sea, and nationalities.[59] The catch limits would be determined through consideration of fishery resource trends based on scientific evidence, Japanese fishing within the zone, and such other factors as actual foreign fishing practice in the zone and Japanese fishing in foreign coastal waters.[60] In other words, the 200-mile law incorporated the principle that the coastal state had the right to determine the allowable catch for foreign fishermen, although the law did not specify "surplus" as the portion of the fishery resources in the 200-mile zone to which foreign access would be accorded. This was a major departure from the Japanese position as late as the New York session in 1976. Lastly, the country to which the foreign applicant belonged should not fail to give due consideration to fishing by Japanese fishermen in the waters adjacent to that country.[61] This criterion was incorporated into the Japanese law on the basis of the reciprocity principle that Japan firmly maintained. Should a state fail to set an acceptable Japanese catch quota in its fishery zone, nationals of that state would have difficulty securing their share of Japan's coastal fish stocks. Given the Japanese government's desire to secure reciprocity vis-à-vis the Soviet Union and the fear among western Japanese fishermen about the possibility of a South Korean or a Chinese 200-mile fishery zone, the reciprocity rule built into the Japanese legislation may be considered a manifestation of thse concerns.

The eighth characteristic of the 200-mile zone law is that it provided for the requirement of payment of fishing fees by foreign nationals engaged in fishing in the zone.[62] No foreigner has actually been required to pay a fishing fee as of 1977, however.[63]

Although the foregoing description of the major features of the 200-mile fishery zone law is by no means exhaustive, it is sufficient to illuminate the basic concerns of the drafters of the law regarding the balance between Japan's domestic legal provisions and those that were either believed to be an international consensus or near-consensus or actually found in the practice of other nations that had established a 200-mile fishery zone. The summary also makes it clear that the Japanese government had come a long way since the early phases of the Third UNCLOS toward accepting some major principles associated with national ocean enclosure. It is to be expected that, as indicated by the provisional nature of the 200-mile fishery zone law, as well as of the territorial sea law, Japan will continue to make adjustments as the international situation changes in the future.

The Japan-Soviet Agreement and Its Repercussions

With a national consensus on and support for the new fishery zone law, the Japanese went back to the negotiating table with the Soviet Union on

May 5, 1977. When the delimitation of the Japanese fishery zone was explained, the Soviets expectedly opposed the inclusion of the area around the four northern islands. On the other hand, the Japanese rejected the Soviet Union's repeated request that its fishermen be allowed in Japan's extended territorial sea. Since they could not come together on this point, the two sides concurred on what was essentially a set of provisions that supported their respective claims without resolving their differences. Article 1 of this agreement stated that Japan recognized the Soviet fishery zone based on the decision of the Soviet Council of Ministers, which included the fishery zone delimitation inclusive of the area around the four contested islands; Article 2 indicated Soviet recognition of Japan's 200-mile fishery zone delimitation.[64] Furthermore, Article 8 provided an escape clause: nothing contained in the agreement should be deemed to affect or prejudice in any manner the positions or views of either government with respect to the questions relating to the mutual relations between the two countries. The questions relating to the mutual relations, the Japanese government argued, included the territorial dispute; but if asked, the Soviet Union would have maintained that such was not the case because there was no such territorial dispute.

The agreement was initialled on May 21 and formally signed on May 27. At the same time, the salmon fisheries negotiations reached an agreement. Japan's total quota outside the Soviet fishery zone was set at 62,000 tons for the year. Other fisheries quotas were also set, and the long, arduous, negotiations came to an end. The Japan-Soviet provisional fisheries agreement went into force on June 10.[65]

The new bilateral fishery regime got off to a troubling start. Due to catch recording errors, Japanese fishermen operating within the new Soviet fishery zone were fined as much as ¥143,470,000 by mid-November, but this problem was largely solved by the end of the year.[66] In comparison, only a few violations were committed by Soviet fishermen operating off Japan's coasts. By August 15, all Soviet fishing boats had left the Japanese fishery zone, with some returning in mid-September. By the end of October, only four Soviet boats had been detained for allegedly violating fishery regulations. They were released after a fine of ¥500,000 each.[67]

As a result of the long negotiations and of the new agreement, Japanese fishing in the North Pacific had to be greatly reduced in scale. For example, the number of Japanese fishing boats operating in the Soviet 200-mile fishery zone went from an estimated 7,400 in 1976 to 6,335 in 1977.[68]

The scaling back of fishing efforts obviously necessitated some difficult decisions on the part of the fishery industry and the MAFF/FA. First, they had to formulate measures to deal with the reduction in the number of fishing boats and the termination of some fishing operations. Second, they had to come up with budgetary and tax measures to implement such measures. Third, the MAFF/FA had to provide administrative guidance for the fishery and other related industries. Lastly, some reorganization of governmental and nongovernmental institutions involved in the implementation of the programs to be developed was necessary.

The industry closely coordinated its efforts with the MAFF/FA, since the needed adjustments clearly required government policy guidance and financial assistance. On March 31, 1977, the Japan Fisheries Association set up a North Pacific Fisheries Emergency Headquarters to coordinate the industry's response to this urgent challenge and to consolidate its requests to the government.[69] On April 4, the MAFF established a counterpart office with the identical name. The ad hoc set-up was headed by MAFF permanent vice-minister Yoshihide Uchimura, aided by FA director-general Makoto Okaysu and other full-time staff. Furthermore, to provide political support for the MAFF/FA programs, the LDP Policy Affairs Research Council decided on April 5 to set up a Special Committee on the North Pacific Fisheries.[70]

The ministry-level organizational response showed the readiness of the MAFF/FA to secure high-level political decisions to assist the fishermen affected by the drastic reduction of fishing in the North Pacific, which was, from the fishermen's perspective, a result of the government's negotiations with the Soviet Union. Indeed, even the highest-level decision-making subunit of the government—the Cabinet—responded to the MAFF/FA request for government assistance. On April 15, a Cabinet understanding was reached on special emergency loans for the fisheries affected by the talks then underway between Japan and the Soviet Union. The Japanese Fisheries Association was designated as the actual distributor of the special-interest loans, which in total amounted to ¥15 billion for the herring fishery industry, which could not operate in March and April, and for *hokutensen* (trawler) and other fisheries that could not operate in April; ¥15 billion for the salmon fishery industry, which gave up its operation in 1977; and ¥10.3 billion for the offshore trawler fisheries, large-sized squid long-lining, and other fisheries.[71]

Furthermore, the Fisheries Agency decided to provide emergency relief loans totalling ¥30 billion for medium- to small-sized fishery processing businesses.[72] Moreover, on April 30, the Labor Ministry announced that employment adjustment benefits were available to fishing gear manufacturers, fishery food and fishmeal producers, fresh seafood retailers, and fishery shipping companies.[73] These early measures were taken to deal with the deadlock of the Japan-Soviet negotiations, which made it impossible for some fishing boats to conduct their seasonal fishing off the Soviet coasts. The deadlock of negotiations and their final bilateral agreement forced a large number of boats to lie idle during the 1977 fishing season. These included 57 Northwest Pacific crab fishery boats, 7 Northwest Pacific *tsubu* (sea snail) fishery boats, 167 *hokutensen*, 70 offshore trawlers, about 200 dragnet and gillnet fishery boats, 146 herring fishing boats, 20 mothership trawl fishery boats, 330 seakelp fishery boats, and 31 West Bering Sea tanner crab fishery boats.[74]

To deal with this crisis situation, the government on June 21 reached a Cabinet understanding outlining a "Basic Plan for Relief Measures." The plan included long-term, low-interest loans for the affected industries; employment adjustment benefits; job-training programs for fishermen and seamen voluntarily taking retirement; transfer of surplus boats for other uses, scrapping of surplus boats, and promotion of the development of coastal fishing grounds, of aquaculture, and of fishery resource research and development.[75] In accordance with the plan, the government on July 28 decided to provide special relief subsidies amounting to a total of ¥79.7 billion to assist in the reduction of an estimated 1,025 fishing boats. The government's measures also included the expansion of government-sponsored loans amounting to ¥54 billion and an additional ¥13.6 billion subsidies for the scrapping of about 380 boats.[76]

Support also came from the Diet. On May 2, the Agriculture, Forestry, and Fisheries Committee of the House of Councillors passed a resolution concerning the promotion of the fishery industry. More specifically, it asked for government action in the following areas:

1. Active fishery diplomacy and overseas fishery cooperation to secure fishery supplies for Japan.

2. Adequate relief measures for fishery and fishery-related industries affected by the reduction of fishing boats and fishing efforts as a result of the Japan-Soviet fishery talks.

3. Financial assistance for Japanese fishermen required to pay fishing fees to foreign coastal governments and for the stabilization of the living and employment of retired seamen, including employment adjustment and insurance benefits.

4. Government assistance for "cooperativization" of small- to medium-sized businesses and reassessment of fishery legislation for the promotion of energy conservation, cost reduction, scale adjustment, and fishery resource conservation.

5. Detailed studies of Japanese coastal fishery resources.

6. Promotion of the patrol system of the Maritime Safety Agency.

7. Development of coastal fishing grounds.

8. Promotion of mariculture in Japan's 200-mile fishery zone and offshore fisheries.

9. Promotion of fishery research and development for efficient utilization of fishery resources.

10. Establishment of a price stabilizing program for fishery products, improvement of fishery product distribution networks, and establishment of a new fishery import system that did not adversely affect the domestic industry.

11. Promotion of water quality conservation, prevention of marine pollution, and revitalization of fishing grounds.

12. Reevaluation of all fishery-related programs, including the financial, insurance, and mutual aid arrangements for the readjustment of the fishery industry.[77]

In short, the appeal touched on every aspect of the domestic fishery adjustment that became necessary as a result of the arrival of the 200-mile age. A month later, the House of Representatives Agriculture, Forestry, and Fisheries Committee also passed a resolution asking the government to undertake a comprehensive review of its fishery policy and to provide support for the hard-hit fishery and fishery-related industries.[78] Japan's success or failure in meeting the many challenges posed by national ocean enclosure depends largely on how effectively the government can respond to the Diet's call for comprehensive reexamination of its policy and how it can coordinate its policy with the fishery industry's efforts to meet Japanese food needs. In this context, the two maritime laws clearly mark a major turning point in Japanese fishery policy, and their importance easily matches that of the postwar development of coastal, offshore, and distant-water fisheries as part of the nation's overall effort to feed itself.

Conclusion

JAPAN'S decisions in 1977 to extend its territorial sea limit to twelve miles and to establish a 200-mile fishery zone marked an important break with its past ocean policy. The past policy clearly stood in favor of narrow coastal state sovereignty and jurisdiction and broad high seas, and it was largely shaped by Japan's extensive dependence on the ocean space and the ocean resources for its economic development. While those interests were protected by the regime of freedom of the seas in postwar global ocean politics, Japan supported it, and when the regime came under heavy attack, Japan defended it through bilateral negotiations and multilateral discussions. However, when the traditional regime was coming apart under global pressure toward national enclosure and when what remained of the status quo began to hurt its own coastal fisheries because of foreign fishing close to its shores, Japan abandoned its long-standing policy of 3-mile territorial waters and adopted instead what had become a part of the new regime: the 12-mile limit. Furthermore, when its non-ocean, that is, territorial, interests became threatened and the protection of these political interests coincided with the defense of its fisheries interests vis-à-vis the Soviet Union, Japan abandoned its opposition to unilateral establishment of 200-mile economic or fishery zones and adopted its own 200-mile fishery zone before the conclusion of UNCLOS.

What became clear in this study is that the process of decision making in the national government had an important impact on both the manner in which the two decisions were made and the content of those decisions. The series of decisions that culminated in the two maritime laws were characterized by incremental adjustment in response to immediate problems rather than as systematic and comprehensive policy evaluation based on long-term calculations.[1] Nonetheless, if we compare the Japanese government's position on law of the sea questions at the beginning of the Third UNCLOS with its eventual decisions in 1977, we see drastic changes in Japan's policy.

The foregoing examination of the two decisions has illuminated several important patterns in Japan's adjustment to the transformation of the global ocean regime. First, it has enabled us to see the varying responses of the foreign policy and the fishery policy subunits of the government to domestic and international events and developments. Prior to the Caracas session of UNCLOS, different responses were observed with respect to the emerging international consensus on the right of coastal states to establish a 200-mile exclusive economic zone. The Ministry of Foreign Affairs was quicker than MAFF/FA in acknowledging the difficulty of opposing the global trends toward the 200-mile zone. During the period between the Caracas and the Geneva sessions, there again emerged important differences between the foreign policy and the fishery policy actors. Although they concurred that Japan had no alternative but to recognize the rights of coastal states to set up 200-mile zones, they disagreed on the question of Japan's territorial sea limit. While the makers of foreign policy adopted a "wait and see" approach, the fishery policy subunit recommended the extension of Japan's territorial sea limit to twelve miles regardless of the outcome of the UNCLOS debate. The disagreement between the two units continued throughout 1976 until it was solved in early 1977 in favor of the recommendation by the fishery policy sector. In contrast, the two sides were generally in agreement on the appropriateness of holding off on Japan's establishment of a 200-mile fishery zone through 1975 and much of 1976. Toward the end of 1976 the MFA came out in favor of a 200-mile fishery zone for Japan as a counterproposal to the recommendation by the MAFF for a 12-mile territorial sea limit. The differences in the two proposals were primarily due to the different goals of the two ministries as well as to a difference in the level of sensitivity and responsiveness to domestic and international developments.

The second observable pattern shows that in the absence of a consensus on major policy issues, the Japanese government largely lacked policy coordinative capacity. The Cabinet simply adopted the least drastic and the least controversial decision each time it had to unify government policy. The least drastic and therefore the least controversial decision in each round of interministerial talks and Cabinet-level discussions was either identical or similar to that which had been adopted during the immediately preceding round. Consequently, the formal government policy response changed only incrementally. With regard to the question of the breadth of the territorial sea, incrementalism may be seen in the following sequence of Cabinet decisions discussed in this study:

1. Oppose territorial waters beyond three miles as a matter of principle.
2. Accept the 12-mile fishery zone as a matter of necessity.
3. Accept the 12-mile territorial sea limit if UNCLOS reached an agreement on the limit as a part of the international legal package.
4. Support the 12-mile territorial sea limit but observe UNCLOS before making a decision on Japan's own territorial sea limit.
5. Extend Japan's territorial sea limit from three to twelve miles but decide on the timing after observing UNCLOS sessions.
6. Extend Japan's territorial sea limit to twelve miles but retain a 3-mile limit in the straits areas.

Likewise, on the question of the 200-mile economic or fishery zone, the Cabinet's decisions changed incrementally as follows:

1. Oppose the 200-mile economic or fishery zone as a matter of principle.
2. Accept the 200-mile economic or fishery zone on the condition that traditional fishing interests would be protected.
3. Wait to establish a 200-mile fishery zone and observe UNCLOS.
4. Establish a 200-mile fishery zone, but exempt western and southwestern waters as well as South Korean and Chinese fishermen.

Our third observation, related to the second, is that the learning capacity of the ministries and the Cabinet was quite limited as far as the territorial sea and the fishery zone questions were concerned. If learning is defined as adaptation of basic goals in response to problems and changes in the environment beyond mere adjustments in strategies to achieve those goals, the present study has shown the Japanese policy-making system lacked learning capacity. Although both foreign and fishery policy sectors of the government demonstrated an ability to adopt different strategies for coping with immediate policy problems, neither abandoned its primary goals themselves. For the foreign policy subunit, the balancing of Cabinet decisions and international law remained one of its utmost concerns throughout the period studied. The MFA's other major concern was how to coordinate Cabinet decisions with the nation's standing foreign policy or domestic policy with foreign policy implications. This is quite understandable, however, for finding some balance between domestic policy and the international status quo is the *raison d'être* of makers of foreign policy.

On the other hand, the fishery policy subunit was keenly concerned with committing the Cabinet to a policy decision that would best protect and promote Japan's distant-water and coastal fisheries. While the MAFF had to accept reluctantly important losses in distant-water fisheries in both bilateral and multilateral negotiations, it insisted throughout that the Cabinet take effective measures to protect Japan's coastal fisheries. Moreover, it never abandoned the goal of securing adequate fisheries for the country. In fact, Japan's search for adequate fisheries has intensified since the implementation of the new maritime laws.

Despite the continuing Japanese interest in foreign fishery resources, there is no denying that the postwar trend away from coastal fisheries to offshore and distant-water fisheries has been reversed and the relative importance of coastal and offshore fisheries is increasing. As greater emphasis is placed on coastal fishing grounds, the problem of policy coordination becomes increasingly pronounced. Competing uses in Japan's coastal sea areas must be coordinated at the national level. But, as this study has amply shown, horizontal policy coordination is largely lacking in the national government. The number of government agencies directly concerned with the uses of coastal areas is even larger than those that directly participated in the decision-making process on the territorial sea and fishery zone problems. The Ministry of Agriculture, Forestry, and Fisheries and the Fisheries Agency will continue to be concerned with the fishery use of the area. The Ministry of Transport will be concerned with marine transportation in the area. The Environment Agency will be in charge of coastal pollution problems, while the Ministry of International Trade and Industry will certainly be involved with the industrial use of the area. The Maritime Safety Agency will deal with marine safety problems that arise form the multiple uses of the coastal marine area. Other interested parties include the Ministry of Health and Welfare, the Ministry of Finance, the Science and Technology Agency, the National Land Agency, and the Defense Agency. Attempts at policy coordination are most likely to be limited and ineffective. Genuine policy innovation will be rare unless a quick and drastic response is required, as was the case with the 200-mile fishery zone problem.

A fourth observation is that only when none of the previously adopted policy options proved irrefutably inappropriate and inadequate to solve an immediate problem did the government initiate a new approach, and even then only reluctantly or as a defensive measure. For example, the shelving formula was proposed by the MAFF as an alternative to a uniform 12-mile limit, which could not be accepted by the MFA and therefore by the Cabinet. The provisional 200-mile fishery zone was also a product of a desperate attempt to defend Japan's interests to the north, the south, and the southwest. The defensive nature of these decisions was evident in the provisional measures that were meant to be eventually deleted when circumstances changed, for example, when UNCLOS agreed on the status of straits used for international navigation and when South Korea and/or China established a 200-mile fishery zone.

Finally, the present study gives us an understanding of Japan's international behavior that cannot be gained if one focused exclusively on the nation's external expressions and actions. While the external manifestations of the status·quo–oriented and defensive posture of Japanese policy in the 1950s, 1960s, and the first part of the 1970s can be readily identified, a closer look at the domestic decision-making process is necessary in order to see that the apparent recalcitrance was a product not only of Japan's dependence on the ocean but of the complex and incremental policy-making process in the government over which no one segment of the system had effective control, much less a monopoly. That is, what may have appeared to outside observers to be obstinance on the part of Japan in the mid-1970s turns out to be not so much a calculated response but a result of the domestic policy-making process. Had the traditional status quo not been subjected to the kind of challenges that it was, Japan's policy-making, with its established government-client relationships, would have served the country's interests well. When the challenge became formidable and then irreversible, however, the incremental nature of the policy process could not but guarantee delays in formulating appropriate new responses.

So, where is Japan in global ocean politics today? The two pillars of Japanese ocean policy continue to be maritime transportation and fishing. With regard to shipping, no major disruptions have occurred yet, despite the perennial fear that Persian Gulf war will cut off the oil supply routes from the Middle East—the lifeline of Japan. Even in the early 1980s, at the height of the conflict in this volatile region and despite the Iranian threat to blockade the Strait of Hormuz and Iranian and Iraqi attacks on oil tankers in the northern war zone in the gulf, Japan has not suffered any major cutoffs in its oil supply.

The protracted war between Iran and Iraq keeps Japanese policymakers on their toes, however, and it is imperative that they take every measure possible to keep the oil flowing to Japan. Given the friendly relations that Japan has maintained with both nations, there have been speculations that Japan may be able to play an important diplomatic role in reducing the hostilities that threaten international shipping in the gulf.[2] Prime Minister Yasuhiro Nakasone has stated that his government would make positive efforts to seek an end to the fighting.[3] Reportedly, in preparation for the seven-nation Western economic summit in London on June 4, 1984, the Japanese prime minister drafted a "blueprint for peace." The plan, heralded by some observers as "Japan's first diplomatic initiative since the end of World War II to mediate an armed conflict," would have called upon the summit participants to adopt a joint cease-fire appeal to Iran and Iraq, a formal cease-fire agreement between the warring nations, and an eventual troop pullback from their border. However, due to internal disagreement in the Japanese government about the practicality of the proposed initiative and lack of international support, the prime minister's idea was not formally presented at the London summit.[4]

At the same time as it searches for a diplomatic role in the conflict, Japan is taking other measures to keep its industrial machine afloat in the ocean of uncertainty. Its stockpile of oil now stands at about 120 days. The Ministry of International Trade and Industry plans to increase its 25-day stockpile of liquefied petroleum gas to a 45-day level by 1988.[5] Development of alternative sources of energy has increased the share of nuclear power in the nation's total energy supply, accounting for just under 20 percent of total electricity generated in 1982 and surpassing hydroelectric energy in relative importance.[6] Diversification of the sources of oil imports has been more difficult. Of the 1,305,104,000 barrels of crude oil that Japan imported in 1982, 953,187,000 barrels or 70.6 percent came from the Middle East, with Iranian and Iraqi crude accounting for 6.2 and 1.8 percent, respectively, of the total imports that year. In comparison, Japan imported 19.6 percent of its total crude imports from Southeast Asia and the Far East, 3.7 percent from North and South America, 1.3 percent from Africa, and 4.8 percent from China.[7] The uncertainties surrounding the outcome of the conflict in the gulf make it impossible to predict with any degree of confidence how vulnerable Japan's energy supply may be in the future.

While the uncertainties in the oil field are beyond Japan's control, Japan has created for itself and for others concerned with its international posture another source of uncertainty. To protect its merchant fleet of about 41 million tons from a potential attack, Japan has recently embarked on a program to expand its maritime defense capabilities, including the protection of its strategic straits areas and sea-lanes out to a thousand miles from its main islands. Together with Prime Minister Nakasone's reference to Japan as an "unsinkable aircraft carrier" in the Pacific during his interview with a *Washington Post* reporter in January 1983, these apparent changes in Japan's defense posture have caused wide-ranging speculations both inside and outside Japan about its real intentions and capabilities.[8] Japan's Asian neighbors, particularly the Southeast Asian nations, have warned about a possible resurgence of Japanese militarism.[9] Japan's real intentions and capabilities regarding the protection of its shipping interests remain ambiguous for the time being, however, and in the foreseeable future, educated guesses as well as wild speculations and conjectures are more likely than articulate pronouncements and concrete policy actions on the part of the Japanese government.

On the fishery side, Japan has been able to meet its domestic needs with only a limited amount of difficulty. Where Japan has lost to foreign 200-mile fishery or economic zones, it continues to search for new forms of access to the fishery resources in foreign coastal waters through means such as bilateral fishery agreements, joint venture arrangements, direct trade, and technical assistance. Japan has been quite successful in these. For example, it has been able to fill the growing gap between its demand for fishery products and domestic production by increasing fishery imports, 1,088,000 tons in 1975, 1,136,000 tons in 1976, 1,848,000 tons in 1977, and 1,479,000 tons in 1978. This means a growing import cost, from slightly less than ¥400 billion in 1975 to nearly ¥900 billion in 1979. Increases in imports have been particularly drastic for those types of fish for which Japan's catch quota in foreign coastal waters has been cut significantly, including salmon, crab, and shrimp.[10] Drastic reductions in distant-water production from 3,168,000 tons in 1975 to 2,132,000 tons in 1978 have also been partially compensated for by increases in coastal and offshore catches, from 2,708,000 tons and 4,469,000 tons in 1975 to 2,907,000 tons and 5,559,000 tons in 1978, respectively.[11]

Japan will not voluntarily reduce its distant-water fishing efforts. It will continue to defend its fishery interests wherever and whenever it meets a threat to its fishery supplies. Japan's quota in the Soviet 200-mile zone went down from 850,000 tons in 1978 to 750,000 tons in 1979. In the U.S. 200-mile fishery zone, Japan was allotted 1,157,635 tons of fish in 1978 and 1,105,144 tons in 1979. Its share in Canada's 200-mile zone dropped from 27,030 tons in 1978 to 15,800 tons in 1979.[12] In the face of these significant reductions in catch quotas in foreign 200-mile zones, Japan will continue efforts to find new access to foreign fishery resources. More recently, on March 10, 1984, the United States established a 200-mile economic zone in which the country exercises exclusive jurisdiction over all resources, including fisheries and minerals. Since Japan's fish quota in the U.S. 200-mile zone had already become part of the bilateral fishery arrangements on the basis of the 1976 Fishery Conservation and Management Act, the establishment of the economic zone was not expected to significantly alter Japan's fishing efforts in the area in the near future.[13] However, if the campaign in the United States to gradually phase out all foreign fishing in its 200-mile zone continues, Japanese fishery interests and policymakers are certain to watch developments in the United States with much concern.

Japan has also concluded new fishery agreements to continue fishing operations in the newly established 200-mile zones of Pacific-rim states in the southern hemisphere, including Kiribati (in June 1978), the Solomon Islands (September 1978), New Zealand (September 1978), Papua New Guinea (November 1978), Palau (April 1979), Federated States of Micronesia (April 1979), and Australia (October 1979). In recent years, the Japanese government initiated six types of programs to assist less developed countries in developing their fishery capabilities: (1) bilateral interest-free loans for purchasing Japanese-made fishery training, research, and survey facilities and equipment; (2) assistance in surveying fishery resources as part of the foreign aid program of the Japan International Cooperation Agency (JICA) established in 1973; (3) cooperative technology transfer projects (with Turkey, Sri Lanka, Peru, Micronesia, Tunisia, Indonesia, and Chile); (4) training of nationals of developing countries and dispatch of Japanese fishery experts and volunteers; (5) loans for fishery development projects in developing countries, including Pakistan, Kenya, Indonesia, and South Korea; and (6) participation in the multilateral assistance programs of the Southeast Asia Fisheries Development Center (SEAFDEC) established in 1967. An important part of the assistance from the Japanese government is the nonrepayment capital that it provides for various fishery infrastructure development projects in the developing countries. Aid of this type ammounted to ¥5 billion in 1977 and 1978 and ¥6 billion in 1979.[14] In addition, the government supports the activities of the Overseas Fisheries Cooperation Foundation, established in 1973 to provide financial aid to private Japanese groups offering technical assistance to developing countries.[15] At the private level, Japanese investment abroad for fishery projects has also shown a dramatic increase in recent years, standing at US $68.75 million as of March 1978. It has so far been concentrated in joint ventures in Asia and Oceania.[16]

These efforts are important in view of the fact that most developing countries will gradually reduce foreign fishing within their coastal waters until their own fish harvesting capacity is fully developed, at which time they may totally eliminate foreign fishing. Until then, or even if they cannot develop their own resource exploitation capabilities, the developing coastal states will take advantage of the economic and technical opportunities that national ocean enclosure has presented to them.

As for the Third UNCLOS, its sixth session was held in New York in 1977 and produced the ICNT. The following, seventh session in 1978 was held first in Geneva and then in New York, with seven negotiating groups tackling "hard core" differences over the ICNT. The eighth session in 1979, first in Geneva and then in New York, produced a revised version of the ICNT and reached the decision to complete the conference's work by 1980. The ninth session in the following year was held first in New York and then in Geneva and produced an informal text of the Draft Convention on the Law of the Sea. The first official text of the Draft Convention was then issued at the tenth session in 1981, held first in New York and then in Geneva. The conference came to a close on December 10, 1982. On that day, 117 nations signed the new United Nations Convention on the Law of the Sea, the final product of the conference, in Montego Bay, Jamaica. Twenty-eight countries, including Japan, the United States, Great Britain, the Federal Republic of Germany, Italy, Belgium, Spain, Switzerland, Israel, Venezuela, and the Republic of Korea decided not to sign the 320-article document at the ceremony, largely because of the U.S. objection to provisions of the new treaty dealing with deep-sea minerals exploration and exploitation. Over the U.S. objection, however, Japan finally signed the treaty on February 7, 1983, becoming the 119th country to do so.[17]

The convention was open for signature until December 9, 1984, and as of November 24, 1984, 138 countries had affixed their official seals on the document.[18] It is scheduled to go into force one year after the 60th country to sign has either ratified the treaty or acceded to it. Due to the slow process of ratifications, it will still be a few more years before the convention will become effective. However, the bulk of the provisions of the convention are already recognized as part of customary international law, including the 12-mile territorial sea, the 200-mile exclusive economic zone, the status of straits used for international navigation, and so forth.

One area where there is some disagreement about the universal applicability of the UN convention is the international seabed regime. The United States, Great Britain, and a few other industrialized Western nations are opposed to various aspects of the regime. Just to name a few of the provisions that are objectionable to these countries, there are those that relate to the control of deep-sea mineral production to protect land-based producers of minerals found on the seabed; mining technology transfer from developed to developing nations to assist the latter in their efforts to develop their own mining capacity; the sharing of revenues generated from the exploitation of seabed minerals; the role and authority of the newly established International Seabed Authority (ISA), which makes and administers policy decisions regarding deep-sea mineral exploitation; and the relationship between private corporations that have already invested substantial amounts of capital in the development of mining technology and in mineral exploration and the Enterprise, the operational arm of the ISA, which will engage in mining alongside private corporations and other state enterprises.

The Reagan administration has repeatedly stated it will not join the convention because of the treaty's provisions concerning deep-sea mining and has urged other industrialized countries not to do so.[19] Against this urging, Japan, France, and the Netherlands have accepted the convention. On August 3, 1984, however, these three countries joined the United States, Britain, Italy, Belgium, and West Germany in concluding an agreement designed as a means to avoid disputes over conflicting claims by companies to mine deep-sea minerals outside territorial waters. The agreement, "Provisional Understanding Regarding Deep Seabed Matters," became necessary when six international deep-sea mining consortia made arrangements concerning their respective mining zones in the area of the sea to the southeast of Hawaii, where they had been exploring for manganese nodules.[20] Japan joined the group of industrialized countries to stay abreast of the deep-sea mining frontier even though developing countries have criticized the move by industrialized countries as invalid in view of the law of the sea convention, which they claim provides the only international legal basis for deep-sea mining.[21]

Caught between the urging by its closest ally, the United States, and the majority of the nations that participated in the Third UNCLOS and accepted the new law of the sea, what will Japan do? Toru Nakagawa, chairman of the Japanese delegation to the signing ceremony for the UN convention in Jamaica, answered this question when he spoke before an international ocean symposium in Tokyo in October 1982. Nakagawa acknowledged that "it would be impossible to create a Convention for the Law of the Sea which will please every country 100%" and that the UN convention that had been produced by nine years of negotiations was "probably the best convention in the present world." Of the convention, he asked:

> Would not the fact that it will seal up the age of maritime lawlessness since World War II and secure a new order of the sea represent a great benefit, more than enough to offset many defects with regard to particular countries? If we pass up this opportunity, the High Seas, whose benefits should be shared by all mankind in common, will be further encroached upon by the sovereignty of the coastal States, and will soon disappear completely."[22]

As the ambassador's statement indicates, Japan has accepted the new order of the sea. Japan supports the new status quo, represented by the UN convention, as clearly more desirable than the "lawlessness" that might result if certain influential states should decide to take unilateral actions in defiance of the new order. Still fresh in the memories of Japanese leaders is the painful and bitter experience in navigating through the roaring tides and rough currents of global ocean politics over the last three decades.

Appendix

Law on the Territorial Sea; Enforcement Order of the Law on the Territorial Sea; Law on Provisional Measures Relating to the Fishing Zone; Enforcement Order of the Law on Provisional Measures Relating to the Fishing Zone

Law on the Territorial Sea
(Law No. 30 of 2 May 1977)

(Extent of the territorial sea)
Article 1

The territorial sea of Japan comprises the areas of the sea extending from the baseline to the line twelve nautical miles seaward thereof. Provided that, where any part of that line as measured from the baseline lies beyond the median line, the median line (or the line which may be agreed upon between Japan and a foreign country as a substitute for the median line) shall be substituted for that part of the line.

2. The median line referred to in the preceding paragraph shall be the line every point of which is equidistant from the nearest point on the baseline and the nearest point on the baseline from which the breadth of the territorial sea pertaining to the foreign coast which is opposite the coast of Japan is measured.

(Baseline)
Article 2

The baseline shall be the low-water line and the straight line drawn across the mouth of or within a bay, or across the mouth of a river. Provided that, with respect to the Seto Naikai, which is internal waters, the baseline shall be the lines prescribed by Cabinet Order as the boundaries with other areas of the sea adjacent thereto.

2. The criteria to be used when employing as the baseline the lines provided for in the main part of the preceding paragraph and any other matters necessary for the drawing of the baseline shall be prescribed by Cabinet Order.

Unofficial translations supplied by the Foreign Ministry of Japan

Appendix

Supplementary Provisions
(Date of entry into force)
1. This Law shall enter into force on the date prescribed by Cabinet Order, which shall be within two months of the date of its promulgation.

(Extent of the territorial sea pertaining to the designated areas)
2. For the time being, the provisions of Article 1 shall not apply to the Sōya Strait, the Tsugaru Strait, the eastern channel of the Tsushima Strait, the western channel of the Tsushima Strait and the Osumi Strait (including areas of the sea which are adjacent to these waters and which are recognized as forming respectively integral parts thereof from the point of view of the course normally used for navigation by vessels; hereinafter referred to as "designated areas"). The territorial sea pertaining to the designated areas shall be respectively the areas of the sea extending from the baseline to the line three nautical miles seaward thereof and to the line drawn connecting with the said line.
3. The limits of the designated areas and the lines referred to in the preceding paragraph shall be prescribed by Cabinet Order.

Enforcement Order of the Law on the Territorial Sea
(Cabinet Order No. 210 of 17 June, 1977)
The Cabinet hereby enacts this Cabinet Order in accordance with the provisions of Article 2 of the Law on the Territorial Sea (Law No. 30 of 1977) and Paragraph 3 of the Supplementary Provisions of the same Law.

(Boundaries of the Seto Naikai with other areas of the sea)
Article 1
The lines prescribed by Cabinet Order provided for in the proviso to Article 2 paragraph 1 of the Law on the Territorial Sea (hereinafter referred to as "the Law") shall be the following:
(1) The line drawn from the Kii Hi-no-Misaki Lighthouse (33°52′42″ North Latitude, 135°3′50″ East Longitude) to the Kamoda Misaki Lighthouse (33°49′50″ North Latitude, 134°45′8″ East Longitude);
(2) The line drawn from the Sada Misaki Lighthouse (33°20′24″ North Latitude, 132°1′ East Longitude) to the Seki Saki Lighthouse (33°15′48″ North Latitude, 131°54′20″ East Longitude);
(3) The line drawn from Daiba Hana (33°56′50″ North Latitude, 130°52′27″ East Longitude) on Takenoko Sima to the Wakamatsu Dōkai Wan Entrance Breakwater Lighthouse (33°56′17″ North Latitude, 130°51′11″ East Longitude).

(Baseline)
Article 2
Excluding the Seto Naikai, which is internal waters, the baseline shall be the low-water line along the coast (or, if a river flows directly into the sea, a straight line across the mouth of the river between points on the low-tide line of its banks; the same shall apply hereinafter). Provided that, with respect to bays, referred to

in each of the following sub-paragraphs, low-water line along the coast which is within the straight line (or lines) prescribed in the sub-paragraphs shall not be used as the baseline, the straight line (or lines) prescribed in the relevant sub-paragraphs being the baseline.

(1) Bays in which the distance between the low-water marks at the natural entrance points (where, because of the presence of islands, there is more than one natural entrance point, the sum total of the distances between the low-water marks at each natural entrance point; the same shall apply in the following sub-paragraph) does not exceed twenty-four nautical miles: the straight line joining the low-water marks at the natural entrance points.

(2) Bays in which the distance between the low-water marks at the natural entrance points exceeds twenty-four nautical miles: the straight line twenty-four nautical miles in length joining two points on the low-water line along the coast within the bay which, with the low-water line along the shore, will enclose the maximum area of water.

2. The low-water line on a low-tide elevation which, when the lines laid down in the sub-paragraphs of the preceding Article and in the preceding paragraph are used as the baseline, is situated wholly or partly within the area of water which is included in the territorial sea shall be the baseline.

3. By bays and islands, in Paragraph 1, and low-tide elevations, in the preceding paragraph, are meant bays, islands, and low-tide elevations as defined in, respectively, Article 7 paragraph 2, Article 10 paragraph 1 and Article 11 paragraph 1 of the Convention on the Territorial Sea and the Contiguous Zone.

4. The low-water line along the coast referred to in Paragraph 1 and the low-water line of a low-tide elevation referred to in Paragraph 2, shall be the lines marked on large-scale charts published by the Maritime Safety Agency.

(Limits of the designated areas)
Article 3

The limits of the designated areas prescribed in Paragraph 2 of the Supplementary Provisions of the Law shall be the limits of the areas of the sea (the territorial sea of a foreign country being excluded therefrom) prescribed in the B sections of the Annexed Schedule.

(Outer limit of the territorial sea pertaining to the designated areas)
Article 4

The lines referred to in Paragraph 2 of the Supplementary Provisions of the Law shall be the lines prescribed in the C sections of the Annexed Schedule.

Supplementary Provisions

This Cabinet Order shall enter into force on the date of entry into force of the Law (1 July, 1977).

Annexed Schedule (with reference to Article 3 and Article 4)

A   Designated area pertaining to the Sōya Strait

B   The area of the sea enclosed by the following lines:
   (1) The line drawn at an angle of 105 degrees from the Sōya Misaki Light-house (45°31′9″ North Latitude, 141°56′25″ East Longitude);
   (2) The line drawn at an angle of 15 degrees from the first intersection of the line referred to in the preceding sub-paragraph with the line which is twelve nautical miles seaward of the baseline (hereinafter referred to as "the twelve-nautical mile line");
   (3) The line drawn at an angle of 285 degrees from the Sōya Misaki Light-house;
   (4) The line drawn at an angle of 15 degrees from the first intersection of the line referred to in the preceding sub-paragraph with the twelve-nautical mile line;
   (5) The line drawn at an angle of 105 degrees from a point on the line referred to in the preceding sub-paragraph so as to be at a tangent to the twelve-nautical mile line.

C   The line within the designated area drawn at a distance of three nautical miles seaward of the baseline (hereinafter referred to as "the three-nautical mile line"), and the lines pertaining to the designated area referred to in sub-paragraph (1) and sub-paragraph (3) above (but limited to those parts between a point of intersection with the three-nautical mile line and a point of intersection with the twelve-nautical mile line).

A   Designated area pertaining to the Tsugaru Strait

B   The area of the sea enclosed by the following lines and the coast:
   (1) The line drawn at an angle of 90 degrees from the Ōma Saki Light-house (41°33′7″ North Latitude, 140°54′55″ East Longitude);
   (2) The line drawn at an angle of 0 degrees from the intersection of the line referred to in the preceding sub-paragraph with the twelve-nautical mile line;
   (3) The line drawn at an angle of 175 degrees from the Ōma Saki Light-house to the Simokita Peninsula;
   (4) The line drawn at an angle of 67.5 degrees from the Tappi Saki Light-house (41°15′21″ North Latitude, 140°20′45″ East Longitude) to the Simokita Peninsula;
   (5) The line drawn at an angle of 235 degrees from the Tappi Saki Light-house;
   (6) The line drawn at an angle of 235 degrees from the Sirakami Misaki Lighthouse (41°23′44″ North Latitude, 140°12′3″ East Longitude);
   (7) The line drawn at an angle of 145 degrees from the intersection of the line referred to in the preceding sub-paragraph with the twelve-nautical mile line;

(8) The line drawn from the Kattosi Misaki Lighthouse (41°44′22″ North Latitude, 140°36′11″ East Longitude) to the southernmost point of Obana Saki;

(9) The line drawn at an angle of 90 degrees from the Siokubi Misaki Lighthouse (41°42′31″ North Latitude, 140°58′4″ East Longitude).

C   The three-nautical mile line within the designated area, and the lines pertaining to the designated area referred to in sub-paragraph (1), sub-paragraph (5), sub-paragraph (6), and sub-paragraph (9) above (but limited to those parts between a point of intersection with the three-nautical mile line and a point of intersection with the twelve-nautical mile line).

A   Designated area pertaining to the eastern channel of the Tsushima Strait

B   The area of the sea enclosed by the following lines:

(1) The line drawn at an angle of 49 degrees from the Wakamiya Lighthouse (33°51′57″ North Latitude, 129°41′20″ East Longitude);

(2) The line drawn at an angle of 229 degrees from the Wakamiya Lighthouse;

(3) The line drawn at an angle of 49 degrees from the Kō Saki Lighthouse (34°4′52″ North Latitude, 129°12′58″ East Longitude);

(4) The line drawn at an angle of 229 degrees from the Kō Saki Lighthouse;

(5) The line drawn from the first intersection of the line referred to in sub-paragraph (1) with the twelve-nautical mile line to the first intersection of the line referred to in sub-paragraph (3) with the twelve-nautical mile line;

(6) The line drawn from the first intersection of the line referred to in sub-paragraph (2) with the twelve-nautical mile line to the intersection of the line referred to in sub-paragraph (4) with the twelve-nautical mile line.

C   The three-nautical mile line within the designated area, and the lines pertaining to the designated area referred to in sub-paragraph (1), sub-paragraph (2), and sub-paragraph (3) above (but limited to those parts between a point of intersection with the three-nautical mile line and a point of intersection with the twelve-nautical mile line).

A   Designated area pertaining to the western channel of the Tsushima Strait

B   The area of the sea enclosed by the following lines and the coast:

(1) The line drawn at an angle of 53 degress from the Mitu Sima Lighthouse (34°43′15″ North Latitude, 129°26′48″ East Longitude);

(2) The line drawn at an angle of 323 degrees from the first intersection of the line referred to in the preceding sub-paragraph with the twelve-nautical mile line;

(3) The line drawn at an angle of 233 degrees from a point on the line referred to in the preceding sub-paragraph so as to be a tangent to the twelve-nautical mile line;

(4) The line drawn from the Mitu Sima Lighthouse to the northernmost point of Kunosita Saki;

(5) The line drawn from the westernmost point of Komatu Saki to the Gō Saki Lighthouse (34°19′41″ North Latitude, 129°12′25″ East Longitude);

(6) The line drawn at an angle of 229 degrees from the Kō Saki Lighthouse;

(7) The line drawn at an angle of 287 degrees from the intersection of the line referred to in the preceding sub-paragraph with the twelve-nautical mile line;

(8) The line drawn at an angle of 17 degrees from a point on the line referred to in the preceding sub-paragraph so as to be at a tangent to the twelve-nautical mile line.

C   The three-nautical mile line within the designated area, and the line pertaining to the designated area referred to in sub-paragraph (1) above (but limited to that part between a point of intersection with the three-nautical mile line and a point of intersection with the twelve-nautical mile line).

A   Designated area pertaining to the Osumi Strait

B   The area of the sea enclosed by the following lines and the coast:

(1) The line drawn at an angle of 60 degrees from the Kisika Saki Lighthouse (30°49′55″ North Latitude, 131°3′30″ East Longitude);

(2) The line drawn from the Kisika Saki Lighthouse to the Mage Sima Lighthouse (30°45′44″ North Latitude, 130°51′30″ East Longitude);

(3) The line drawn from the southwesternmost point of Mage Sima to the southeasternmost point of Kuti-no-Erabu Sima;

(4) The line drawn at an angle of 240 degrees from the westernmost point of Kuti-no-Erabu Sima;

(5) The line drawn at an angle of 330 degrees from the intersection of the line referred to in the preceding sub-paragraph with the twelve-nautical mile line;

(6) The line drawn at an angle of 240 degrees from the southernmost point of Yu Se (30°44′40″ North Latitude, 130°6′24″ East Longitude);

(7) The line drawn from the southernmost point of Yu Se to the southernnmost point of Yakuro Se (30°43′16″ North Latitude, 130°19′14″ East Longitude);

(8) The line drawn from the southernmost point of Yakuro Se to the southeasternmost point of Take Sima;

(9) The line drawn from the southeasternmost point of Take Sima to the

Sata Misaki Lighthouse (30°59′19″ North Latitude, 130°39′42″ East Longitude);
(10) The line drawn from the Hi Saki Lighthouse (31°16′39″ North Latitude, 131°8′2″ East Longitude) to the Toi Misaki Lighthouse (31°21′49″ North Latitude, 131°20′53″ East Longitude);
(11) The line drawn at an angle of 60 degrees from the Toi Misaki Lighthouse;
(12) The line at an angle of 150 degrees from the first intersection of the line referred to in the preceding sub-paragraph with the twelve-nautical mile line.

C   The three-nautical mile line within the designated area, and the lines pertaining to the designated area referred to in sub-paragraph (1), sub-paragraph (2), sub-paragraph (3), sub-paragraph (4), sub-paragraph (6), sub-paragraph (7), sub-paragraph (8), sub-paragraph (9), and sub-paragraph (11) above (but limited to those parts between a point of intersection with the three-nautical mile line and a point of intersection with the twelve-nautical mile line or another point of intersection with the three-nautical mile line).

Law on Provisional Measures relating to the Fishing Zone
(Law No. 31 of 2 May 1977)

(Purposes)
Article 1
This Law, in line with factors such as the recent rapid developments in the international community toward a new order of the sea and other significant changes in the international environment relating to fisheries, and to ensure proper conservation and management of fishery resources, shall prescribe provisional measures necessary for the exercise of jurisdiction over fisheries and similar activities within the fishing zone.

(Jurisdiction within the fishing zone)
Article 2
Japan has jurisdiction over fisheries (The term "fisheries" means the undertaking involving the catching and taking or culturing of marine animals and plants. The same shall apply hereinafter.) within the fishing zone.
2. Japan also has jurisdiction over the catching and taking of marine animals and plants (Other than that which falls under "fisheries." The same shall apply hereinafter.) within the fishing zone.
3. In exercising its jurisdiction provided for in the preceding two paragraphs, Japan shall respect the recommendations relating to the conservation and management of fishery resources of international organizations of which Japan is a member.

(Definitions)
Article 3

In this Law, the term "the baseline of Japan" means the baseline provided for in Article 2 Paragraph 1 of the Law on the Territorial Sea (Law No. 30 of 1977).

2. In this Law, the term "median line" means the line every point of which is equidistant from the nearest point on the baseline of Japan and the nearest point on the baseline from which the breadth of the territorial sea pertaining to the foreign coast which is opposite the coast of Japan is measured.

3. In this Law, the term "fishing zone" means the areas of the sea (excluding the territorial sea and such areas of the sea as prescribed by Cabinet Order) which extend from the baseline of Japan to the line every point of which is two hundred nautical miles from the nearest point on the baseline of Japan. Provided that, where any part of that line as measured from the baseline of Japan lies beyond the median line, the median line (or the line which may be agreed upon between Japan and a foreign country as a substitute for the median line) shall be substituted for that part of the line.

4. In this Law, the term "foreigner" means the following:

(1) Persons who are not Japanese nationals, with the exception of persons lawfully resident in Japan and designated by the Minister of Agriculture and Forestry;

(2) Foreign countries, public organizations of a foreign country or similar organizations, or juridical persons and other organizations established under foreign laws.

(Application of Laws and Regulations within the fishing zone)
Article 4

The Laws and Regulations of Japan shall apply, as prescribed by Cabinet Order, with respect to the fisheries and the catching and taking of marine animals and plants in which foreigners engage within the fishing zone. The technical modifications necessary for the application of these Laws and Regulations shall be prescribed by Cabinet Order.

(Prohibition of fisheries, etc.)
Article 5

Foreigners shall not engage in fisheries or in the catching and taking of marine animals and plants in the following areas of the sea within the fishing zone, except in so far as such catching and taking of marine animals and plants is of insignificant nature as prescribed by Ministry of Agriculture and Forestry Ordinance.

(1) Areas of the sea within the designated areas provided for in Paragraph 2 of the Supplementary Provisions of the Law on the Territorial Sea but limited to that part of the sea which extends from the baseline of Japan to the line every point of which is twelve nautical miles from the baseline of Japan;

(2) Areas of the sea designated by the Minister of Agriculture and Forestry as necessary for the protection of fishery resources and for fisheries adjustment.

(Permission to engage in fisheries, etc.)
Article 6

Foreigners shall not engage in fisheries or in the catching and taking of marine animals and plants within the fishing zone (The areas prescribed in each of the sub-paragraphs in the preceding article are excluded therefrom. The same shall apply in the next article and in Article 9 Paragraph 1.), without obtaining permission from the Minister of Agriculture and Forestry as prescribed by Ministry of Agriculture and Forestry Ordinance, except in so far as the case falls under one of the following sub-paragraphs:

(1) Where the fisheries or the catching and taking of marine animals and plants pertain to highly migratory species prescribed by Cabinet Order;

(2) Where the catching and taking of marine animals and plants is conducted with the approval provided for in Article 9 Paragraph 1;

(3) Where the catching and taking of marine animals and plants is of insignificant nature as prescribed by the Ministry of Agriculture and Forestry Ordinance referred to in the proviso of the preceding article.

2. Where the Minister of Agriculture and Forestry grants the permission provided for in the preceding paragraph, the Minister shall issue a permit to the foreigner concerned, as prescribed by Ministry of Agriculture and Forestry Ordinance.

3. The foreigner, having obtained the permission provided for in Paragraph 1, shall display a prominent sign to that effect on the vessel pertaining to the fisheries or the catching and taking of marine animals and plants in which he engages and shall keep the permit provided for in the preceding paragraph on the vessel, as prescribed by Ministry of Agriculture and Forestry Ordinance.

(Criteria for permission, etc.)
Article 7

When an application for the permission provided for in the first paragraph of the preceding article is made, the Minister of Agriculture and Forestry shall not grant the permission of the aforesaid paragraph unless it is considered certain that the fisheries or the catching and taking of marine animals and plants pertaining to the application will be conducted properly in accordance with an international agreement or other arrangements, that such activities will not exceed the limit of catch laid down by the Minister of Agriculture and Forestry for each of the classifications prescribed by Ministry of Agriculture and Forestry Ordinance for the fisheries or the catching and taking of marine animals and plants in which foreigners engage within the fishing zone, and that such activities will be in conformity with other criteria prescribed by Cabinet Order.

2. Decisions on the limit of catch pursuant to the provisions of the preceding paragraph shall be made, as prescribed by Cabinet Order, on the basis of fishery resources trends supported by scientific evidence and of the actual situation with respect to fishing by Japanese fishermen within the fishing zone, and with overall consideration of factors such as the actual situation with respect to fishing by foreigners within the fishing zone and the situation with respect to Japanese fisheries in the waters adjacent to a foreign country.

(Fishing fees)
Article 8
Where a foreigner is granted a permit pursuant to the provisions of Article 6 Paragraph 2, he shall pay to the State fishing fees the amount of which shall be prescribed by Cabinet Order.

2. Where a special reason justifies it, the fishing fees provided for in the preceding paragraph may be reduced or remitted, as prescribed by Cabinet Order.

3. In addition to what is prescribed in the preceding two paragraphs, other necessary matters relating to fishing fees shall be prescribed by Cabinet Order.

(Approval relating to the catching and taking of marine animals and plants for the purposes of experiment, research, etc.)
Article 9
A foreigner who wishes to engage in the catching and taking of marine animals and plants within the fishing zone for the purposes of experiment or research, or for other purposes prescribed by Ministry of Agriculture and Forestry Ordinance, shall obtain approval from the Minister of Agriculture and Forestry as prescribed by Ministry of Agriculture and Forestry Ordinance, except in so far as the catching and taking of marine animals and plants pertains to highly migratory species prescribed by the Cabinet Order referred to in Article 6 Paragraph 1 Sub-paragraph 1, or is of insignificant nature as prescribed by the Ministry of Agriculture and Forestry Ordinance referred to in the proviso of Article 5.

2. A foreigner who applies for the approval provided for in the preceding paragraph shall, as prescribed by Cabinet Order, pay to the State fees the amount of which shall be prescribed by Cabinet Order.

3. The provisions of Paragraph 2 and Paragraph 3 of Article 6 shall apply mutatis mutandis to the approval provided for in Paragraph 1, and the provisions of Paragraph 2 of the preceding article shall apply mutatis mutandis to the fees provided for in the preceding paragraph.

(Conditions and restrictions)
Article 10
The permission provided for in Article 6 Paragraph 1 or the approval provided for in Paragraph 1 of the preceding article may be made subject to conditions or restrictions, which may be subsequently altered.

(Revocation, etc., of permission and approval)
Article 11
Where a foreigner who has obtained the permission provided for in Article 6 Paragraph 1 contravenes Laws and Regulations, or conditions or restrictions provided for in the preceding article, the Minister of Agriculture and Forestry may order the suspension of fisheries or of the catching and taking of marine animals and plants for a fixed period of time or may revoke the permission provided for in the aforesaid paragraph.

2. Where a foreigner who has obtained the approval provided for in Article 9 Paragraph 1 contravenes Laws and Regulations, or conditions or restrictions provided for in the preceding article, the Minister of Agriculture and Forestry may revoke the approval provided for in the aforesaid paragraph.

(Conservation and management of anadromous species)
Article 12

From the standpoint that in areas of the sea beyond the fishing zone also (excluding the internal waters, the territorial sea and the areas of the sea equivalent to the fishing zone of a foreign country) Japan has jurisdiction over the anadromous species which spawn in fresh waters of Japan, Japan shall endeavor to achieve, through international cooperation, proper conservation and management of anadromous species in the aforesaid areas of the sea.

(Delegation of powers to Cabinet Orders, etc.)
Article 13

Where Cabinet Orders or Ministry of Agriculture and Forestry Ordinances are enacted, amended or abrogated in accordance with the provisions of this Law, such Orders or Ordinances may prescribe necessary transitional measures (including transitional measures relating to penal provisions), in so far as they are considered reasonably necessary for such enactment, amendment or abrogation.

Article 14

Exemption from the provisions of Articles 5 to 11 may be granted by a Cabinet Order to the foreigner and for the areas of the sea designated by that Order with respect to one or more of the aforesaid provisions.

Article 15

Unless otherwise provided for in this Law, procedures necessary for the implementation of this Law and other matters necessary therefor shall be prescribed by Ministry of Agriculture and Forestry Ordinance.

(Effect of treaties)
Article 16

Where a treaty provides otherwise for matters provided for in this Law, the provisions of the treaty shall apply.

(Penal provisions)
Article 17

A person who falls under one of the following sub-paragraphs shall be liable to a fine not exceeding ten million yen.

(1) A person who has contravened the provisions of Article 5 or of Article 6 Paragraph 1;

(2) A person who has contravened conditions and restrictions to which the permission provided for in Article 6 Paragraph 1 is made subject pursuant to the provisions of Article 10, including those altered pursuant to the provisions of Article 10;

(3) A person who has contravened an order issued pursuant to the provisions of Article 11 Paragraph 1.

Article 18

A person who has contravened the conditions and restrictions to which the approval provided for in Article 9 Paragraph 1 is made subject pursuant to the provisions of Article 10, including those altered pursuant to the provisions of Article 10, shall be liable to a fine not exceeding five hundred thousand yen.

Article 19

In cases which fall under the two preceding articles, any catch and its products, any vessel or any fishing gear or other objects which may be used for fisheries or for the catching and taking of marine animals and plants owned or possessed by the offender may be forfeited. Provided that, where the forfeiture of the whole or part of the aforesaid objects owned by the offender is impracticable, the monetary value thereof may be forfeited.

Article 20

A person who has contravened the provisions of Article 6 Paragraph 3 (including cases where the paragraph shall apply mutatis mutandis under Article 9 Paragraph 3) shall be liable to a fine not exceeding two hundred thousand yen.

Article 21

Where a representative of a juridical person or an agent, employee or other worker of a juridical person or of a person has acted, with respect to the business activities or properties of the juridical person or the persons, in contravention of Article 17, Article 18 or the preceding article, not only shall such offender be liable, but the juridical person or the person shall also be liable to the penalty provided for in whichever article is relevant.

(Exception relating to the jurisdiction of the first instance)
Article 22

The jurisdiction of the first instance with respect to legal proceedings pertaining to offenses under the provisions of this Law shall also be conferred upon District Courts.

Supplementary Provisions
(Date of entry into force)
1. This Law shall enter into force on the date prescribed by Cabinet Order, which shall be within two months of the date of its promulgation.

(Partial amendment of the Law on Regulation
of Fisheries of Foreigners)
2. The Law on Regulation of Fisheries of Foreigners (Law No. 60 of 1967) shall be partially amended as follows:

The heading of Article 3 shall be amended to read "Prohibition of fisheries etc." and in the same article the words "shall not engage in fisheries" shall be amended to read "shall not engage in fisheries or in the catching and taking of marine animals and plants (Other than that which falls under "fisheries." The same shall apply hereinafter.), except in so far as such catching and taking of marine animals and plants is of insignificant nature as prescribed by Ministry of Agriculture and Forestry Ordinance."

Sub-paragraph 2 of the same article shall be amended to read as follows:

(2) Foreign countries, public organizations or a foreign country or similar organizations, or juridical persons and other organizations established under foreign laws.

The following article shall follow Article 6:

(Transitional measures)
Article 6–2

Where the Cabinet Orders or Ministry of Agriculture and Forestry Ordinances are enacted, amended or abrogated in accordance with the provisions of this Law, such Orders or Ordinances may prescribe necessary transitional measures (including transitional measures relating to penal provisions), in so i.. as they are considered reasonably necessary for such enactment, amendment or abrogation.

The word "or the catching and taking of marine animals and plants" shall follow the words "fisheries" in Article 9 Paragraph 2.

Enforcement Order of the Law on Provisional
Measures relating to the Fishing Zone
(Cabinet Order No. 212 of 17 June, 1977)

The Cabinet hereby enacts this Cabinet Order in accordance with the provisions of Article 3 Paragraph 3, Article 4, Article 6 Paragraph 1 Sub-paragraph 1, Article 7 and Article 14 of the Law on Provisional Measures relating to the Fishing Zone (Law No. 31 of 1977).

(Areas of the sea prescribed by Cabinet Order provided for in Article 3 Paragraph 3 of the Law on Provisional Measures relating to the Fishing Zone)
Article 1

The areas of the sea prescribed by Cabinet Order provided for in Article 3 Paragraph 3 of the Law on Provisional Measures relating to the Fishing Zone (hereinafter referred to as "the Law") shall be those areas of the sea to the west of the line formed by the lines enumerated hereunder (excluding areas of the sea which are fishery zones of Japan in accordance with the provisions of the Cabinet Order relating to the Establishment of Fishery Zones provided for in Article 1 Paragraph 1 of the Agreement on Fisheries between Japan and the Republic of Korea (Cabinet Order No. 373 of 1965).

(1) The line 135° East Longitude (but limited to that part north of its point of intersection in the Sea of Japan (referred to as "point A" in the next sub-paragraph) with the line every point of which is twelve nautical miles from the nearest point on the baseline of Japan (hereinafter referred to as "the twelve-nautical mile line").

(2) The twelve-nautical mile line extending from point A and passing north of Mishima Island to the first point (referred to as "point B" in the next sub-para-

graph) at which the line drawn from the southernmost point of Yokoatejima Island (28°47′15″ North Latitude, 128°59′40″ East Longitude) to the Sotsuko-zaki Lighthouse (28°15′3″ North Latitude, 129°8′20″ East Longitude) intersects with the twelve-nautical mile line.

(3) The line drawn from the southernmost point of Yokoatejima Island to the Sotsukozaki Lighthouse (but limited to that part from point B to the other point (referred to as "point C" in the next sub-paragraph) at which it intersects with the twelve-nautical mile line).

(4) The twelve-nautical mile line extending from point C and passing north of Okinawajima Island to the first point (referred to as "point D" in the next sub-paragraph) at which the line drawn from the Nishimezaki Lighthouse (26°21′40″ North Latitude, 126°42′40″ East Longitude) to the Fudeiwa Lighthouse (24°58′40″ North Latitude, 125°21′36″ East Longitude) intersects with the twelve-nautical mile line.

(5) The line drawn from the Nishimezaki Lighthouse to the Fudeiwa Light-house (but limited to that part from point D to the other point—referred to as "point E" in the next sub-paragraph—at which it intersects with the twelve-nau-tical mile line).

(6) The twelve-nautical mile line extending from point E and passing north of Ishigakijima Island to the first point (referred to as "point F" in the next sub-par-agraph) at which the line drawn from the Funauke Harbor Lighthouse (24°20′39″ North Latitude, 123°42′12″ East Longitude) to the Agarisaki Light-house (24°27′24″ North Latitude, 123°2′31″ East Longitude) intersects with the twelve-nautical mile line.

(7) The line drawn from the Funauke Harbor Lighthouse to the Agarisaki Lighthouse (but limited to that part from point F to the other point (referred to as "point G" in the next sub-paragraph) at which it intersects with the twelve-nauti-cal mile line).

(8) The twelve-nautical mile line extending from point G and passing north of Yonakunijima Island to the point 24°17′15″ North Latitude, 122°47′42″ East Longitude.

(9) The line drawn at an angle of 131 degrees from the point 24°17′15″ North Latitude, 122°47′42″ East Longitude.

(Application of Laws and Regulations within the fishing zone)
Article 2
The Laws and Regulations of Japan other than the following Laws (including Orders enacted thereunder) shall apply with respect to the fisheries and the catch-ing and taking of marine animals and plants in which foreigners engage within the fishing zone.

(1) The Law to Control Hunting of Sea Otters and Fur Seals (Law No. 21 of 1912)

(2) The Fisheries Law (Law No. 267 of 1949) (excluding Article 74, and those parts of Article 141 and Article 145 which refer to Article 74)

(3) The Fishery Resources Conservation Law (Law No. 313 of 1951)

2. With respect to the application of the provisions of Article 74 of the Law on Regulation of Fisheries of Foreigners, in Paragraph 1 of that article, the words

"the competent Minister or Prefectural Governor" shall be modified to read "the competent Minister," and the words "fisheries inspector or fisheries inspection official" shall be modified to read "fisheries inspector."

(Highly migratory species prescribed by Cabinet Order)
Article 3
The highly migratory species prescribed by Cabinet Order provided for in Article 6 Paragraph 1 Sub-paragraph 1 of the Law shall be the following:

(1) skipjack *(Katsuwonus pelamis)*, black skipjack *(Euthynnus affinis yaito)*, frigate mackerel *(Auxis thazard)* and bullet mackerel *(Auxis tapeinosoma)*;

(2) albacore *(Thunnus alalunga)*, yellowfin tuna *(Thunnus albacares)*, bluefin tuna *(Thunnus thynnus)*, bigeye tuna *(Thunnus obesus)*, and longtail tuna *(Thunnus tonggol)*;

(3) broadbill swordfish *(Xiphias gladius)*, blue marlin *(Makaira mazara)*, black marlin *(Makaira indica)*, striped marlin *(Tetrapturus audax)*, sailfish *(Istiophorus platypterus)*, and shortbill spearfish *(Tetrapturus angustirostris)*.

(Criteria for permission)
Article 4
The criteria prescribed by Cabinet Order provided for in Article 7 Paragraph 1 of the Law shall be that the foreign country to which a foreigner making an application belongs shall not be a country which fails to give due consideration to fishing by Japanese fishermen in the waters adjacent to that foreign country.

(Hearing of opinions)
Article 5
In laying down the limits of catch provided for in Article 7 Paragraph 1 of the Law, the Minister of Agriculture and Forestry shall hear the opinion of persons of learning and experience, fishermen, and other parties concerned, with respect to factors such as fishery resources trends and the actual situation with respect to fishing within the fishing zone (excluding the areas of the sea designated in each of the sub-paragraphs of Article 5 of the Law; the same shall apply hereinafter), and the situation with respect to Japanese fishing in the waters adjacent to a foreign country.

(Exceptions with regard to application)
Article 6
The provisions of the Law shown in the top section of the following schedule shall not apply with respect to the fisheries or the catching and taking of marine animals and plants in which the foreigners as set forth in the middle section of the schedule engage in the areas of the sea as set forth in the bottom section of the schedule.

Article 5	Articles 6 to 11	
Nationals of the Republic of Korea (including the Republic of Korea, its public organizations or similar organizations, or juridical persons and other organizations established under its laws and regulations; the same shall apply hereinafter)	Nationals of the Republic of Korea	Nationals of the People's Republic of China (including the People's Republic of China, its public organizations or similar organizations, or juridical persons and other organizations established under its laws and regulations)
Areas of the sea which are fishery zones of Japan established in accordance with the provisions of the Cabinet Order relating to the Establishment of Fishery Zones provided for in Article 1 Paragraph 1 of the Agreement on Fisheries between Japan and the Republic of Korea	The fishing zone	The fishing zone

Supplementary Provisions

This Cabinet Order shall enter into force on the date of entry into force of the Law (1 July, 1977).

Notes

Introduction

1. Robert L. Friedheim, "Satisfied and Dissatisfied States Negotiate International Law: A Case Study," *World Politics* 18 (October 1965): 20–41.
2. "Dai Sanji Kokuren Kaiyōhō Kaigi Nyū Yōku Kaiki o Maenishite" [The Third UNCLOS: As we approach the New York session], *Sekai no Ugoki* 308 (February 1976): 9 (hereafter cited as "The Third UNCLOS").
3. Calculated from statistics in Gaimushō Jōhō Bunkakyoku, *200-Kairi no Gyogyō. Saikin no Taigai Gyogyō Mondai to Kokusai Kyōryoku* [Fisheries in the 200-mile age. Recent external fishery issues and international cooperation], p. 6.
4. Tsūsanshō, *Shōwa 57-nendo Tsūsan Hakusho* [White paper on international trade and industry, 1982].
5. Ibid.
6. "The Third UNCLOS," p. 9.
7. Takeo Iguchi, "Dai Sanji Kokuren Kaiyōhō Kaigi Dai Yon-kaiki: Atarashii Kaiyō Chitsujo no Keisei Katei" [The fourth session of the Third UNCLOS: The process of a new ocean order formation], *Gaikō Jihō* (July 1976): 10–11.
8. Mamoru Koga, "Developing a Manganese Nodule Policy for Japan," in *Japan and the New Ocean Regime*, ed. Robert L. Friedheim et al., p. 271.
9. "The Third UNCLOS," p. 11.
10. Tsūsanshō, *Shōwa 57-nendo Tsūsan Hakusho*.
11. Ko Nakamura, "Kaiyō Kokka Nihon wa Ikinokoreruka" [Can maritime nation Japan survive?], *Keizai Orai* (July 1976): 58–65.
12. Kazuo Sumi, "Umi kara Shimedasareru Nihon" [Japan squeezed out of the sea], *Asahi Jānaru*, August 13–20, 1976, pp. 28–33.
13. Eishiro Shoshi, "Hokuyō Gyogyō wa Kaimetsu no Kiki ni" [North Pacific fisheries face a crisis of total devastation], *Sekai Shūhō*, May 25, 1976, pp. 28–33.

Chapter 1

1. M. Grant Gross, *Oceanography*, p. 119.
2. Ibid., p. 122. Figures are from 1968 statistics.
3. For discussion of these approaches to ocean management, see, for example, Seyom Brown et al., *Regime for the Ocean, Outer Space, and Weather*, pp. 19–

34; Robert L. Friedheim, "The Political, Economic and Legal Ocean," in *Managing Ocean Resources: A Primer*, ed. Robert L. Friedheim, pp. 26–42.

4. Friedheim, "Political, Economic and Legal Ocean," pp. 30–32; Brown et al., *Regime for the Ocean*, p. 31.

5. This does not mean that the regime of open access and free use is no longer practiced. It is practiced both at the international and at the subnational levels. At the international level, for example, freedom of the high seas fisheries and freedom of the high seas navigation are still maintained. At the subnational level, most coastal states have only recently begun to limit their nationals' access to coastal areas and marine resources.

6. Friedheim, "Political, Economic and Legal Ocean," pp. 35–36.

7. Kenzo Kawakami, *Sengo no Kokusai Gyogyo Seido* [The postwar international fisheries regime], pp. 788–789.

8. Gaimushō Jōhō Bunka Kyoku, *Dai Sanji Kaiyōhō Kaigi—Dai Roku Kaiki* [The Third UNCLOS—The sixth session], November 1977, pp. 88–90, 94.

9. Kaiyō Sangyō Kenkyūkai, ed., *Kaiyō Kaihatsu Sangyōkai* [Ocean development industry], p. 199.

10. Ibid.

11. Ibid.

12. Lewis Alexander, "Indices of National Interest in the Ocean," *Ocean Development and International Law Journal* 1 (Spring 1973): 40.

13. Francis Njenga, "Regional Approaches to the Law of the Sea," *Perspectives on Ocean Policy*, Conference on Conflict and Order in Ocean Relations, Ocean Policy Project, Johns Hopkins University, p. 91.

14. M. A. Robinson, "World Fisheries to 2000: Supply, Demand, and Management," *Marine Policy* 4 (January 1980): 23.

15. Ibid.

16. United Nations General Assembly, Committee on the Peaceful Uses of the Seabed and the Ocean Floor Beyond Limits of National Jurisdiction, *Economic Significance, in Terms of Seabed Mineral Resources, of the Various Limits Proposed for National Jurisdiction: Report of the Secretary-General* (A / AC.138 / 87), June 4, 1973, p. 33.

17. Frederick W. Bell, *Food from the Sea: The Economics and Politics of Ocean Fisheries*, pp. 174–175.

18. Gaimushō Jōhō Bunkakyoku, *200-Kairi no Gyogyo. Saikin no Taigai Gyogyo Mondai to Kokusai Kyōryoku*, pp. 72–73.

19. Bell, *Food from the Sea*, p. 174.

20. Ibid., pp. 176–177.

21. Ibid., p. 178.

22. Willard Bascom, "The Disposal of Waste in the Ocean," *Ocean Science*, p. 281.

23. Cited in Yoshio Hiyama, ed., *Kaiyō Kaihatsu to Shakai Kankyō Mondai* [Ocean development and social-environmental problems], Kaiyō Kaihatsu Mondai Kōza, no. 5, p. 267.

24. For an analysis of Japan's effort to legislate measures to protect one of its most polluted coastal areas, see Tsuneo Akaha, "Conservation of the Environment of the Seto Inland Sea," *Coastal Zone Management Journal* 1 (1984): 83–136.

25. Robert L. Friedheim, "Factor Analysis as a Tool in Studying the Law of the Sea," in *The Law of the Sea: Offshore Boundaries and Zones*, ed. Lewis M. Alexander, pp. 45–70.

26. Ibid., p. 57.

27. Ibid., p. 60.

28. Ibid., pp. 64–65.

29. For analyses of the complex structure and dynamic process of the Third UNCLOS negotiations, see, for example, Edward Miles, "The Dynamics of Global Ocean Politics," in *Marine Policy and the Coastal Community*, ed. Douglas M. Johnston, pp. 147–181; R. L. Friedheim and J. B. Kadane, with the assistance of J. K. Gamble, Jr., "Quantitative Content Analysis of the United Nations Seabed Debate: Methodology and a Continental Shelf Case Study," *International Organization* 33 (Summer 1970): 479–502.

30. Garret Hardin, "The Tragedy of the Commons," *Science* 162 (December 18): 1243–1248; Mancur Olson, *The Logic of Collective Action: Public Goods and the Theory of Groups*.

31. For "security dilemma," see Bruce M. Russett, *Prisoner of Insecurity*.

32. Arvid Pardo, "An Opportunity Lost," in *Law of the Sea: U.S. Diplomacy Dilemma*, ed. Bernard H. Oxman, David D. Coron, and Charles L. O. Buderi, p. 9.

33. For recent trends in Japanese shipbuilding, see George O. Totten III, "The Reconstruction of the Japanese Shipbuilding Industry," in *Japan and the New Ocean Regime*, ed. Robert L. Friedheim et al., pp. 130–172.

34. For recent studies of Japanese continental shelf petroleum development, deep sea mineral development, and scientific research, see Masayuki Takeyama, "Japan's Foreign Negotiations over Offshore Petroleum Development: An Analysis of Decision-Making in the Japan-Korea Continental Shelf Joint Development Program"; Mamoru Koga, "Developing a Manganese Nodule Policy for Japan"; and Mamoru Koga and Hiroyuki Nakahara, "Japanese Ocean Science and Technology Policy and the National Budget," in ibid., pp. 276–313, 227–275, and 108–129, respectively.

35. "Shīrēn Bōei to Sono Haikei" [Sealane defense and its background], *Bōei Nenkan 1983* [Defense yearbook 1983], pp. 29–32.

36. Ibid., p. 32.

37. *Unyushō* [Ministry of Transport], Gyōsei Kikō Shirīzu, no. 109, p. 62.

38. "Shīrēn Bōei to Sono Haikei," p. 47. The shipping distance from Japan to the oil fields in the Persian Gulf is 6,800 miles via the Straits of Malacca and Singapore, 8,000 miles via the Sunda-Lomboc Straits, and 14,000 miles via the route around Australia.

39. Ibid.

40. The prewar record was established in 1936, when Japan caught 4,330,000 tons of fish. The total catch plummeted in the war years, for example, 1,820,000 tons in 1945.

41. "Coastal fisheries" include fisheries operating without fishing boats, those operated with nonpowered boats, and those operated with powered boats of less than 10 gross tons, and include shellfish and seaweed collection, set net, and beach seine. "Offshore fisheries" include fisheries operating with powered boats of more than 10 gross tons, excepting fisheries in distant waters, shellfish and sea-

weed collection, set net, and beach seine. "Distant-water fisheries" include mothership-type fisheries, large trawl in the East China Sea, distant-water trawl, tuna longline in distant waters, skipjack pole-and-line in distant waters, North Pacific tanner crab fishery, and North Pacific longline and gill net. In other words, the distinction is not necessarily based on the distance from the coastline, but the three types of fisheries roughly represent fairly distinct areas of concentration in Japanese fisheries.

42. Fisheries Agency, *Statistics of Fisheries Production.*
43. Ibid.
44. Suisanchō, *Shōwa 52 nendo Gyogyō Hakusho* [Fisheries white paper 1977], p. 76.
45. For an overview of coastal fisheries programs in Japan, see Suisanchō, Kikakuka, *Engan Gyojō Seibi Kaihatsuhō no Kaisetsu* [A guide to the coastal fisheries ground engineering and development act].
46. Yutaka Hirasawa, *Nihon Suisan Dokuhon* [Japanese fisheries reader], p. 6.
47. Suisanchō, *Shōwa 53 nendo Gyogyō Hakusho* [Fisheries white paper 1978], p. 14.
48. Japan Fisheries Association, *Fisheries of Japan,* p. 40.

Chapter 2

1. United Nations General Assembly, Eleventh Session, Official Records, Supp. 17 (A/3572).
2. United Nations General Assembly, Eleventh Session, Official Records, Supp. 9, *International Law Commission Report,* (A/3159).
3. Arthur H. Dean, "The Geneva Conference on the Law of the Sea: What Was Accomplished," *American Journal of International Law* 52 (October 1958): 608.
4. Ibid., p. 610.
5. Ibid., pp. 610–611.
6. Ibid., p. 612.
7. Ibid., pp. 612–613.
8. Ibid., p. 614.
9. Ibid., p. 615.
10. Shigeru Oda, "Japan and the United Nations Conference on the Law of the Sea," *Japanese Annual of International Law* (1959): 67.
11. Ibid., pp. 67–68. See UNCLOS, A/CONF.13/39, p. 149.
12. Oda, "Japan and UNCLOS," p. 68. See UNCLOS, A/CONF.13/39, p. 149.
13. Oda, "Japan and UNCLOS," p. 69.
14. United Nations General Assembly, *International Law Commission Report,* p. 39.
15. UNCLOS, A/CONF.13/39, p. 248.
16. Ibid., p. 181.
17. UNCLOS A/CONF.13/38, p. 40.
18. Reproduced in U.S. Congress, Senate Committee on Commerce, Science, and Transportation, *Treaties and Other International Agreements on Fisheries,*

Oceanographic Resources, and Wildlife Involving the United States (Washington, D.C.: GPO, 1977), p. 341.

19. Oda, "Japan and UNCLOS," pp. 70–71.
20. UNCLOS, A/CONF.13/39, p. 238.
21. Quoted in Oda, "Japan and UNCLOS," p. 71. See UNCLOS, A/CONF.13/39, p. 156.
22. UNCLOS, A/CONF.13/39, p. 160.
23. UNCLOS, A/CONF.13/38, p. 63.
24. Quoted in Oda, "Japan and UNCLOS," p. 72.
25. Ibid., p. 73. See UNCLOS, A/CONF.13/40, p. 11.
26. Oda, "Japan and UNCLOS," p. 74.
27. United Nations General Assembly, *International Law Commission Report*, p. 24.
28. UNCLOS, A/CONF.13/40, p. 134.
29. Oda, "Japan and UNCLOS," p. 75.
30. Quoted in Oda, "Japan and UNCLOS," p. 11. See UNCLOS, A/CONF.13/39, p. 24.
31. Oda, "Japan and UNCLOS," pp. 66–67.
32. Ibid., p. 76.
33. Ibid. See UNCLOS, A/CONF.13/41, p. 143.
34. Oda, "Japan and UNCLOS," p.77.
35. United Nations General Assembly, *International Law Commission Report*, p. 144.
36. Oda, "Japan and UNCLOS," p. 78.
37. United Nations, Convention on Fishing and Conservation of the Living Resources of the High Seas, A/CONF.13/L.54, Article 6, paragraphs 1–2.
38. Ibid., paragraphs 3–5.
39. Oda, "Japan and UNCLOS," p. 81.
40. Ibid., p. 84.
41. United Nations, Convention on the Continental Shelf, A/CONF.13/L.55, Article 1.
42. Ibid., Article 6.
43. Dean, "The Geneva Conference," p. 621.
44. United Nations, Convention on the Continental Shelf, A/CONF.13/L.55, Article 2.
45. Respectively, UN conventions on the Territorial Sea and the Contiguous Zone (A/CONF.13/L.52); on the High Seas (A/CONF.13/L.53 and Correction 1); on Fishing and Conservation of the Living Resources of the High Seas (A/CONF.13/L.54 and Addendum 1); and on the Continental Shelf (A/CONF.13/L.55).
46. Oda, "Japan and UNCLOS," p. 73.
47. Arthur H. Dean, "The Second Geneva Conference on the Law of the Sea: The Fight for Freedom of the Seas," *American Journal of International Law* 54 (October 1960): 752.
48. UNCLOS, Committee I, A/CONF.19/C.I/L.10.
49. UNCLOS, Committee I, A/CONF.19/C.I/L.1.
50. UNCLOS, Committee I, A/CONF.19/C.I/SR. 27, p. 8; Dean, "The Second Geneva Conference," pp. 774–775.

51. UNCLOS, Committee I, A/CONF.19/C.I/L.2/Rev. 1.
52. UNCLOS, A/CONF.19/L.9.
53. Dean, "The Second Geneva Conference," p. 776.
54. UNCLOS, Committee I, A/CONF.19/C.I/SR.13, pp. 10–11.
55. UNCLOS, Committee I, A/CONF.19/C.I/SR. 38.
56. Dean, "The Second Geneva Conference," pp. 777–778.
57. UNCLOS, A/CONF.13/L.54 and Add. 1. For a concise summary of the negotiations regarding the Canada-U.S. proposal, see Dean, "The Second Geneva Conference," pp. 777–785.
58. UNCLOS, A/CONF.19/L.12.
59. UNCLOS, Committee I, A/CONF.19/C.I/SR. 13, p. 7.
60. Dean, "The Second Geneva Conference," pp. 781–782.
61. UNCLOS, Committee I, A/CONF.19/C.I/SR. 13, p. 8.
62. Ibid.
63. Ibid.

Chapter 3

1. For example, see Yutaka Hirasawa, *Nihon Suisan Dokuhon*, pp. 234–236.
2. These statistics are from the Fisheries Agency and are cited in Hirasawa, *Nihon Suisan Dokuhon*, p. 235.
3. Kenzo Kawakami, *Sengo no Kokusai Gyogyō Seido*, p. 789.
4. Ibid., pp. 790–791.
5. Ibid., pp. 789, 791. Guatemala had established a 12-mile territorial sea as early as 1934. Honduras followed suit in 1965.
6. Earlier, in 1955, Ecuador had claimed a 200-mile fishery zone. Venezuela decided in 1956 to establish a 12-mile territorial sea.
7. Kawakami, *Sengo no Kokusai Gyogyō Seido*, pp. 789, 791.
8. Territorial claims were laid by Gabon, 1963 (25-mile territorial sea in 1970); Madagascar, 1963; Ghana, 1963; Algeria, 1963; Togo, 1964; Sierra Leone, 1965; Dahomey, 1965; Mauritania, 1967; Nigeria, 1967; Somalia, 1967; Sudan, date unknown; Senegal, 1968; Liberia, 1968; Kenya, 1969; and Gambia, 1969. Twelve-mile fishery jurisdiction was claimed by Tunisia, 1963; South Africa, 1963; Ivory Coast, 1967; and Morocco, 1967. Ibid., pp. 786–788.
9. Ibid., pp. 786–787.
10. Parties to the agreement were Belgium, Denmark, France, West Germany, Ireland, Italy, Luxemburg, the Netherlands, Portugal, Spain, Sweden, and Great Britain. Ibid., p. 853.
11. Ibid., p. 857.
12. Ibid., pp. 785–788.
13. Pakistan and India also claimed 100-mile fishery zones beyond their territorial sea limits. See ibid., pp. 786–789.
14. Ibid., p. 785.
15. Shigeru Oda, *The Law of the Sea in Our Time: 1. New Developments, 1966–1975*, p. 119.
16. Choon-ho Park, "Marine Resource Conflicts in the North Pacific," in

Marine Policy and the Coastal Community: The Impact of the Law of the Sea ed.
Douglas M. Johnston, p. 221.
 17. Kawakami, *Sengo no Kokusai Gyogyō Seido*, p. 253.
 18. Ibid., p. 238.
 19. Ibid., p. 239.
 20. Ibid., pp. 239–240.
 21. Ibid., p. 242.
 22. Ibid., pp. 244, 246.
 23. Ibid., pp. 247–248.
 24. Ibid., p. 248.
 25. Ibid., pp. 248–249. Although Korea did not refer to the Rhee Line in its
proposal, it had not repealed the law establishing the controversial line and,
therefore, the line was presumably still in force as far as the Korean government
was concerned despite Japan's consistent and persistent rejection of it.
 26. Ibid., p. 249.
 27. Ibid., pp. 249–250.
 28. Ibid., p. 250.
 29. Ibid.
 30. Ibid., pp. 250–252.
 31. Ibid., p. 272.
 32. Ibid.
 33. Ibid., pp. 272–273.
 34. Ibid., p. 273.
 35. Ibid., p. 274.
 36. Ibid., pp. 274–276.
 37. Ibid., p. 448.
 38. Ibid., p. 450.
 39. Ibid.
 40. Ibid., p. 452.
 41. Ibid., p. 453.
 42. Ibid., p. 454.
 43. Ibid., pp. 454–458.
 44. The International Convention for the Fisheries of the North Pacific, signed
by Japan, the United States, and Canada in May 1952 had established this line
eastward of which Japanese salmon fishing was banned.
 45. Kawakami, *Sengo no Kokusai Gyogyō Seido*, p. 460.
 46. Ibid., p. 451.
 47. Ibid., pp. 467–468.
 48. Ibid., pp. 468–469.
 49. Ibid., p. 469.
 50. Ibid., p. 470.
 51. Ibid.
 52. Ibid., pp. 476–477.
 53. Ibid., pp. 486–487.
 54. The year 1968 was chosen by the Mexican government because the belief
was that it would take about a year to negotiate and conclude fishery agreements
with foreign governments after the new fishery zone law went into effect on Janu-

ary 1, 1967. The same arrangement had been incorporated into the U.S.-Mexican fishery treaty concluded on October 27, 1967. Ibid., p. 487.
55. Ibid., pp. 491–492.
56. Ibid., p. 502.
57. Ibid., pp. 502–505.
58. Ibid., pp. 507–508.
59. Ibid., p. 508.
60. Ibid., p. 509.
61. Ibid.
62. Ibid., pp. 509–510.
63. Ibid., p. 515.
64. Ibid., pp. 522–523.
65. Ibid., pp. 521–522.
66. Ibid., p. 515.
67. Ibid., pp. 515–516, 523.
68. Ibid., pp. 516–517, 523.
69. Ibid., p. 516.
70. Ibid., p. 519.
71. Ibid., p. 520.

Chapter 4

1. United Nations General Assembly, Twenty-second Session, First Committee, *Provisional Verbatim Records,* 1515th Meeting, A/C.1/PV.1515, and 1516th Meeting, A/C.1/PV.1516.
2. Ibid.
3. Ibid.
4. Ibid.
5. Ibid.
6. United Nations General Assembly, *Provisional Verbatim Records,* A/C.1/PV.1529, p. 61.
7. For a review of the Ad Hoc Seabed Committee work see Shigeru Oda, *The Law of the Sea in Our Time: 1. New Developments, 1966–1975.*
8. "Examination of the Question of the Preservation Exclusively for Peaceful Purposes of the Seabed and the Ocean Floor and the Subsoil thereof, Underlying the High Seas Beyond the Limits of Present National Jurisdiction, and the Use of Their Resources in the Interests of Mankind," (A/RES/2467 XXIII). The full text of the resolution is found in United Nations General Assembly, Twenty-third Session, Official Records, Supplement 18, Resolutions Adopted by the General Assembly during Its Twenty-third Session (A/7218), pp. 15–17.
9. Oda, *Law of the Sea in Our Time,* p. 65.
10. Ibid., p. 23.
11. Ibid., p. 67.
12. Ibid., p. 73.
13. Ibid.
14. Ibid., p. 74.

15. Ibid., pp. 74–75.

16. The resolution did not clearly define the area to which its call for freezing of jurisdictional claims would apply but simply referred to "the area . . . beyond the limits of national jurisdiction." United Nations General Assembly, Twenty-fourth Session, *Provisional Verbatim Records*, A/C.1/PV.1709, p. 31.

17. Oda, *Law of the Sea in Our Time*, p. 75.

18. Ibid., pp. 76–77.

19. United Nations General Assembly, 21st Plenary Session, A/AC.138/SR.21, pp. 32–33.

20. United Nations General Assembly, 33rd Plenary Session, A/AC.138/SR.33, p. 43.

21. The full text of Resolution 2749 (XXV) appeared in the United Nations, Press Release GA/4355, December 17, 1970.

22. United Nations General Assembly, Twenty-fifth Session, *Provisional Verbatim Records*, A/C.1/PV.1787, p. 12.

23. Ibid.

24. Ibid.

25. Ibid.

26. Ibid., pp. 19–20. The same position was reiterated by another Japanese delegate, Motoo Ogiso, in the First Committee of the General Assembly on December 14 (*Provisional Verbatim Records*, A/C.1/PV.1796, pp. 56–62).

27. United Nations General Assembly, Twenty-fifth Session, *Provisional Verbatim Records*, A/C.1/PV.1787, p. 16. The statement was made in the First Committee of the General Assembly on December 7, 1970.

28. "Grooved thinking" refers to the thinking pattern of a person or organization attending to a small number of variables pertinent to the task at hand and according to the ranges of values on those variables, placing the critical variables in certain preestablished categories and responding to them accordingly. In the present case, for example, Japanese fishery policymakers would habitually categorize other governments as anti-status quo on the question of freedom of high seas fishing if the latter suggested any changes in the ocean regime, changes that would give expanded jurisdiction to coastal states. They had a preprogrammed response, that is, to oppose any changes proposed by emphasizing the "universal utility" of the existing maritime order. On the other hand, they saw other maritime powers as basically supporting the status quo. So grooved was their thinking until about 1974 that they failed to respond effectively to changes made by other traditional users of the ocean, such as the United States and the Soviet Union when they decided to accept the 200-mile economic zone concept proposed by developing coastal states in return for the latter's recognition of the right of free passage through straits used for international navigation.

"Theoretical thinking" refers to the mode of thinking in which the decision maker adopts very abstract and extensive belief patterns that are internally consistent and stable over time and to which he displays a great deal of commitment. The decision maker typically becomes so committed to one alternative that forms part of his general values that he can easily ignore or deny incoming information that contradicts his established belief system. The present study shows how defensive Japanese foreign policymakers were of the "package approach" to the law of the sea questions; in the absence of a comprehensive UNCLOS agreement, they would not readily accept the 12-mile territorial sea alternative proposed initially by the Ministry of Agriculture and Forestry. The package approach had become part of their strongly held belief system that supported the adoption by the international community of a new ocean regime that would establish a balance among the various uses of the seas and among the many users of the ocean space and resources. For an elaborate discussion of "grooved thinking" and "theoretical thinking," see John D. Steinbruner, *Cybernetic Theory of Decision: New Dimensions in Political Analysis,* pp. 125–128 and 131–136, respectively.

29. United Nations General Assembly, 34th Plenary Session, A/AC.138/ SR.34, pp. 3–4.

30. "Latin American Meeting on Aspects of the Law of the Sea: Declaration and Resolutions," *International Legal Materials* 10 (January 1971): 207.

31. United Nations General Assembly, 34th Plenary Session, A/AC.138/ SR.34, p. 7.

32. Ibid.

33. United Nations General Assembly, Twenty-seventh Session, *Report of the Committee on the Peaceful Uses of the Seabed and the Ocean Floor beyond the Limits of National Jurisdiction,* A/8721, Supp. 21, p. 74.

34. Ibid., p. 75.

35. United Nations, Third Conference on the Law of the Sea, A.CONF.62.33, p. 3.

36. United Nations General Assembly, *Report on Peaceful Uses of Seabed and Ocean Floor,* A/8721, p. 71.

37. Ibid.

38. Ibid.

39. United Nations General Assembly, Subcommittee II, A/AC.138/SC.II/ L.11.

40. United Nations General Assembly, Subcommittee II,A/AC.138/SC.II/ SR.27.

41. Shigeru Oda, "Toward a New Regime for Ocean Development," *Ocean Development and International Law Journal* 3 (1973): 296.

42. Ibid., p. 297.

43. Ibid., p. 295.

44. United Nations General Assembly, Subcommittee II, A/AC.138/SC.II/ SR.60, p. 21.

45. See United Nations General Assembly, Subcommittee II, A/AC.138/85.

46. Statement by Sugihara at the seventy-fourth meeting of the Second Subcommittee on August 14, 1973 (United Nations General Assembly, A/AC.138/ SC.II/SR.74, pp. 15–16).

47. This argument was presented by Ambassador Ogiso during the plenary session of the enlarged Seabed Committee on March 19, 1971; see United Nations, "Statement by Ambassador Ogiso, Representative of Japan at the March Session of the Sea-Bed Committee held at Geneva," n.d. (mimeo.), pp. 5–7. Y. Okawa, Acting Representative of Japan, made a similar statement in the Second Subcommittee on July 27, 1971; see United Nations, "Statement by Minister Y. Okawa, Acting Representative of Japan, in Subcommittee II of the Committee on the

Peaceful Uses of the Seabed and the Ocean Floor beyond the Limits of National Jurisdiction, Geneva, July 27, 1971" (mimeo.), pp. 5–9.

48. United Nations General Assembly, Subcommittee II, A/AC.138/SC.II/L.9, p. 175.

49. See Ogiso's remark at the sixtieth meeting of the Second Subcommittee on April 4, 1973. United Nations General Assembly, Subcommittee II, A/AC.138/SC.II/SR. 60, p. 20.

50. See the statement made by Ogiso at the forty-third meeting of the Second Subcommittee on August 18, 1972. United Nations General Assembly, Subcommittee II, A/AC.138/SC.II/SR.43, p. 4.

51. See ibid., p. 2.

52. Statement by Ogiso at the thirty-first meeting of the Second Subcommittee on April 3, 1972. United Nations General Assembly, Subcommittee II, A/AC.138/SC.II/SR.31, p. 6.

53. See Ogiso's statement in ibid., p. 7.

54. United Nations General Assembly, Subcommittee II, A/AC.138/SC.II/L.12.

55. By this time Japan had shown readiness to agree to twelve miles as the uniform breadth of the territorial sea if the international community agreed to it.

56. "Proposals for a Regime of Fisheries on the High Seas Submitted by Japan," United Nations General Assembly, Subcommittee II, A/AC.138/SC.II/L.12, pp. 1–3.

57. For a similar observation, see Kazuomi Ouchi, "A Perspective on Japan's Struggle for Its Traditional Rights on the Oceans," *Ocean Development and International Law Journal* 5, 1 (1978): 107–134, particularly pp. 116–121.

58. The Japanese position on this question had not yet been clearly developed. Oda, "Toward a New Regime for Ocean Development," pp. 301–302.

59. See Ogiso's statement at the thirty-eighth meeting of the First Subcommittee on March 16, 1972. United Nations General Assembly, Subcommittee I, A/AC.138/SC.I/SR.38, p. 7.

60. United Nations, "Note Verbale Dated 22 November 1971 from the Permanent Mission of Japan Addressed to the Secretariat of the United Nations," A/AC.138/63, p. 6. See Ogiso's statement at the thirty-eighth meeting of the First Subcommittee on March 11, 1972. United Nations General Assembly, Subcommittee I, A/AC.138/SC.I/SR.38, p. 8.

61. United Nations, "Note Verbale," p. 4.

62. United Nations General Assembly, Subcommittee II, A/AC.138/SC.II/L.56. The document was submitted to the Second Subcommittee on August 15, 1973.

63. United Nations, "Statement by Okawa," p. 5.

64. The statement made by the Mexican representative in the Second Subcommittee in 1971. United Nations General Assembly, Subcommittee II, A/AC.138/SC.II/SR.11.

65. United Nations, Twenty-seventh Session, *Report of the Committee on the Peaceful Uses of the Seabed and the Ocean Floor beyond the Limits of National Jurisdiction,* A/8721, Supp. no. 21, p. 71.

66. Ibid., p. 75.

67. United Nations General Assembly, 34th Plenary Session, A/AC.138/SR.34, p. 7.

68. United Nations General Assembly, Twenty-sixth Session, Official Records, Supplement 21, _Report of the Committee on the Peaceful Uses of the Seabed and the Ocean Floor beyond the Limits of National Jurisdiction_, A/8421 (1971).

69. Article II of the U.S. Draft Articles, ibid.

70. United Nations, "Statement by Okawa," pp. 4–5.

71. United Nations, "Statement by Okawa," p. 4.

72. United Nations General Assembly, Subcommittee II, A/AC.138/SC.II/SR.36, p. 2.

73. United Nations General Assembly, Subcommittee II, A/AC.138/SC.II/L.18.

74. United Nations General Assembly, Twenty-eighth Session, Official Records, Supplement 21, _Report of the Committee on the Peaceful Uses of the Seabed and the Ocean Floor Beyond the Limits of National Jurisdiction, Volume III_ (A/9021), pp. 102–105.

75. Ibid., pp. 99–100. Cited in John R. Stevenson and Bernard H. Oxman, "The Preparations for the Law of the Sea Conference," _American Journal of International Law_ 68 (January 1974): 12.

76. United Nations General Assembly, Subcommittee II, A/AC.138/SC.II/SR.74, p. 15.

77. Ibid.

78. Ibid.

79. United Nations General Assembly, Subcommittee II, A/AC.138/SC.II/SR.60, pp. 20–21.

80. See Sugihara's statement made at the seventy-fourth meeting of the Second Subcommittee on August 14, 1973. United Nations General Assembly, Subcommittee II, A/AC.138/SC.II/SR.74, pp. 13–14.

81. Ibid., p. 13.

82. Ibid.

83. United Nations General Assembly, Subcommittee II, A/AC.138/SC.II/L.56.

84. United Nations General Assembly, Subcommittee III, A/AC.138/SC.III/SR.23, p. 9.

85. Ibid.

86. Ibid., pp. 9–10.

87. Ibid., p. 10.

88. Ibid.

89. Ibid.

90. Ibid., p. 11. These approaches were incorporated into Japan's "Proposal on Enforcement Measures by Coastal States for the Purpose of Preventing Marine Pollution," submitted to the Third Subcommittee on August 13, 1973. United Nations General Assembly, Subcommittee III, A/AC.138/SC.III/L.49.

91. United Nations General Assembly, Subcommittee III, A/AC.138/SC.III/SR.28, p. 12.

92. Ibid., p. 13.

93. Ibid., pp. 13–14.

94. Ibid., p. 14.

95. Ibid.
96. Ibid., p. 16.
97. Ibid., pp. 15–16.
98. United Nations, Third Conference on Law of the Sea, A/CONF.62/30/Rev.1.
99. For the concept of "open system," see Ludwig von Bertalanffy, *General System Theory: Foundations, Development, Applications*, pp. 139–154.

Chapter 5

1. *Asahi Shimbun*, April 25, 1970.
2. *Nihon Keizai Shimbun*, May 13, 1971.
3. *New York Times*, March 19, 1969, sec. c, p. 6.
4. *Nihon Keizai Shimbun*, September 29, 1972.
5. "U.N. Law of the Sea Confab," *Japan Times Weekly*, editorial, December 15, 1973, p. 12; *Japan Economic Journal* 12 (June 25, 1974).
6. *Nihon Keizai Shimbun*, June 13, 1974.
7. *Nihon Keizai Shimbun*, May 18, 1974.
8. *Nihon Keizai Shimbun*, May 29, 1974. In fact as early as the late 1960s, the MFA was aware of the growing tide of 200-mile economic zones and expected that they would eventually become one of the key trends of global ocean politics. Author interview with Kazunari Nomura, director-general of the MFA Office for the Law of the Sea Conference, September 1979.
9. Yutaka Hirasawa, *Nihyaku-Kairi Jidai to Nihon Gyogyō—Sono Henkaku to Kaisei no Michi* [The 200-mile age and Japan's fishing—its road to reform and renovation], pp. 100–102.
10. *Nihon Keizai Shimbun*, June 19, 1974.
11. Author interview with Akira Matsuura, director-general of the Oceanic Fisheries Department, Fisheries Agency, and with Kunio Yonezawa, councillor, Fisheries Agency, October 1979.
12. *Asahi Shimbun*, June 20, 1974.
13. For a discussion of the historical significance of the Third UNCLOS, see Elizabeth Mann Borgese, "The Law of the Sea," *The Center Magazine* 12 (November/December 1974): 25–34.
14. United Nations, Third Conference on the Law of the Sea, A/CONF.62/SR.41, pp. 12–13.
15. Ibid., p. 13.
16. Ibid.
17. Ibid., p. 14.
18. Ibid.
19. Ibid.
20. Ibid.
21. United Nations, Third Conference, Second Committee, A/CONF.62/C.2/SR.17, p. 7.
22. See John R. Stevenson and Bernard H. Oxman, "The Third United Nations Conference on the Law of the Sea: The 1974 Caracas Session," *American Journal of International Law* 69 (January 1975): 13.

23. See Ogiso's statement at the seventh meeting of the Second Committee on July 22, 1974. United Nations, Third Conference, Second Committee, A/CONF.62/C.2/SR.7, p. 7. Article 12 of the Geneva Convention on the Territorial Sea and the Contiguous Zone stated: "Where the coasts of two States are opposite or adjacent to each other, neither of the two States is entitled, failing agreement between them to the contrary, to extend its territorial sea beyond the median line every point of which is equidistant from the nearest points on the baselines from which the breadth of the territorial sea of each of the two States is measured," *The Law of the Sea: The Final Act and Annexes of the United Nations Conference on the Law of the Sea, Geneva, 1958, together with a Synoptical Table of Claims to Jurisdiction over the Territorial Sea, the Contiguous Zone and the Continental Shelf,* London: The Society of Comparative Legislation and International Law, 1958, p. 7.

24. See Ogiso's statement at the seventeenth meeting of the Second Committee on July 30, 1974. United Nations, Third Conference, Second Committee, A/CONF.62/C.2/SR.17, pp. 6–7. Article 6 of the Geneva Convention on the Continental Shelf stated: "Where the same continental shelf is adjacent to the territories of two or more States whose coasts are opposite each other, the boundary of the continental shelf appertaining to such States shall be determined by agreement between them. In the absence of agreement, and unless another boundary line is justified by special circumstances, the boundary is the median line, every point of which is equidistant from the nearest points of the baselines from which the breadth of the territorial sea of each State is measured." It further stated: "Where the same continental shelf is adjacent to the territories of two adjacent States, the boundary of the continental shelf shall be determined by agreement between them. In the absence of agreement, and unless another boundary line is justified by special circumstances, the boundary shall be determined by application of the principle of equidistance from the nearest points of the baselines from which the breadth of the territorial sea of each State is measured," *The Law of the Sea: The Final Act and Annexes of the United Nations Conference on the Law of the Sea, Geneva, 1958,* p. 26.

25. Japan also maintained the median line principle vis-à-vis its immediate neighbors. For example, Japan held this position against the South Korean assertion that it had sovereign rights over all of the continental shelf protruding from its coast. In 1974, the two governments set aside this jurisdictional dispute and concluded an agreement to jointly develop the continental shelf petroleum lying between the two countries.

26. See Ogiso's statement at the twentieth meeting of the Second Committee on August 8, 1974. United Nations, Third Conference, Second Committee, A/CONF.62/C.2/SR.28, p. 3.

27. Ibid., p. 2.

28. Ibid., pp. 2–3.

29. Stevenson and Oxman, "Third United Nations Conference, 1974," p. 17.

30. See Ogiso's statement in United Nations, Third Conference, Second Committee, A/CONF.62/C.2/SR.28, p. 4; Japan's draft articles are found in United Nations, Third Conference, Second Committee A/CONF.62/C.2/L.46.

31. Stevenson and Oxman, "Third United Nations Conference, 1974," pp. 14–15.

32. Ibid., p. 15.

33. United Nations, Third Conference, Second Committee, A/CONF.62/C.2/SR.36, p. 5.

34. Ibid.

35. Ibid., p. 6.

36. Ibid.

37. The Fisheries Agency recognized that Japan was quite an anomaly at the Caracas session. For example, see Akira Matsuura, "200-Kairi Gyogyō Senkan Suiiki Mondai to Nihon Gyogyō" [The problem of 200-mile exclusive fishery zones and Japanese fisheries], *AFF* [Agriculture, Forestry and Fisheries] 7 (April 1976): 4–10. The MFA recognized the same fact; see Koichiro Seki, "Kaiyōhō Kaigi—Karakasu kara Junēbu e" [Law of the Sea Conference—from Caracas to Geneva], *Keizai Hyōron* 24 (1974): 69–80.

38. "Chōki Shokuryō Seisaku no Ikkan de Kakuritsu o: Kaiyōhō e Gyōkai Hōshin, Jisseki Kakuho no Sesshō nado Santen" [Let's establish (policy) as part of a long-term food policy: The industry's position on the Law of the Sea, three points including negotiations for ensuring past (fish catch) levels], *Suisankai*, no. 1084 (April 1975): 52–54.

39. For details of the Law of the Sea Headquarters, see "Kaiyōhō Taisaku Honbu o Setchi: Junēbu Kaigi Taisaku e Katsudō o Kyōka" [The establishment of the Law of the Sea Headquarters: Strengthening of activities toward the Geneva session], *Suisankai*, no. 1082 (February 1975): 78–79.

40. "Chōki Shokuryō Seisaku no Ikkan de Kakuritsu o," pp. 52–54.

41. For a general summary of the Foreign Ministry's assessment of the Caracas session, see Gaimushō Jōhō Bunkakyoku, *Dai-Sanji Kaiyōhō Kaigi* [The third law of the sea conference], no. 2 (1975): 51–70.

42. "Agreement between the Government of Japan and the Government of the Union of Soviet Socialist Republics Concerning Fishing Operation" (author's translation of "Gyogyō Sogyō ni Kansuru Nihonkoku Seifu to Sobieto Shakaishugi Kyōwakoku Rempō Seifu tono Aida no Kyōtei").

43. A Soviet Air Force lieutenant landed at Hakodate Airport in Hokkaidō on September 6 and asked for asylum in the United States. The pilot was admitted to the U.S. on the ninth, but the MiG 25 he had flown to Japan was thoroughly checked by Japanese and U.S. military personnel before being returned to the Soviet Union on November 12. There was widespread speculation in Japan that the expanded Soviet fishing operation during the following months was in retaliation for the Japanese refusal to return the aircraft to the Soviet Union immediately in response to repeated demands.

44. *Suisan Shūhō*, July 30, 1975.

45. *Asahi Shimbun*, February 28, 1975.

46. For a discussion of the three nonnuclear principles and their implications for Japan's near-future policy vis-à-vis U.S.-Japanese security ties, see Tsuneo Akaha, "Japan's Nonnuclear Policy," *Asian Survey* 24, 8 (August 1984): 852–877.

47. *Asahi Shimbun*, February 28, 1975.

48. *Asahi Shimbun,* March 15, 1975.
49. The ISNT is found in United Nations, Third Conference on Law of the Sea, A/CONF.62/WP.8/Parts I, II, III (hereafter cited as ISNT). For the development of the Evensen document, see Edward Miles, "An Interpretation of the Geneva Proceedings, Part II," *Ocean Development and International Law Journal* 3 (1976): 303–326; John R. Stevenson and Bernard H. Oxman, "The Third United Nations Conference on the Law of the Sea: The 1975 Geneva Session," *American Journal of International Law* 69 (October 1975): 763–797; and Shigeru Oda, "The Law of the Sea Conference—Recent Developments, Present Status, and Future Implications," *Japanese Annual of International Law* 19 (1975): 80–101.
50. ISNT, Part II, Art. 2.
51. Ibid., Art. 16.
52. Miles, "Geneva Proceedings," pp. 305–308. Fiji, as an island country and a moderate state, was in two coalitions.
53. Ibid., p. 306.
54. Ibid.
55. ISNT, Part II, Art. 38.
56. Ibid.
57. Ibid., Art. 41.
58. For an extended discussion of the competing approaches to the definition of the economic zone, see Miles, "Geneva Proceedings," pp. 308–318.
59. Stevenson and Oxman, "Third UN Conference, 1975," p. 778.
60. ISNT, Part II, Art. 51.
61. Ibid., Art. 50.
62. Ibid.
63. Ibid.
64. Ibid.
65. Miles, "Geneva Proceedings," p. 309.
66. ISNT, Part II, Art. 53.
67. Ibid., Art 54.
68. Ibid.
69. Ibid.
70. Ibid.
71. Ibid., Art. 55.
72. Matsuura, "200-Kairi Gyogyō Senkan Suiiki Mondai to Nihon Gyogyō," pp. 5–7.
73. Ibid.
74. Article 63 of the ISNT provided that the natural resources on the continental shelf, subject to the provisions of the text, consist of the mineral and other nonliving resources of the seabed and subsoil together with living organisms belonging to sedentary species. The sedentary species were then defined as organisms that at the harvestable stage either were immobile on or under the seabed or were unable to move except in constant physical contact with the seabed or the subsoil.
75. ISNT, Art. 53.
76. Ibid., Art. 124.
77. Ibid.

78. Ibid., Arts. 124, 125, and 128.
79. Ibid., Art. 123.
80. Ibid., Art. 118.
81. Ibid.
82. For a study of the complex coalition politics in the Second Committee, see Miles, "Geneva Proceedings."
83. Author interview with Shunji Yanai, director of the Legal Affairs Division, Treaties Bureau, Ministry of Foreign Affairs, September 1979.
84. *Asahi Shimbun,* July 9, 1975.
85. *Asahi Shimbun,* May 9, 1975.
86. Shūgiin Nōrin Suisan Iinkai Chōsashitsu, *Ryōkai-hōan ni tsuite* [On the territorial sea law], April 1977, p. 64.
87. "Ryōkai 12-Kairi no Sōki Sengen ni Kansuru Shitsumonsho" [Questionnaire concerning early declaration of the 12-mile territorial sea], *Suisankai,* no. 1093 (January 1976): 66–83.
88. Henshūbu, "Yamaba Mukaeta Gyogyō Keiei Antei Taisaku: Suisan Gyōkai, Kessokushite Koto ni Atarō" [Fishery management stabilization measures at a crucial point: The fishery industry, let's unify its action], *Suisankai,* no. 1089 (September 1975): 25–37.
89. "Sapporo de Seidai ni Higashi Nihon Suisan Shinkō Kaigi: Keiei Antei ni Shinken na Iken, Shisaku no Sokuji Kakuritsu o Kakunin" [Large-scale East Japan Fisheries Promotion Conference in Sapporo: Earnest opinions for management stabilization, affirms prompt establishment of policy measures], *Suisankai,* no. 1090 (October 1975): 72–84.
90. "Keiei Kiki Dakai eno Nekki Minagiru: Nishi Nihon Suisan Shinkō Kaigi Hiraku" [Full of fervor for overcoming management crisis: West Japan Fisheries Promotion Conference held], *Suisankai,* no. 1092 (December 1975): 38–44.
91. Author interview with Shunji Yanai. Difficulties in horizontal policy coordination are frequently pointed out by observers of the Japanese policy-making process. For an interesting case study of this problem, see Chalmers Johnson, "MITI and Japanese International Economic Policy," in *The Foreign Policy of Contemporary Japan,* ed. Robert A. Scalapino, pp. 227–280.
92. *Asahi Shimbun,* January 31, 1975.

Chapter 6

1. Author interview with Akira Matsuura, director-general of the Oceanographic Fisheries Department, Fisheries Agency, October 1979.
2. *Nihon Keizai Shimbun,* October 16, 1975.
3. *Nihon Keizai Shimbun,* October 17, 1975.
4. *Asahi Shimbun,* October 24, 1975.
5. *Asahi Shimbun,* November 12, 1975.
6. *Asahi Shimbun,* April 1, 1976.
7. *Nihon Keizai Shimbun,* May 29, 1976.
8. *Asahi Shimbun,* July 23, 1976.
9. *Asahi Shimbun,* July 27, 1976.

10. "Seidai ni Nihon Gyogyō Shinkō Taisaku Kaigi: Kiki Dakai e Kokuminteki Sōi de Katsudō, Nihon Gyogyō no Shinkō o Hakarukai ga Hossoku" [Grand Japan Fisheries Promotion Conference: Activities to overcome the crisis with the will of all people of the country, Association for the Promotion of Japanese Fisheries established], *Suisankai*, no. 1103 (November 1976): 7–22.

11. Takeo Iguchi, "Shin Kaiyōhō no Sōki Daketsu ga Kokueki ni Gatchi" [Early settlement of the new law of the sea will meet the national interests], *Sekai Shūhō* 12 (1976): 14.

12. The relevant provisions are in Article 50 of the two texts. The ISNT is found in United Nations, Third Conference on the Law of the Sea, A/CONF.62/WP.8/Parts I, II, and III (hereafter cited as ISNT); the RSNT is found in United Nations, Third Conference on the Law of the Sea, A/CONF.62/WP.8/Rev.1/Part II (hereafter cited as RSNT).

13. See Article 51 of the two texts.

14. See Article 53 of the two texts.

15. See Article 54 of the ISNT and Article 55 of the RSNT.

16. See David L. Gantz, "The United Nations and the Law of the Sea," *International and Comparative Law Quarterly* 26 (January 1977): 37–38. For discussions of the juridical status of the exclusive economic zone and of the rights and duties of the coastal and other states with regard to the zone, see Bernard H. Oxman, "The Third United Nations Conference on the Law of the Sea: The 1976 New York Sessions," *American Journal of International Law* 71 (April 1977): 259–268; J. C. Phillips, "The Exclusive Economic Zone as a Concept in International Law," *International and Comparative Law Journal* 26 (July 1977): 585–618.

17. RSNT, Part II, Art. 18; ISNT, Part II, Art. 16, respectively.

18. RSNT and ISNT, Art. 37 and Art. 38, respectively.

19. RSNT and ISNT, Art. 38 and Art. 39, respectively.

20. RSNT and ISNT, Art. 39 and Art. 40, respectively.

21. RSNT and ISNT, Art. 40 and Art. 41, respectively.

22. Ibid.

23. RSNT and ISNT, Art. 42 and Art. 43, respectively.

24. A number of Japanese observers, critical of the U.S. unilateral 200-mile decision, attributed the wave of unilateral moves that took place in 1976 and 1977 to the U.S. decision. For example, see Kazuo Sumi, "Umi kara Shimedasareru Nihon" [Japan squeezed out of the Sea], *Asahi Jānaru* (August 13–20, 1976), p. 28. The FA also believed that the U.S. action caused the chain reactions among other states. Author interview with Matsuura.

25. Akira Matsuura, "200-Kairi Keizai Suiiki wa Dōnaru—Nichibei Gyogyō Kōshō o Furikaette" [What will become of the 200-mile economic zone?—A reflection on Japan-U.S. fishery negotiations], *Gekkan Jiyū Minshu*, no. 253 (February 1977): 93–99.

26. Soviet recognition of the U.S. 200-mile zone was considered the most decisive factor in Japan's turnaround by Akira Matsuura, one of the chief Japanese negotiators with the U.S. See ibid., p. 97.

27. *Asahi Shimbun*, December 11, 1976.

28. Author interview with Ichiro Nakamura, director of the International Division, Japan Fisheries Association, October 1979.

29. *Suisan Nenkan,* 1977 [Fisheries yearbook, 1977], p. 32.
30. Ibid.
31. "Seidai ni Nihon Gyogyō Shinkō Taisaku Kaigi."
32. Author interviews with Shunji Yanai, director of Legal Affairs Division, Treaties Bureau, Ministry of Foreign Affairs, September 1979, and Kazunari Nomura, director-general of the Office for the Law of the Sea Conference, Ministry of Foreign Affairs, September 1979.
33. Interview with Yanai.
34. "Ryōkai 12-Kairi no Sōki Sengen ni Kansuru Shitsumonsho" [Questionnaire concerning early declaration of the 12-mile territorial sea], *Suisankai,* no. 1093 (January 1976): 66–83.
35. The provisions of the Geneva Convention cited here are found in *The Law of the Sea: The Final Act and Annexes of the United Nations Conference on the Law of the Sea, Geneva, 1958, together with a Synoptical Table of Claims to Jurisdiction over the Territorial Sea, the Contiguous Zone and the Continental Shelf,* London: The Society of Comparative Legislation and International Law, 1958, pp. 7–8. For an analysis of the controversy over the relationship between the law of the sea and Japan's nonnuclear principles, see Tadao Kuribayashi, "The Basic Structure of the New Regime of Passage through International Straits: An Emerging Trend in the Third UNCLOS and Japan's Situation," *Japanese Annual of International Law* 21 (1977).
36. Later in 1980, he attained the highest political post in the country, that of the prime minister, on account of becoming the chairman of the LDP. The importance of his role in interministerial discussion was recognized within his ministry. Author interview with Ken Mihori, director-general of the Cabinet Councillor's Office Cabinet Secretariat, October 1979.
37. *Asahi Shimbun,* December 26, 1976. The active role that Suzuki took upon himself is quite understandable given his background and the interests of his constituency. It is nonetheless remarkable because his strong personal commitment is not typical of Japanese politicians who find themselves faced with a policy problem for which there is no easy consensus among the parties whose interests are directly affected by government policy. For a critical view of this aspect of decision making, see, for example, Shinkichi Eto, "Foreign Policy Formation in Japan," *Japan Interpreter* (Winter 1976): 251–266; Chihiro Hosoya, "Characteristics of the Foreign Policy Decision-Making System in Japan," *World Politics* 26 (April 1974): 353–369; Akira Watanabe, "Foreign Policy Making Japanese Style," *International Affairs* 54 (January 1978): 75–88; and Kan Ori, "Political Factors in Post-War Japan's Foreign Policy Decisions," in *Japan, America, and the Future World Order,* ed. Morton Kaplan and Kinhide Mushakoji, pp. 145–174.
38. The Soviet action was perceived by many Japanese observers as being targeted against Japan. For example, see Sadaaki Isoda, "Kyokutō Gyojō o 'Jikoku no Niwa' ni—200-Kairi no Taisei ni Junnō" [Turning the Far East fishing grounds into (the Soviet Union's) "own yard"—Adaptation to the dominant trend of 200-mile (zones)], *Sekai Shūhō* (January 1977): 23–24; Motokichi Morisawa, "200-Kairi Mondai no Yukue to Kongo no Nihon no Suisangyō no Arikata" [The direction of the 200-mile issue and the future of Japanese fisheries], *Keidanren Geppō* 25 (1977): 52–56.

39. *Asahi Shimbun,* December 16, 1976.
40. Author interview with Kunio Yonezawa, councillor, Fisheries Agency, October 1979.
41. *Asahi Shimbun,* January 8, 1977.
42. Author interview with Yonezawa.
43. *Asahi Shimbun,* January 8, 1977; author interview with Nomura.
44. *Akahata,* February 25, 1977.
45. Katsu Kawamura, "Ryōkai 12-Kairi ni Taisuru Minshatō no Kangae" [Democratic Socialist Party's position on the 12-mile territorial sea], *Kakushin* 80 (1977): 70–71.
46. *Asahi Shimbun,* January 27, 1977.
47. Ibid.
48. Ibid.
49. Shūgiin Nōrin Suisan Iinkai Chōsashitsu, *Kaiyō-hōan ni tsuite,* p. 67.
50. *Asahi Shimbun,* January 27, 1977.
51. For discussions of "consensus decision making" in the Japanese policymaking process, see Albert M. Craig, "Functional and Dysfunctional Aspects of Bureaucracy," in *Modern Japanese Organization and Decision Making,* ed. Ezra F. Vogel, pp. 3–31; Eto, "Foreign Policy Formation"; Hosoya, "Characteristics of Decision-Making System in Japan"; I. M. Destler et al., *Managing An Alliance: The Politics of U.S.-Japanese Relations,* pp. 101–108; Watanabe, "Foreign Policy Making Japanese Style"; Ori, "Political Factors"; and Edwin O. Reischauer, *The Japanese,* pp. 286–297.
52. *Asahi Shimbun,* January 27, 1977.
53. Ibid.
54. Ibid.
55. Ibid.
56. Ibid.
57. Author interview with Mihori.
58. Author interview with Yanai. The setup was called *Kankei Kakuryō Kondankai.*
59. The executive committee was called *Kyokuchō Kaigi* and the working-level office *Ryōkaihō Jumbishitsu.*
60. For technical details of the delimitation, see Shunji Yanai and Kuniaki Asomura, "Japan and the Emerging Order of the Sea: Two Maritime Laws of Japan," *Japanese Annual of International Law* (1977): 53–65.
61. For the exhaustive list of the sixty-nine straits, see Shūgiin Nōrin Suisan Iinkai Chōsashitsu, *Ryōkai-hōan ni tsuite* [On the territorial sea law], April 1977, pp. 70–71.
62. *Asahi Shimbun,* February 14, 1977.
63. *Asahi Shimbun,* February 24, 1977.
64. Author interview with Yanai and with Nomura.
65. *Asahi Shimbun,* January 19, 1977
66. *Asahi Shimbun,* January 27, 1977.
67. *Asahi Shimbun,* February 18, 1977.
68. Ibid.
69. Kaijō Hoanchō, *Shōwa 54-nenban, Kaijō Hoan Hakusho* [Maritime safety white paper, 1979], p. 19.

Chapter 7

1. "200-Kairi Jidai no Makuake to Natta Sangatsu, Nisso Gyogyō Kōshō" [March marks the dawning of the 200-mile age, the Japan-Soviet fisheries talks], *Suisankai*, no. 1108 (May 1977): 52–53.
2. *Asahi Shimbun*, December 14, 1976.
3. Author interview with Seiichi Yoshida, Fisheries Administration Department, Fisheries Agency, October 1979.
4. *Nihon Keizai Shimbun*, December 26, 1976.
5. "Kamenaga Kaichō, Gyōkai Shunō, Shin Kaiyō Chitsujo Taisaku de Yōbō" [President Kamenaga, industry leaders request new ocean order measures], *Suisankai*, no. 1105 (January 1977): 59–60.
6. Author interview with Ken Mihori, director-general of the Councillors' Office, Cabinet Secretariat, October 1979.
7. The Council of Ministers' decision stated that the outer limit of the new fishery zone was the median line between the southern group of the Kurile Islands (the disputed islands) and the Japanese territories. For a legal discussion of the territorial dispute, see Yuichi Takano, "Ryōdo Mondai" [Territorial problems], *Jūristo*, no. 647 (September 1977): 43–52; Kanae Taijudo, "Ryōdo Mondai —Hoppō Ryōdo, Takeshima, Senkaku Shotō no Kizoku" [Territorial problems— reversion of the Northern Territories, Takeshima, Senkaku Islands], *Jūristo*, no. 647 (September 1977): 53–59.
8. *Asahi Shimbun*, February 25, 1977.
9. For a summary review of Japan-Soviet fishery and territorial disputes in the postwar period, see, for example, William H. MacKenzie, "Japan-USSR Negotiations on Safe Fishing and the Reversion of Disputed Islands in the North-Pacific, 1945–1977," *Marine Affairs Journal*, no. 5 (January 1978): 1–31.
10. "200-Kairi Jidai no Makuake to Natta Sangatsu," pp. 52–53.
11. Author interviews with Kuniaki Asomura, director of the Fishing Division, Economic Affairs Bureau, Ministry of Foreign Affairs, September 1979, and with Akira Matsuura, director-general of the Oceanographic Fisheries Department, Fisheries Agency, October 1979.
12. "Nisso Gyogyō Kōshō ni Kansuru Kokkai Daihyō Giindan Hōkokusho" [Report of the Dietmen's delegation concerning Japan-Soviet fisheries negotiations], submitted to the Diet by Yoshio Sakurauchi, head of the delegation, May 1977, p. 12.
13. Ibid.
14. The delegation visited Moscow from April 16 to 21, 1977, and met with several Soviet leaders including Fisheries Minister Ishkov. Their report is cited above in note 12.
15. "Hokuyō Kiki Toppa Kokumin Sōkekki Taikai Hiraku: Chihō Jichitai Dai Nihon Suisankai Soren no Kyōken Shisei ni Kōgi" [All People's Conference to Overcome the North Pacific Crisis held: Local governments and the Japan Fisheries Association protest the aggressive posture of the Soviet Union], *Suisankai*, no. 1109 (June 1977): 103.
16. *Asahi Shimbun*, March 14, 1977.
17. *Asahi Shimbun*, March 30, 1977.
18. Ko Nakatate, "Keizai Suiiki 200-Kairi to Nishi Nihon Suisangyō" [200-

mile fishery zones and the fishery industry of western Japan], *Kyūshū Keizai Tōkei Geppō* (March 1977): 3–14; *Suisan Nenkan, 1979,* pp. 151–154 and 157.

19. Author interview with Yoshida.
20. Ibid.
21. Ibid.
22. Ibid.
23. Ibid.
24. Author interview with Asomura.
25. Author interview with Matsuura.
26. Author interview with Yoshida.
27. *Nishi Nihon Shimbun,* April 17, 22, and 24, 1977.
28. *Asahi Shimbun,* April 1, 1977.
29. Author interview with Shunji Yanai, director of the Legal Affairs Division, Treaties Bureau, Ministry of Foreign Affairs, September 1979.
30. Shūgiin Nōrin Suisan Iinkai Chōsashitsu, *Ryōkai-hōan Kankei Shiryō* [Documents concerning the territorial sea bill], April 1977, pp. 3–6 (mimeo.).
31. *Asahi Shimbun,* April 20, 1977.
32. Ibid.
33. "Gyogyō Suiiki ni Kansuru Zantei Sochihō: Shūgiin no Teian Riyū to Nōshō, Chōkan no Setsumei" [The Law on Provisional Measures Relating to the Fishing Zone: Reasons for the introduction to the House of Representatives and the explanation by the agriculture minister and the Fisheries Agency director-general], *Suisankai,* no. 1108 (May 1977): 40.
34. An MFA bureaucrat acknowledged that the territorial question was indeed central to Japan's decision to set up a 200-mile fishery zone. Author interview with Asomura.
35. *Asahi Shimbun,* April 20, 1977.
36. Enforcement Order of the Law on the Territorial Sea, Supplementary Provisions.
37. Law on the Territorial Sea, Article 2; Enforcement Order of the Law on the Territorial Sea, Articles 1 and 2.
38. Law on the Territorial Sea, Supplementary Provisions 2 and 3; Enforcement Order of the Law on the Territorial Sea, Articles 3 and 4.
39. The Law on Provisional Measures Relating to the Fishing Zone, Article 5.
40. Enforcement Order of the Law on Provisional Measures Relating to the Fishing Zone, Supplementary Provisions.
41. Shunji Yanai and Kuniaki Asomura, "Japan and the Emerging Order of the Sea: Two Maritime Laws of Japan," *Japanese Annual of International Law* (1977): 71.
42. Section 401 of the U.S. Fishery Conservation and Management Act of 1976 provided that if the United States ratifies a comprehensive treaty including provisions with respect to fishery conservation and management jurisdiction, as a result of any UNCLOS agreement, the secretary of commerce, after consultation with the secretary of state, may promulgate any amendment to the regulations promulgated under this act if such amendment is necessary and appropriate to conform such regulations to the provisions of such treaty, in anticipation of the date when such treaty shall come into force and effect for, or otherwise be applicable

to, the United States. The Decree of the Presidium of the Supreme Soviet, dated December 10, 1976, stipulated in the Preamble and Article 1 that pending the conclusion of comprehensive international conventions, provisional measures should be implemented within the Soviet 200-mile fishery zone. Article 8 further stipulated that the decree would be effective until the Soviet Union adopted other legislation prescribing the regime for the sea areas concerned, taking into account the work of the Third UNCLOS.

The full text of the U.S. legislation and an English translation of the Soviet legislation are found, respectively, in *International Legal Materials* 15 (May 1976): 634–650, and 15 (November 1976): 1381–1383. A Japanese translation of the Soviet law is found in Masao Shimada, "Sobieto no 200-kairihō" [The 200-mile Law of the Soviet Union], *Jūristo,* September 1, 1977, p. 81.

43. Law on Provisional Measures Relating to the Fishing Zone, Articles 3 and 14; Enforcement Order of the Law on Provisional Measures Relating to the Fishing Zone, Articles 1 and 6.

44. The exclusion of certain areas of the sea from a fishery zone is not necessarily unique to Japan. According to MFA officials who participated in the drafting of the Japanese fishery zone law, Denmark, Norway, the United Kingdom, and member states of the EEC have established fishing zones with varying distances around specific coasts. See Yanai and Asomura, "Japan and the Emerging Order," p. 79, n. 66.

45. Gaimushō Jōhō Bunkakyoku, *200-Kairi Jidai no Gyogyō: Saikin no Taigai Gyogyō Mondai to Kokusai Kyōryoku* [Fisheries in the 200-mile age: Recent external fishery issues and international cooperation], Tokyo: Sekai no Ugokisha, 1980, p. 80.

46. Law on Provisional Measures Relating to the Fishing Zone, Article 2.

47. Yanai and Asomura, "Japan and the Emerging Order," pp. 76–77.

48. Ibid., p. 77.

49. Law on Provisional Measures Relating to the Fishing Zone, Article 3.

50. Author interview with Kazunari Nomura, director-general of the Law of the Sea Office, Ministry of Foreign Affairs, September 1979.

51. Law on Provisional Measures Relating to the Fishing Zone, Article 12.

52. RSNT, United Nations, Third Conference on the Law of the Sea, A/CONF.62/WP.8/Rev.1/ Part II, Art. 55, and ICNT, United Nations, Third Conference on the Law of the Sea, A/CONF.62/WP.10 and Add. 1, Part II, Art. 66. The U.S. and Soviet legislative provisions went even further by establishing their "exclusive fishery management authority" (in the U.S. case) and "sovereign rights" (in the Soviet case) over all anadromous species throughout the migratory range of such species beyond their respective fishery zones. See the U.S. Fishery Conservation and Management Act of 1976, Section 102, and the Decree of the Presidium of the Supreme Soviet Concerning Provisional Measures in Regard to the Conservation of Living Resources and Fisheries Regulations in the Area of Sea Adjacent to the Coasts of the Soviet Union, Article 1, *International Legal Materials* 15 (May 1976) and (November 1976).

53. Yanai and Asomura, "Japan and the Emerging Order," p. 82.

54. Enforcement Order of the Law on Provisional Measures Relating to the Fishing Zone, Article 3.

55. See the RSNT, Part II, Art. 51, and the ISNT, Part II, Art. 62.
56. Law on Provisional Measures Relating to the Fishing Zone, Article 6.
57. Ibid.
58. Ibid., Article 7.
59. Ibid. See also Ministry of Agriculture and Forestry Ordinance No. 28 of 1977, Art. 7.
60. Law on Provisional Measures Relating to the Fishing Zone, Article 6.
61. Enforcement Order of the Law on Provisional Measures Relating to the Fishing Zone, Article 4.
62. Law on Provisional Measures Relating to the Fishing Zone, Article 8.
63. Yanai and Asomura, "Japan and the Emerging Order," p. 86.
64. Referred to here is the Agreement between the Government of Japan and the Government of the Union of Soviet Socialist Republics Concerning Fisheries in 1977 Off the Coasts of the Union of Soviet Socialist Republics (author's translation of the Japanese name of the agreement). The full Japanese text is found in Gaimushō Jōhō Bunkakyoku, *Nisso Gyogyō Zantei Kyōtei* [The provisional fishery agreement between Japan and the Soviet Union], Tokyo: Gaimushō Jōhō Bunkakyoku, 1977, pp. 30–35.
65. The ratification bill was unanimously approved by both houses, indicating the shared concern among Diet members of all political parties that the agreement should go into effect as soon as possible, so that Japanese fishermen could leave for their fishing operations in the North Pacific off the Soviet coasts.
66. *Suisan Nenkan, 1978,* pp. 29–30.
67. Ibid.
68. "Nisso Gyogyō Zantei Kyōtei Yōyaku Chōin: Ryōdo ga Hikkakatta Kōshō" [Japan-Soviet provisional fishery agreement finally signed: Negotiations affected by the (northern) territories], *Suisankai,* no. 1109 (June 1977): 66.
69. "Hokuyō Kyūsai ni Seifu Futan 933-oku en" [¥93 billion in government relief for North Pacific fisheries], *Suisankai,* no. 1111 (August 1977): 10.
70. Ibid., pp. 9–10.
71. *Suisan Nenkan, 1978,* p. 28.
72. "Hokuyō Gyogyō Kinkyū Taisaku no Keika to Sono Hōkō: Seifu Kinkyū Yūshi Sochi o Kimeru" [The progress and direction of the North Pacific fisheries emergency measures: Government adopts emergency loan measures], *Suisankai,* no. 1108 (May 1977): 69–70.
73. Ibid., p. 70.
74. "Soren 200-Kairi Suiiki nai 1,065-seki o Gensen" [Reduction of boats in the Soviet 200-mile zone by 1,065], *Suisankai,* no. 1109 (June 1977): 84–85.
75. Ibid., pp. 78–79.
76. "Hokuyō Kyūsai ni Seifu Futan 933-oku en," pp. 21–24. The total amount of government relief was far smaller than the amount requested by the fishery industry which amounted to ¥38 billion. Ibid., pp. 17–19.
77. Sangiin Nōrin Suisan Iinkai Chōsashitsu, *Sangiin Nōrin-Suisan Iinkai Shingi Yōroku* [Summary record of the proceedings of the House of Councillors Agriculture, Forestry, and Fisheries Committee], pp. 141–143.
78. Ibid., pp. 146–149.

Conclusion

1. The process of policy making in the present case closely resembles the "organizational model" described by Graham T. Allison and the "cybernetic theory" presented by John D. Steinbruner. See, respectively, Graham T. Allison, *Essence of Decision: Explaining the Cuban Missile Crisis,* and John D. Steinbruner, *The Cybernetic Theory of Decision: New Dimensions of Political Analysis.*

2. For a brief analysis of Japan's shipping and energy policy concerns in connection with the Iran-Iraq war, see Tsuneo Akaha, "Japan: Energy, Sea Lanes, and Security," *Marine Policy Reports* 7 (December 1984): 1–6.

3. *New York Times,* June 5, 1984, p. 5.

4. *Christian Science Monitor,* June 13, 1984, p. 13.

5. Jon Choy, "The Energy Situation in Japan," *Japan Economic Institute (JEI) Report,* no. 22B (June 8, 1984): 8.

6. Ibid., p. 6.

7. Ibid., p. 7.

8. For a report on Nakasone's remark and the waves of "mini-shocks" it has created at home and abroad, see, for example, *Asahi Shimbun,* January 22, 1983, p. 1. For a review of the recent trends in Japanese defense policy, see, for example, Tsuneo Akaha, "Japan's Nonnuclear Policy," *Asian Survey* 24,8 (August 1984): 852–877.

9. For reports of Asian fears of Japan's remilitarization, see, for example, *Asahi Shimbun,* January 1, 1983, p. 11, January 25, 1983, p. 2, March 29, 1983, p. 2; *Yomiuri Shimbun,* April 12, 1983, pp. 1, 5.

10. Nōrin Tōkei Kyōkai, *Shōwa 54-nendo Gyogyō Hakusho* [Fishery White Paper, 1979], pp. 26, 32–34.

11. Ibid., p. 8.

12. These figures are from *Suisan Nenkan* [Fisheries yearbook] 1978 and 1979, and Gaimushō Jōhō Bunkakyoku, *200-Kairi Jidai no Gyogyō: Saikin no Taigai Gyogyō Mondai to Kokusai Kyōryoku.*

13. *Asahi Shimbun,* March 11, 1984 (evening ed.).

14. *Fisheries of Japan 1980* (Tokyo: Japan Fisheries Association, 1980), p. 12.

15. Gaimushō Jōhō Bunkakyoku, *200-Kairi Jidai no Gyogyō,* pp. 130–137.

16. Ibid., pp. 137–138.

17. Gaimushō Keizaikyoku Kaiyōka, "Kokuren Kaiyōhō Jōyaku no Shomei, Hijun Jōkyō" [The status of signatures and ratifications of the UN Convention on the Law of the Sea], September 7, 1983 (mimeo.).

18. *New York Times,* November 24, 1984.

19. For the Reagan administration's position on the UN Convention on the Law of the Sea, see, for example, James L. Malone, "Who Needs the Sea Treaty?" *Foreign Policy* 54 (Spring 1984): 44–63; Daniel S. Cheever, "The Politics of the UN Convention on the Law of the Sea," *Journal of International Affairs* 37,2 (Winter 1984): 247–252; and Marian Nash Leich, "Contemporary Practice of the United States," *The American Journal of International Law* 77 (1983): 616–623.

20. *Asahi Shimbun,* August 4, 1984. The full texts of the agreement and accompanying documents are found in " 'Belgium–France–Federal Republic of

Germany–Italy–Japan–Netherlands–United Kingdom–United States: Provisional Understanding Regarding Deep Seabed Mining' (Done at Geneva, August 3, 1984; entered into force, September 2, 1984)," *International Legal Materials* 23 (November 1984): 1354–1365.

21. *Christian Science Monitor,* August 16, 1984.

22. Toru Nakagawa, "Keynote Speech: On the Eve of the Final Adoption of the Convention of the Law of the Sea," *Exclusive Economic Zone, 1982: Proceedings of the 7th International Ocean Symposium,* October 21–22, 1982 (Tokyo: Ocean Association of Japan, 1983), p. 7.

Selected Bibliography

Publications in English

Akaha, Tsuneo. "Conservation of the Environment of the Seto Inland Sea." *Coastal Zone Management Journal* 12 (1984): 83–136.
——. "Japan's Nonnuclear Policy." *Asian Survey* 24 (August 1984): 852–877.
——. "Japan: Energy, Sea Lanes, and Security." *Marine Policy Reports* 7 (December 1984): 1–6.
Alexander, Lewis. "Indices of National Interest in the Ocean." *Ocean Development and International Law Journal* 1 (Spring 1973): 40.
Allison, Graham T. *Essence of Decision: Explaining the Cuban Missile Crisis.* Boston: Little Brown and Company, 1971.
Bascom, Willard. "The Disposal of Waste in the Ocean." In *Ocean Science,* 276–285. San Francisco: W. H. Freeman & Co., 1977.
" 'Belgium–France–Federal Republic of Germany–Italy–Japan–Netherlands–United Kingdom–United States: Provisional Understanding Regarding Deep Seabed Mining' (Done at Geneva, August 3, 1984; entered into force, September 2, 1984)." *International Legal Materials* 23 (November 1984): 1354–1365.
Bell, Frederick W. *Food from the Sea: The Economics and Politics of Ocean Fisheries.* Boulder, Colorado: Westview Press, 1978.
Bertalanffy, Ludwig von. *General System Theory: Foundations, Development, Applications.* Rev. ed. New York: George Braziller, 1968.
Borgese, Elizabeth Mann. "Law of the Sea." *The Center Magazine* 12 (November/December 1974): 25–34.
Brown, Seyom, Nina W. Cornell, Larry L. Fabian, and Edith Brown Weiss. *Regimes for the Ocean, Outer Space, and Weather.* Washington, D.C.: The Brookings Institution, 1977.
Cheever, Daniel S. "The Politics of the UN Convention on the Law of the Sea." *Journal of International Affairs* 37 (Winter 1984): 247–252.
Choy, Jon. "The Energy Situation in Japan." *Japan Economic Institute (JEI) Report,* no. 22B (June 8, 1984): 6–8.
Craig, Albert M. "Functional and Dysfunctional Aspects of Bureaucracy." In *Modern Japanese Organization and Decision Making,* edited by Ezra F. Vogel, 3–32. Berkeley: University of California Press, 1975.

Dean, Arthur H. "The Geneva Conference on the Law of the Sea: What Was Accomplished." *American Journal of International Law* 52 (October 1958): 607–728.

————. "The Second Geneva Conference on the Law of the Sea: The Fight for Freedom of the Seas." *American Journal of International Law* 54 (October 1960): 751–789.

Destler, I. M., Hideo Sato, Priscilla Clapp, and Haruhiro Fukui. *Managing an Alliance: The Politics of U.S.-Japanese Relations.* Washington, D.C.: The Brookings Institution, 1976.

Eto, Shinkichi. "Foreign Policy Formation in Japan." *Japan Interpreter* (Winter 1976): 251–266.

Friedheim, Robert L. "Satisfied and Dissatisfied States Negotiate International Law: A Case Study." *World Politics* 18 (October 1965): 20–41.

————. "Factor Analysis as a Tool in Studying the Law of the Sea." In *The Law of the Sea: Offshore Boundaries and Zones,* edited by Lewis M. Alexander, 45–70. Columbus: Ohio State University Press, 1967.

————. "The Political, Economic, and Legal Ocean." In *Managing Ocean Resources: A Primer,* edited by Robert L. Friedheim, 26–42. Boulder, Colorado: Westview Press, 1979.

Friedheim, R. L., and J. B. Kadane, with the assistance of J. K. Gamble, Jr. "Quantitative Content Analysis of the United Nations Seabed Debate: Methodology and a Continental Shelf Case Study." *International Organization* 33 (Summer 1970): 479–502.

Friedheim, Robert L., George O. Totten, Haruhiro Fukui, Tsuneo Akaha, Masayuki Takeyama, Mamoru Koga, and Hiroyuki Nakahara. *Japan and the New Ocean Regime.* Boulder, Colorado: Westview Press, 1984.

Gantz, David L. "The United Nations and the Law of the Sea." *International and Comparative Law Quarterly* 26 (January 1977): 1–53.

Gross, M. Grant. *Oceanography.* 3rd ed. Columbus, Ohio: Charles E. Merrill, 1976.

Hardin, Garrett. "The Tragedy of the Commons." *Science* 162 (December): 1243–1248.

Hosoya, Chihiro. "Characteristics of the Foreign Policy Decision-Making System in Japan." *World Politics* 26 (April 1974): 353–369.

Japan Fisheries Association. *Fisheries of Japan.* Tokyo: Japan Fisheries Association, 1980.

Johnson, Chalmers. "MITI and Japanese International Economic Policy." In *The Foreign Policy of Modern Japan,* edited by Robert A. Scalapino, 227–280. Berkeley: University of California Press, 1977.

Koga, Mamoru. "Developing a Manganese Nodule Policy for Japan." In *Japan and the New Ocean Regime,* edited by Robert L. Friedheim et al., 227–275. Boulder, Colorado: Westview Press, 1984.

Koga, Mamoru, and Hiroyuki Nakahara. "Japanese Ocean Science and Technology Policy and the National Budget." In *Japan and the New Ocean Regime,* edited by Robert L. Friedheim et al., 108–129. Boulder, Colorado: Westview Press, 1984.

Kuribayashi, Tadao. "The Basic Structure of the New Regime of Passage Through

International Straits: An Emerging Trend in the Third UNCLOS and Japan's Situation." *Japanese Annual of International Law* 21 (1977): 29–47.

"Latin American Meeting on Aspects of the Law of the Sea: Declarations and Resolutions." *International Legal Materials* 10 (January 1971): 207.

The Law of the Sea: The Final Act and Annexes of the United Nations Conference on the Law of the Sea, Geneva, 1958, together with a Synoptical Table of Claims to Jurisdiction over the Territorial Sea, the Contiguous Zone and the Continental Shelf. London: The Society of Comparative Legislation and International Law, 1958.

Leich, Marian Nash. "Contemporary Practice of the United States." *The American Journal of International Law* 77 (1983): 616–623.

MacKenzie, William H. "Japan-USSR Negotiations on Safe Fishing and the Reversion of Disputed Islands in the North-Pacific, 1945–1977." *Marine Affairs Journal*, no. 5 (January 1978): 1–31.

Malone, James L. "Who Needs the Sea Treaty?" *Foreign Policy* 54 (Spring 1984): 247–252.

Miles, Edward. "The Dynamics of Global Ocean Politics." In *Marine Policy and the Coastal Community*, edited by Douglas M. Johnston, 147–181. New York: St. Martin's Press, 1976.

———. "An Interpretation of the Geneva Proceedings, Part II." *Ocean Development and International Law Journal* 3 (1976): 303–327.

Nakagawa, Toru. "Keynote Speech: On the Eve of the Final Adoption of the Convention on the Law of the Sea." In *Exclusive Economic Zone, 1982: Proceedings of the 7th International Ocean Symposium, October 21–22, 1982, Tokyo*, 3–7. Tokyo: Ocean Association of Japan, 1983.

Njenga, Francis. "Regional Approaches to the Law of the Sea." *Perspectives on Ocean Policy*, 87–105. Conference on Conflict and Order in Ocean Relations, October 1974, Ocean Policy Project, Johns Hopkins University. Washington, D.C.: GPO, 1975.

Oda, Shigeru. "Japan and the United Nations Conference on the Law of the Sea." *Japanese Annual of International Law* (1959): 65–86.

———. "Toward a New Regime for Ocean Development." *Ocean Development and International Law Journal* 3 (1973): 291–302.

———. "The Law of the Sea Conference: Recent Developments, Present Status, and Future Implications." *Japanese Annual of International Law* 19 (1975): 80–101.

———. *The Law of the Sea in Our Time: 1. New Developments, 1966–1975.* Leyden: A. W. Sijthoff, 1977.

Olson, Mancur. *The Logic of Collective Action: Public Goods and the Theory of Groups.* Cambridge: Harvard University Press, 1977.

Ori, Kan. "Political Factors in Post-War Japan's Foreign Policy Decisions." In *Japan, America, and the Future World Order*, edited by Morton Kaplan and Kinhide Mushakoji, 145–174. New York: Free Press, 1976.

Ouchi, Kazuomi. "A Perspective on Japan's Struggle for Its Traditional Rights on the Oceans." *Ocean Development and International Law Journal* 5, 1 (1978): 107–134.

Oxman, Bernard H. "The Third United Nations Conference on the Law of the
    Sea: The 1976 New York Sessions." *American Journal of International
    Law* 71 (April 1977): 247–268.
Pardo, Arvid. "An Opportunity Lost." In *Law of the Sea: U.S. Diplomacy
    Dilemma,* edited by Bernard H. Oxman, David D. Coron, and Charles
    L. O. Buderi. San Francisco: ICS Press, 1983.
Park, Choon-ho. "Marine Resource Conflicts in the North Pacific." In *The Impact
    of the Law of the Sea,* edited by Douglas M. Johnston, 215–232. Lon-
    don: Croom Helm, 1976.
Phillips, J. C. "The Exclusive Economic Zone as a Concept in International Law."
    International and Comparative Law Journal 26 (July 1977): 585–618.
Reischauer, Edwin O. *The Japanese.* Tokyo: Charles E. Tuttle, 1977.
Robinson, M. A. "World Fisheries to 2000: Supply, Demand, and Management."
    Marine Policy 4 (January 1980): 19–32.
Russett, Bruce M. *Prisoner of Insecurity.* San Francisco: H. F. Freeman, 1983.
Steinbruner, John D. *The Cybernetic Theory of Decision: New Dimensions of
    Political Analysis.* Princeton, N.J.: Princeton University Press, 1974.
Stevenson, John R., and Bernard H. Oxman. "The Preparations for the Law of
    the Sea Conference." *American Journal of International Law* 68 (Janu-
    ary 1974): 1–12.
————. "The Third United Nations Conference on the Law of the Sea: The 1974
    Caracas Session." *American Journal of International Law* 69 (January
    1975): 1–30.
————. "The Third United Nations Conference on the Law of the Sea: The 1975
    Caracas Session." *American Journal of International Law* 69 (October
    1975): 763–797.
Takeyama, Masayuki. "Japan's Foreign Negotiations over Offshore Petroleum
    Development: An Analysis of Decision-Making in the Japan-Korea
    Continental Shelf Joint Development Program." In *Japan and the New
    Ocean Regime,* edited by Robert L. Friedheim et al., 276–313. Boulder,
    Colorado: Westview Press, 1984.
Totten, George O. "The Reconstruction of the Japanese Shipbuilding Industry."
    In *Japan and the New Ocean Regime,* edited by Robert L. Friedheim et
    al., 130–72. Boulder, Colorado: Westview Press, 1984.
Watanabe, Akio. "Foreign Policy Making Japanese Style." *International Affairs*
    (London) 54 (January 1978): 75–88.
Yanai, Shunji, and Kuniaki Asomura. "Japan and the Emerging Order of the
    Sea: Two Maritime Laws of Japan." *Japanese Annual of International
    Law,* 1977, pp. 48–114.

Newspapers

Christian Science Monitor. June 13, 1984; August 16, 1984.
Japan Economic Journal (Tokyo). Vol. 12, June 25, 1984.
Japan Times Weekly (Tokyo). December 15, 1973.
New York Times. March 19, 1969; June 5, 1984; November 24, 1984.

United Nations Documents

"Note Verbale Dated 22 November 1971 from the Permanent Mission of Japan addressed to the Secretariat of the United Nations." A/AC.138/63. 1971.

United Nations. Convention on the Territorial Sea and the Contiguous Zone. A/CONF.13/L.52.

———. Convention on the High Seas. A/CONF.13/L.53.

———. Convention on Fishing and Conservation of the Living Resources of the High Seas. A/CONF.13/L.54.

———. Convention on the Continental Shelf. A/CONF.13/L.55.

———. Press Release. December 17, 1970. GA/4355.

———. "Statement by Ambassador M. Ogiso, Representative of Japan at the March Session of the Sea-Bed Committee held at Geneva." N.d. (Mimeographed)

———. "Statement by Minister Y. Okawa, Acting Representative of Japan, in Subcommittee II of the Committee on the Peaceful Uses of the Sea-Bed and the Ocean Floor Beyond the Limits of National Jurisdiction, Geneva." July 27, 1971 (mimeographed).

United Nations Conference on the Law of the Sea (UNCLOS). A/CONF.13/34. 1958.

———. A/CONF.13/38. 1958.

———. A/CONF.13/39. 1958.

———. A/CONF.13/40. 1958.

———. A/CONF.13/41. 1958.

———. A/CONF.13/L.52. 1958.

———. A/CONF.13/L.53. 1958.

———. A/CONF.13/L.54 and Add. 1. 1958.

———. A/CONF.13/L.55. 1958.

———. A/CONF.19/L.4 and Annex. 1960.

———. A/CONF.19/L.9. 1960.

———. A/CONF.19/L.12. 1960.

———, Committee I. A/CONF.19/C.I/L.1. 1960.

———, Committee I. A/CONF.19/C.I/L.2/Rev.1. 1960.

———, Committee I. A/CONF.19/C.I/L.10. 1960.

———, Committee I. 13th Meeting. A/CONF.19/C.I/SR.13. 1960.

———, Committee I. 27th Meeting. A/CONF.19/C.I/SR.27. 1960.

———, Committee I. 38th Meeting. A/CONF.19/C.I/SR.38. 1960.

United Nations General Assembly. Committee on the Peaceful Uses of the Seabed and the Ocean Floor Beyond Limits of National Jurisdiction. *Economic Significance, in Terms of Seabed Mineral Resources, of the Various Limits Proposed for National Jurisdiction: Report of the Secretary General.* A/AC.138/87. 1973.

———, Committee on the Peaceful Uses of the Seabed and the Ocean Floor Beyond Limits of National Jurisdiction. 21st Plenary Meeting. A/AC.138/SR.21. 1970.

————. 33rd Plenary Meeting. A/AC.138/SR.33. 1970.
————. 34th Plenary Meeting. A/AC.138/SR.34. 1971.
————. 53rd Plenary Meeting. A/AC.138/SR.53. 1971.
————. Subcommittee I. 9th Meeting. A/AC.138/SC.I/SR.9. 1971.
————. Subcommittee I. 38th Meeting. A/AC.138/SC.I/SR.38. 1972.
————. Subcommittee II. A/AC.138/SC.II/L.9. 1972.
————. Subcommittee II. A/AC.138/SC.II/L.11. 1972.
————. Subcommittee II. A/AC.138/SC.II/L.12. 1972.
————. Subcommittee II. A/AC.138/SC.II/L.15. 1972.
————. Subcommittee II. A/AC.138/SC.II/L.18. 1972.
————. Subcommittee III. A/AC.138/SC.III/L.49. 1973.
————. Subcommittee II. 11th Meeting. A/AC.138/SC.II/SR.11. 1971.
————. Subcommittee II. 27th Meeting. A/AC.138/SC.II/SR.27. 1972.
————. Subcommittee II. 31st Meeting. A/AC.138/SC.II/SR.31. 1972.
————. Subcommittee II. 36th Meeting. A/AC.138/SC.II/SR.36. 1972.
————. Subcommittee II. 43rd Meeting. A/AC.138/SC.II/SR.43. 1972.
————. Subcommittee II. 56th Meeting. A/AC.138/SC.II/SR.56. 1972.
————. Subcommittee II. 60th Meeting. A/AC.138/SC.II/SR.60. 1973.
————. Subcommittee II. 74th Meeting. A/AC.138/SC.II/SR.74. 1973.
————. Subcommittee III. 23rd Meeting. A/AC.138/SC.III/SR.23. 1972.
————. Subcommittee III. 28th Meeting. A/AC.138/SC.III/SR.28. 1972.
United Nations General Assembly, Eleventh Session. Official Records, Supplement 9. *International Law Commission Report.* A/3159. 1956.
————, Eleventh Session. Official Records, Supplement 17. A/3572.
————, Twenty-second Session. First Committee. 1515th Meeting. *Provisional Verbatim Records.* A/C.1/PV.1515. 1967.
————, Twenty-second Session. First Committee. 1516th Meeting. *Provisional Verbatim Records.* A/C.1/PV.1516. 1967.
————, Twenty-second Session. First Committee. 1529th Meeting. *Provisional Verbatim Records.* A/C.1/PV.1529. 1967.
————, Twenty-third Session. Official Records, Supplement 18. *Resolutions Adopted by the General Assembly during Its Twenty-Third Session.* A/7218. 1968.
————, Twenty-fourth Session. First Committee. 1709th Meeting. *Provisional Verbatim Records.* A/C.1/PV.1709. 1969.
————, Twenty-fifth Session. First Committee. 1787th Meeting. *Provisional Verbatim Records.* A/C.1/PV.1787. 1970.
————, Twenty-fifth Session. First Committee. 1796th Meeting. *Provisional Verbatim Records.* A/C.1/PV.1796. 1970.
————, Twenty-fifth Session. First Committee. 1798th Meeting. *Provisional Verbatim Records.* A/C.1/PV.1798. 1970.
————, Twenty-sixth Session. Official Records, Supplement 21. *Report of the Committee on the Peaceful Uses of the Seabed and the Ocean Floor Beyond the Limits of National Jurisdiction.* A/8421. 1971.
————, Twenty-seventh Session. Official Records, Supplement 21. *Report of the Committee on the Peaceful Uses of the Seabed and Ocean Floor Beyond the Limits of National Jurisdiction.* A/8721. 1972.

————, Twenty-eighth Session. Official Records, Supplement 21. *Report of the Committee on the Peaceful Uses of the Seabed and the Ocean Floor Beyond the Limits of National Jurisdiction, Volume III.* A/9021. 1972.

United Nations Third Conference on the Law of the Sea. Plenary Session. 41st Meeting. A/CONF.62/SR.41. 1974.

————. Plenary Session. A/CONF.62/30/Rev.1. 1974.

————. Plenary Session. A/CONF.62/33. 1974.

————. Plenary Session. A/CONF.62/WP.8/Parts I, II, and III. (ISNT). 1975.

————. Plenary Session. A/CONF.62/WP.8/Rev.1/Part II. (RSNT). 1976.

————. Plenary Session. A/CONF.62/WP.10 and Add. 1. (ICNT). 1977.

————. Second Committee. 7th Meeting. A/CONF.62/C.2/SR.7. 1974.

————. Second Committee. 17th Meeting. A/CONF.62/C.2/SR.17. 1974.

————. Second Committee. 28th Meeting. A/CONF.62/C.2/SR.28. 1974.

————. Second Committee. 36th Meeting. A/CONF.62/C.2/SR.36. 1974.

————. Second Committee. 41st Meeting. A/CONF.62/C.2/SR.41. 1974.

————. Second Committee. 46th Meeting. A/CONF.62/C.2/L.46. 1974.

United States Government Documents

U.S. Senate Committee on Commerce, Science, and Transportation. *Treaties and Other International Agreements on Fisheries, Oceanographic Resources, and Wildlife Involving the United States.* Washington, D.C.: GPO, 1977.

Publications in Japanese

"Chōki Shokuryō Seisaku no Ikkan de Kakuritsu o: Kaiyōhō e Gyōkai Hōshin, Jisseki Kakuho no Sesshō nado Santen" [Let's establish (policy) as part of a long-term food policy: The industry's position for the law of the sea, three points including negotiations for ensuring past (fish catch) levels]. *Suisankai,* no. 1084 (April 1975): 52–54.

"Dai Sanji Kokuren Kaiyōhō Kaigi Nyū Yōku Kaiki o Maenishite" [The Third UNCLOS: As we approach the New York session]. *Sekai no Ugoki,* no. 308 (February 1976): 9–11.

"Gyogyō Suiiki ni Kansuru Zantei Sochihō: Shūgiin no Teian riyū to Nōshō, Chōkan no Setsumei" [The Law on Provisional Measures Relating to the Fishing Zone: Reasons for the Introduction to the House of Representatives and the explanation by the agriculture minister and the Fisheries Agency director-general]. *Suisankai,* no.1108 (May 1977): 40.

Henshūbu. "Yamaba Mukaeta Gyogyō Keiei Antei Taisaku: Suisan Gyōkai, Kessokushite Koto ni Atarō" [Fishery management stabilization measures at a crucial point: The fishery industry, let's unify our action]. *Suisankai,* no. 1089 (September 1975): 25–37.

Hirasawa, Yutaka. *Nihon Suisan Dokuhon* [Japanese fisheries reader]. Tokyo: Tōyō Keizai Shimpōsha, 1976.

————. *Nihyaku-Kairi Jidai to Nihon Gyogyō—Sono Henkaku to Kaisei no*

Michi [The 200-mile age and Japanese fisheries—its road to reform and renovation]. Tokyo: Hokuto Shobō, 1978.

Hiyama, Yoshio, ed. *Kaiyō Kaihatsu to Shakai Kankyō Mondai* [Ocean development and social-environmental problems]. Kaiyō Kaihatsu Mondai Kōza, no. 5. Tokyo: Kashima Kenkyūjo Shuppankai, 1974.

"Hokuyō Gyogyō Kinkyū Taisaku no Keika to Sono Hōkō: Seifu Kinkyū Yūshi Sochi o Kimeru" [The progress and direction of the North Pacific fisheries emergency measures: Government adopts emergency loan measures]. *Suisankai,* no. 1108 (May 1977): 69–70.

"Hokuyō Kiki Toppa Kokumin Sōkekki Taikai Hiraku: Chihō Jichitai Dai Nihon Suisankai Soren no Kyoken Shisei ni Kōgi" [All People's Conference to Overcome the North Pacific Crisis held: Local governments and the Japan Fisheries Association protest the aggressive posture of the Soviet Union]. *Suisankai,* no. 1109 (June 1977): 103.

Iguchi, Takeo. "Dai Sanji Kokuren Kaiyōhō Kaigi Dai Yon-kaiki: Atarashii Kaiyō Chitsujo no Keisei Katei" [The Fourth Session of the Third UNCLOS: The process of a new ocean order formation]. *Gaikō Jihō* (July 1976): 3–30.

————. "Shin Kaiyōhō no Sōki Daketsu ga Kokueki ni Gatchi" [Early settlement of the new law of the sea will meet the national interest]. *Sekai Shūhō* 12 (1976): 12–21.

Isoda, Sadaaki. "Kyokutō Gyojō o Jikoku no Niwa ni—200-kairi no Taisei ni Junnō" [Turning the Far East fishing grounds into (the Soviet Union's) "own yard"—Adaptation to the dominant trend of 200-mile (zones)]. *Seikai Shūhō* 1 (January 1977): 23–24.

"Kaiyōhō Taisaku Honbu o Setchi: Junēbu Kaigi Taisaku e Katsudō o Kyōka" [The establishment of the Law of the Sea Headquarters: Strengthening of activities toward the Geneva session]. *Suisankai,* no. 1082 (February 1975): 78–79.

"Kaiyō Sangyō Kenkyūkai, ed. *Kaiyō Kaihatsu Sangyōkai* [Ocean development industry]. Tokyo: Kyōikusha, 1977.

————, ed. *200-Kairi Jidai no Sekaito Nihon* [The world in the 200-mile age and Japan]. Kaiyō Kaihatsu Mondai Kōza, supp. Tokyo: Kashima Shuppankai, 1977.

"Kamenaga Kaichō, Gyōkai Shunō, Shin Kaiyō Chitsujo Taisaku de Yōbō" [President Kamenaga, industry leaders request new ocean order measures]. *Suisankai,* no. 1105 (January 1977): 59–60.

Kawakami, Kenzo. *Sengo no Kokusai Gyogyō Seido* [The postwar international fisheries regime]. Tokyo: Dai Nihon Suisankai, 1972.

Kawamura, Katsu. "Ryōkai 12-Kairi ni Taisuru Minshatō no Kangae" [Democratic Socialist Party's position on the 12-mile territorial sea]. *Kakushin* 80 (1977): 70–71.

"Keiei Kiki Dakai eno Nekki Minagiru: Nishi Nihon Suisan Shinkō Kaigi Hiraku" [Earnest fervor for overcoming management crisis: West Japan fisheries promotion conference held]. *Suisankai,* no. 1092 (December 1975): 38–44.

Matsuura, Akira. "200-Kairi Keizai Senkan Suiiki Mondai to Nihon Gyogyō"

[The problem of the 200-mile exclusive fishery zone and Japan's fisheries]. *AFF* [Agriculture, forestry, and fisheries] 7 (April 1976): 4–10.

―――. "200-Kairi Keizai Suiiki wa Dōnaru—Nichibei Gyogyō Kōshō o Furikaette" [What will become of the 200-mile economic zone? A reflection on Japan-U.S. fishery negotiations]. *Gekkan Jiyū Minshu*, no. 253 (February 1977): 93–99.

Morisawa, Motokichi. "200-Kairi Mondai no Yukue to Kongo no Nihon no Suisangyō no Arikata" [The direction of the 200-mile issue and the future of Japanese fisheries]. *Keidanren Geppō* 25 (1977): 52–56.

Nakamura, Ko. "Kaiyō Kokka Nihon wa Ikinokareruka" [Can maritime nation Japan survive?] *Keizai Orai* (July 1976): 58–65.

Nakatate, Ko. "Keizai Suiiki 200-Kairi to Nishi Nihon Suisangyō" [200-mile fishery zones and the fishery industry of western Japan]. *Kyūshū Keizai Tōkei Geppō* (March 1977): 3–14.

"200-Kairi Jidai no Makuake to Natta Sangatsu, Nisso Gyogyō Kōshō" [March marks the dawning of the 200-mile age, the Japan-Soviet fisheries talks]. *Suisankai*, no. 1108 (May 1977): 52–53.

Nōrin Tōkei Kyōkai, *Shōwa 54-nendo Gyogyō Hakusho* [Fishery white paper, 1979], Tokyo: Nōrin Tōkei Kyōkai, 1979.

"Ryōkai 12-Kairi no Sōki Sengen ni Kansuru Shitsumonsho" [Questionnaire concerning early declaration of the 12-mile territorial sea]. *Suisankai*, no. 1093 (January 1976): 66–83.

"Sapporo de Seidai ni Higashi Nihon Suisan Shinkō Kaigi: Keiei Antei ni Shinken na Iken, Shisaku no Sokuji Kakuritsu o Kakunin" [Large-scale East Japan Fisheries Promotion Conference in Sapporo: Earnest opinions for management stabilization, affirms prompt establishment of policy measures]. *Suisankai*, no. 1090 (October 1975): 72–84.

"Seidai ni Nihon Gyogyō Shinkō Taisaku Kaigi: Kiki Dakai e Kokuminteki Sōi de Katsudō, Nihon Gyogyō no Shinkō o Hakarukai ga Hossoku" [Grand Japan Fisheries Promotion Conference: Activities to overcome the crisis with the will of all people of the country, Association for the Promotion of Japanese Fisheries established]. *Suisankai*, no. 1103 (November 1976): 7–22.

Seki, Koichiro. "Kaiyōhō Kaigi–Karakasu kara Junēbu e" [Law of the Sea Conference—from Caracas to Geneva]. *Keizai Hyōron* 24 (1974): 69–80.

Shimada, Masao. "Sobieto no 200-kairihō" [The 200-mile law of the Soviet Union]. *Jūristo*, September 1, 1977, p. 81.

"Shīrēn Bōei to Sono Haikei" [Sea lane defense and its background]. *Bōei Nenkan 1983* [Defense yearbook 1983], 1–169. (Tokyo: Bōei Nenkan Kankōkai, 1983).

Shoshi, Eishiro. "Hokuyō Gyogyō wa Kaimetsu no Kiki ni" [North Pacific fisheries face a crisis of total devastation]. *Sekai Shūhō*, May 25, 1976, pp. 22–27.

"Soren 200-Kairi Suiiki nai 1,065-seki o Gensen" [Reduction of boats in the Soviet 200-mile zone by 1,065]. *Suisankai*, no. 1109 (June 1977): 84–85.

Suisan Nenkan, 1977 [Fisheries yearbook, 1977]. Tokyo: Suisansha, 1977.

Suisan Nenkan, 1978 [Fisheries yearbook, 1978]. Tokyo: Suisansha, 1978.
Suisan Nenkan, 1979 [Fisheries yearbook, 1979]. Tokyo: Suisansha, 1979.
Sumi, Kazuo. "Umi kara Shimedasareru Nihon" [Japan squeezed out of the sea].
    Asahi Jānaru, August 13–20, 1976, pp. 28–33.
Unyushō [The Ministry of Transport]. Gyōsei Kikō Shirīzu, no. 109. Tokyo:
    Kyōikusha, 1979.

Japanese Government Documents

Fisheries Agency. *Statistics of Fisheries Production*. Annual.
Gaimushō Jōhō Bunkakyoku. *Dai Sanji Kaiyōhō Kaigi* [The third law of the sea
    conference] 2. Tokyo: Gaimushō Jōhō Bunkakyoku, 1975.
———. *Dai Sanji Kaiyōhō Kaigi—Dai Roku Kaiki* [The Third United Nations
    Conference on the Law of the Sea—the sixth session] 9. Tokyo:
    Gaimushō Jōhō Bunkakyoku, 1977.
———. *200-Kairi Jidai no Gyogyō: Saikin no Taigai Gyogyō Mondai to Kokusai
    Kyōryoku* [Fisheries in the 200-mile age: Recent external fishery issues
    and international cooperation]. Tokyo: Sekai no Ugokisha, 1980.
———. *Nisso Gyogyō Zantei Kyōtei* [The provisional fishery agreement between
    Japan and the Soviet Union]. Tokyo: Gaimushō Jōhō Bunkakyoku,
    1977.
Gaimushō Keizaikyoku Kaiyōka. "Kokuren Kaiyōhō Jōyaku no Shomei, Hijun
    Jōkyō" [The status of signatures and ratifications of the UN Convention
    on the Law of the Sea], September 7, 1983 (mimeographed).
Kaijō Hoanchō. *Shōwa 54-nenban, Kaijō Hoan Hakusho* [Maritime safety white
    paper, 1979]. Tokyo: Ōkurashō Insatsukyoku, 1979.
"Nisso Gyogyō Kōshō ni Kansuru Kokkai Daihyō Giindan Hōkokusho" [Report
    of the Dietmen's delegation concerning Japan-Soviet fisheries negotia-
    tions]. Submitted to the Diet by Yoshio Sakurauchi, head of the delega-
    tion, May 1977.
Sangiin Nōrin Suisan Iinkai Chōsashitsu. *Sangiin Nōrin Suisan Iinkai Shingi
    Yōroku* [Summary record of the proceedings of the House of Councillors
    Agriculture, Forestry, and Fisheries Committee], 1977.
Shūgiin Nōrin Suisan Iinkai Chōsashitsu. *Kaiyō-hōan ni tsuite*. [On the maritime
    bills]. 1977.
———. Ryōkai-hōan Kankei Shiryō [Documents concerning the territorial sea
    bill]. April 1977.
———. *Ryōkai-hōan ni tsuite* [On the territorial sea law]. April 1977.
Suisanchō. *Gyogyō Hakusho* [Fisheries white paper]. Tokyo: Nōrin Tōkei Kyōkai.
    Annual.
———. Kikakuka [Fisheries Agency Planning Division]. *Engan Gyojō Seibi
    Kaihatsuhō no Kaisetsu* [A guide to the Coastal Fisheries Ground Engi-
    neering and Development Act]. Tokyo: Chikyūsha, 1974.
Tsūsanshō. *Shōwa 57-nendo Tsūsan Hakusho* [White paper on international
    trade and industry, 1982]. Tokyo: Ōkurashō Insatsukyoku, 1982.

Japanese Laws

Enforcement Order of the Law on Provisional Measures Relating to the Fishing Zone. Cabinet Order No. 212 of June 17, 1977.
Enforcement Order of the Law on the Territorial Sea. Cabinet Order No. 210 of June 17, 1977.
Law on Provisional Measures Relating to the Fishing Zone. Law No. 31 of May 2, 1977.
Law on the Territorial Sea. Law No. 30 of May 2, 1977.
Ministry of Agriculture and Forestry Ordinance No. 28 of 1977.

Periodicals

Akahata (Tokyo). February 25, 1977.
Asahi Shimbun (Tokyo). April 15, 1970–April 22, 1977; January 1, 1983; January 22, 1983; January 25, 1983; March 29, 1983; August 4, 1984; March 11, 1985, (evening ed.).
Nihon Keizai Shimbun (Tokyo). May 13, 1971–May 29, 1976.
Nishi Nihon Shimbun (Fukuoka). February 17–24, 1977.
Suisan Shūhō (Tokyo). July 30, 1975.
Yomiuri Shimbun (Tokyo). April 12, 1983.

Index

About the Author

Tsuneo Akaha was born in Japan, where he received his early education. After earning a B.A. in political science at Oregon State University, where he was an exchange student, and another B.A. in political science at Waseda University in Tokyo, he pursued graduate studies in international relations at the University of Southern California, from which he received his M.A. and Ph.D. degrees, the latter in 1981. He is the author of "A Cybernetic Analysis of Japan's Fishery Policy Process" and coauthor with Robert L. Friedheim of "Japan and the Ocean," both of which appeared in *Japan and the New Ocean Regime,* edited by Robert L. Friedheim et al. (1984). He has also published articles in *Asian Survey, Coastal Zone Management Journal,* and *Marine Policy Reports.* He teaches political science at Bowling Green State University in Ohio and is presently conducting research on the impact of threats to international shipping and the consequences of U.S.-Soviet strategic competition in Asia on Japan's defense and foreign policies.

Production Notes

This book was designed by Roger Eggers. Composition and paging were done on the Quadex Composing System and typesetting on the Compugraphic 8400 by the design and production staff of University of Hawaii Press.

The text and display typeface is Garamond.

Offset presswork and binding were done by Vail-Ballou Press, Inc. Text paper is Writers R Offset, basis 50.